Women
at
Work

Harry C. Trexler Library
Muhlenberg College

Women
at
Work

Mary Frank Fox

THE UNIVERSITY OF MICHIGAN

Sharlene Hesse-Biber

BOSTON COLLEGE

MAYFIELD PUBLISHING COMPANY

Library of Congress Catalog Card Number: 83-061533
International Standard Book Number: 0-87484-525-4

Sponsoring editor: Franklin Graham
Manuscript editor: Linda Purrington
Managing editor: Pat Herbst
Art director: Nancy Sears
Illustrator: Gina Abeles
Cover designer: Deborah Hopping
Production manager: Cathy Willkie
Compositor: G & S Typesetters
Printer and binder: Bookcrafters

Credits

Pages 60, 61   Reprinted by permission of the publisher from *The Undergraduate Woman: Is-
sues in Educational Equality*, edited by Pamela J. Perun (Lexington, Mass.: Lexington
Books, D. C. Heath and Company, 1982). Copyright © 1982 by D. C. Heath and
Company.

Page 73   Excerpted from *Wising Up: The Mistakes Women Make in Business and How to
Avoid Them* by Jo Foxworth. Copyright © 1980 by Jo Foxworth. Reprinted by permission
of Delacorte Press.

Page 82   Excerpt from *The Managerial Woman* by Margaret Hennig and Anne Jardim. Copyright © 1976, 1977 by Margaret Hennig and Anne Jardim. Reprinted by permission of
Doubleday & Company, Inc.

Pages 88, 89   Reprinted from Albie Sacks and Joan Hoff Wilson, *Sexism and the Law: A
Study of Male Beliefs and Legal Bias in Britain and the United States*, p. 114. Copyright
© 1978 by Albie Sacks and Joan Hoff Wilson.

Page 104   From *Not Servants, Not Machines: Office Workers Speak Out* by Jean Tepperman.
Copyright © 1976 by Jean Tepperman. Reprinted by permission of Beacon Press.

Page 106   "Education and Income of Clerical Workers, 1970," from *The Women's Movement:
Political, Socioeconomic, and Psychological Issues*, 3rd edition, by Barbara Sinclair Deckard. Copyright © 1983 by Harper & Row, Publishers, Inc. Reprinted by permission of the
publisher.

Page 108   Reprinted by permission of Westview Press from *Working Women: A Study of
Women in Paid Jobs*, edited by Ann Seidman. Copyright © 1978 by Westview Press, Boulder, Colorado.

Page 123   Reprinted from Terry Wetherby, *Conversations: Working Women Talk About
Doing a Man's Job*, pp. 163–164. Reprinted by permission of Celestial Arts.

Contents

Preface

With the recent surge in women's labor-force participation, and the publicity and commentary that surround the most notable cases of female attainment in business, professions, and government, popular media give the impression of significant advancement and opportunity for women in work, economy, and society. This message is particularly salient for the young people who have "come of age" amidst the reemergence of the women's movement and the redefinitions of sex roles during the 1970s. Compared to their peers of even ten years ago, young women today feel more secure about their chances for active and full participation in areas that have been male domains (see Katz, 1980). In their career expectations, and their expectations for work and family lives, young women now have ambitious hopes and plans—closer to those traditionally held by young men of the same age group.

Among our students in courses on men and women at work and in society, we similarly find optimistic expectations. When students were asked to predict what their lives would be at age 40, a young woman said: "At age 40 I can see myself as a wife and mother and as a successful lawyer working in a well-established firm." Another predicted: "By the time I reach age 40, I hope to be at the peak of success. By success, I mean I have been able to happily integrate the career-marriage-family triad. As my career objectives, I am interested in going into either personnel administration or else becoming a management consultant." Among our students, these are not unrepresentative responses, and, moreover, they are consistent with reports from other campuses (see Katz, 1980; Leland, 1980).

In most recent years, especially, our female students report that they expect to have careers in professions and management and that they look forward to good pay, high status, and rapid advancement. Most assume that they will not only work, but also marry, and in doing so, combine home, employment, and children with little conflict or discord (see Hesse-Biber, 1983; Katz, 1980). In contrast, none of our students report that they expect at age 40 to be working as a secretary or clerk with low ceiling on pay and no chances for promotion. Few expect any difficulty in combining work and family demands.

Of course, these reports are from college students at good institutions, and, as such, they are likely to represent "high" aspirations. We would be surprised if our students predicted that they would be employed as retail clerks, secretaries and bookkeepers, or factory operatives. After all, if they are headed for such employment, why would they be in college? Who needs a college education for such jobs?

Many of our women students today intend to go on to graduate and professional school—where female enrollment has grown dramatically in the last decade. They accept the fact that they must work hard, and they assume that, in doing so, they will be rewarded with rank and earnings commensurate with their education, training, and ability. In short, they accept the American creed about equal opportunity, advancement, and reward for performance.

Yet, profoundly and painfully, the expectations of these students simply are not grounded in reality. And, in fact, they are countered by the reality of the labor force and its effects on women's employment possibilities and career options. The empirically verified fact is that while ability, training, and experience do produce "returns" of pay, power, and prestige in employment, they provide these payoffs at a much lower rate for women than for men. Beyond factors of performance, achievement, and credentials, labor-force locations and rewards are determined by gender, and in every occupational classification women get less. Even in areas such as social work, librarianship, and elementary education, which have long been considered women's domain, the higher ranking positions are held disproportionately by men, and at each rank, the women earn less. When women do enter the highest status occupations—law, medicine, and other professions—they are clustered in low ranking and low paying positions and in areas and fields with limited power and influence. Moreover, the sex segregation of occupations and the salary gap between the sexes show no signs of decline; in fact, the disparities have increased in the past decade.

Yet the myth continues that with their increasing labor-force participation, women are also gaining their share of labor-force rewards, and that with hard work and training women will obtain commensurate rank and location in employment. This book was prepared to combat such stereotypes about women and work and, more fundamentally, to overcome a neglect of the topic, especially in the college curricula.

The sociology of work literature has been based traditionally upon the occupational histories of men. Sociological studies of the work force have used the phrase "head of household" to refer exclusively to men, while women workers have been identified as "secondary earners" or "female head of household." The studies have overlooked women, or they included them only as marginal, secondary figures. At other times, working women are regarded as a "social problem"—with the researchers pondering the consequences of female employment for child care, the survival of the family, or the status of the economy.

Within the past few years, however, the study of gender has become a growing concern of students and scholars in the social sciences, and women's participation and position in the labor force is an acknowledged aspect of that study. With this "new scholarship," social science is beginning to be shaken out of oversight, and biased study, of women at work. Yet, while the literature on women and work has grown, there has been no single book available that analyzes for the student and scholar the broad range of knowledge on the subject. This volume is a response to that need.

In the work toward this book, we appreciate the help of a number of people who supported the endeavor. For their early encouragement and support of the project, we thank Larry Reynolds, Malkah Notman, and Lewis Kirshner. For their thoughtful reading and comments on the preliminary draft of the manuscript, we are grateful to Elizabeth M. Almquist of North Texas State University, Jeanne E. Gullahorn of Michigan State University, Barbara Melosh of the University of Wisconsin at Madison, and Elizabeth Ness Nelson of California State University at Fresno. At Mayfield Publishing, Judith Ziajka, Liz Currie, Frank Graham, and Pat Herbst worked skillfully and patiently toward production of the book, and their intelligence, deftness, and fortitude are greatly appreciated.

In addition, Mary Frank Fox thanks Sandra Baxter, Linda Grant, Judith Hammond, Jane Hood, and Ann Wood for careful reading and comments on chapters. Finally, for unfailing support, for colleagueship, and for the company of their academic standards and personal integrity, Mary Frank Fox extends deepest appreciation to Daniel J. Fox and to Catherine A. Faver.

Sharlene Hesse-Biber wishes to express her appreciation to Michael Peter Biber for his consistent and reliable intellectual and emotional support, and to her daughters Sarah Alexandra and Julia Ariel for their bountiful patience and grace. Special thanks are also due to all the day-care providers (Cheryl Albert Deyle, Debbie Banks, Shari Berkowitz, Ann Lade, Joanne Rice, Mrs. S. Asch, and the staff of the Yal-Day-New Day Care Center) who were instrumental in enabling her to combine work and family life.

Thanks also to the secretarial and administrative staff at Boston College (Lorraine Bone, Alice Close, Shirley Urban, and Sara White) for their help in typing many drafts of the manuscript, and to Ellen Kelly, Jane Annick, Patricia Gagnon, and Sue Kennearly, who provided important research assistance. Special thanks go to Gina Abeles for her intellectual contributions, emotional support, and editorial advice.

M.F.F.
S.H.-B.

Women
at
Work

1 ◆ Introduction: The Study of Work

The dramatic increase in the labor-force participation of women has been called the "single most outstanding phenomenon of our century" (Ginzberg, *New York Times*, September 12, 1976). Women's participation in the labor force affects every aspect of life, including child-rearing patterns, trends in fertility, marriage and divorce, patterns of marital power and decision making, and demand for supportive services in the economy. For this reason, it is said that the greatest changes of the twentieth century may result not from atomic energy, the conquest of space, or the depletion of resources—but rather from the tremendous increase in the proportion of women working outside the home (Rozen, 1979).

Looking over the past century, we find that less than 20 percent of all American women were in the labor force in 1890. That percentage grew very slowly until the outbreak of World War II, when large proportions of women went out to work, and it hit a wartime high of 38 percent in 1945. After the war, women's labor-force participation declined and did not start increasing again until the early 1950s. Then, in the 1960s and 1970s, female labor-force participation made sharp gains, and by the 1980s a clear majority of American women were working outside the home.

Yet women's labor-force participation, in itself, is hardly a cause for celebration. The vast proportion of women are working in a restricted number of jobs and in low-paying, low-prestige, and low-power positions. But, before analyzing those patterns, we need to understand the concepts of work and occupation.

THE CONCEPT AND MEANING OF WORK

Work is any activity, or expenditure of energy, that produces services and products of value to other people. An occupation is the particular work activity—and social role—that an adult assumes on a regular basis. Although work can certainly be performed without wages, salaries, or income, in the following section we refer primarily to labor-market work—or work that is performed for pay.

People work both because they "have to" and because they "want to" (Hall, 1975). In a market economy, we need money to obtain food, clothing, and other goods and services; and, for the most part, that money derives from the wages and salaries of labor-force work. Consequently, people work out of necessity. But beyond meeting economic needs, work also performs social functions and provides social and emotional rewards.

In modern society particularly, work is a source of personal identity. In preindustrial society, by contrast, family and locale operate as the primary sources of identity, and two strangers who meet identify themselves as belonging to a certain village and kinship network (Pavalko, 1971). But in industrial society, people introduce themselves by indicating the kind of work they do, and what one "does" becomes an important basis of who one "is." Thus, one's work and employment are an important part of the definition and evaluation of self.

Correspondingly, work and occupation are important bases of social evaluation, or of rank and standing in society. In America, work is an especially important determinant of social standing, because our ideology of opportunity gets interpreted as opportunity for choice, training, and advancement in occupation. With this emphasis, work and occupation are important determinants of the way one is regarded and evaluated, and occupation is a very good indicator of income level, place of residence, and style of consumption. Hence, whether sociologists approach stratification from a functional perspective stressing division of labor or from a Marxist position emphasizing relation to production, they tend to agree that work and occupation are "solid social facts that condition life chances" (Coleman and Rainwater, 1978:47).

In another of its functions, work also gives content and meaning to our lives. Carrying out work tasks provides a sense of accomplishment, or the intrinsic satisfaction of having successfully manipulated some part of the environment. Experimental psychology indicates that, even as infants, humans are motivated by mastery over environment (Kohlberg, 1966) and will carry on tasks for the sake of doing so, without external rewards (Vroom, 1964). Likewise, people stress that their work occupies them, gives them something to do, and provides purpose in life (Morse and Weiss, 1962; Veroff, Douvan, and Kulka, 1981).

Except for a few occupations such as night security guard or lighthouse keeper, work roles also put people into contact and association with others—customers, clients, and co-workers. Work, then, provides social satisfactions of interacting, influencing, and being appreciated by others. Consequently, friends and acquaintances often result from contacts made at work. And through such patterns of interaction and association, work links individuals with others outside of their private spheres (Pavalko, 1971). In this way, work roles help anchor individuals in the larger society and thus integrate community and society.

In addition, work and employment order and regulate our behavior and activities. Work claims a large proportion of our energy and, in doing so, orders the time available for both work and nonwork activities such as recreation and travel. The rhythm and demands of work—over the day, the week, months, and seasons—then determine our schedule not just on but also off the job (Slocum, 1966). This scheduling of time and energy provides structure and regularity for people's lives.

The various social and emotional functions of work become apparent when we observe the effects of unemployment and retirement. Even though adequate income may be provided by pension or insurance, loss of work still brings feelings of boredom, uselessness, and lowered esteem. As an indication of the centrality of work, 80 percent of a sampled group of employees reported that they would want to keep on working even if they inherited enough money to live comfortably (Morse and Weiss, 1962). And among male auto workers, who are supposed to be the group most alienated from their jobs, the majority still say that they would prefer to work at their jobs than to be guaranteed their present wages without working (Form, 1973).

Nonetheless, beyond certain satisfactions and rewards, work also generates tensions, conflicts, and dissatisfactions. For many, work is a daily confrontation with powerlessness and subordination, estrangement from both self and others, and detachment from both the process and products of their labor (Blauner, 1964; Mills, 1951; Rubin, 1976). In fact, throughout most of human history, leisure rather than work has been the valued and esteemed activity.[1]

To the ancient Greeks, for example, work was a curse imposed on humans because the gods hated them. Grecian thinkers regarded all labor with abhorrence, believing that work brutalized the mind and made it unfit for contemplation or virtue. As in most things, the Romans followed the Greeks. Cicero, the Roman orator, said that only two occupations—agriculture and business—were honorable pursuits. All others were vulgar undertakings to be relegated to slaves.

The Hebrews, likewise, regarded work as painful drudgery. But they differed from the Greeks and Romans in their belief that labor was a penance for the original sin committed in Paradise. As we might expect, the early

Christians shared the Hebrew view. However, they did attribute one positive function to work—as a means to charity or sharing with the needy.

These disdainful views of work persisted generally throughout the Middle Ages. With the Protestant Reformation, the value changed. By defining
work as a means of serving God, Luther's Protestant movement transformed
the value of work and endowed all labor—not just pious work inside the
walls of monasteries and convents—with spiritual meaning and dignity.
This change swept away the distinction between religious piety and worldly
activity, and work and occupation became a "calling" and a means toward
salvation. To these ideas, Calvinism added the doctrine of predestination:
that one's fate (salvation or damnation) is determined by God, not by one-
self. This creed then made a virtue of certain work characteristics such as
austerity, rationality, and discipline; by exercising these characteristics, one
could seek signs of God's ultimate favor.

MEN, WOMEN, AND WORK

Particular values and functions of work are specific to time and place,
and the meaning of work responds to variations in social structure. In contemporary society, the functions and motivations of work vary with particular jobs and settings. For example, holders of middle-class jobs, such
as civil servants and business managers, tend to react more markedly, either positively or negatively, to their current position than do holders of
working-class jobs, such as service workers. And in autonomous (independent and self-directed) occupations, such as farming and the professions,
people report that their work is particularly important (Kohn and Schooler,
1973; Morse and Weiss, 1962).

Still, by and large, people approach work with similar motives: the desire
for economic sustenance and social and emotional satisfaction. This is true
of both men and women. Contrary to popular lore, women do not work for
"extras" or for "a little something to do." Rather, economic need is an important motive. In fact, among women employed in 1978, the majority were
either heads of households themselves or were married to men who had incomes under $10,000 a year (U.S. Department of Labor, Bureau of Labor
Statistics, 1979).

However, although men and women have similar motivations for working, their status and location in the labor force are very different. Women
work at a limited number of jobs, at lower ranks, and with less pay, power,
and prestige than do men. Yet, in their rates of participation in the work
force, men and women are becoming increasingly alike, indicating that
labor-force work is becoming a fact of life for American women as it is for
men.[2]

Women have always made products and performed services within the home. But contemporary American society is a market- and capital-based economy, in which work is assessed in wages, output, and employment, and in which productivity is defined in terms of capital (money and wealth) created. Hence, labor outside the market is not recorded or regarded in the same way as paid labor. For example, in our economy, paid teaching is regarded as labor-market work, but volunteer teaching is not. And telephone canvassing to sell Avon products gets recorded as work, but volunteer phoning to sell UNICEF Christmas cards does not. Only partly in contrast, in developing countries the gross national product (GNP) does include some nonmarket activities such as hunting or handicraft production. But it never encompasses child care, meal preparation, food processing, or other work that is done exclusively by women. In fact, certain work such as water carrying is assigned economic value only if it is performed by men (Newland, 1980).

Consequently, some observers charge that the economic data reflect a sexist attitude regarding certain work (namely men's) as important, and other work (community and domestic, which is predominantly women's) as unimportant, of low status, and hence unworthy of record or analysis. Moreover, the invisibility of women's work has extended beyond house and community labor to the labor market as well. While we fully acknowledge the importance of nonmarket labor, in this book we focus on women's work in the labor force. We focus on labor-market work because women's employment has increased so dramatically that employment is becoming the "average experience" for women, as it has been for men. Furthermore, women's depressed status in the labor force is one of the most significant aspects of their subordination, and it is an area that can be pointed to, analyzed, and evaluated: "In the labor force, we find a microcosm of all the dimensions of sex-related inequality—in power, prestige, and wealth" (Fox, 1978:7). Yet until recently women's role in the labor force has been understudied and misanalyzed, so that little was known about the actual nature, structure, and functioning of women's labor-force work.

BIAS AND OVERSIGHT IN THE STUDY
OF WOMEN'S LABOR-FORCE WORK

To begin with, studies of work and society have been undertaken by men, who in the myopia of their own interests and perspectives have focused on the activities of their male group. Men have attended to, regarded as significant, and recorded that which is said, done, and thought by other men: "The circle of men whose writing and talk was significant to one another extends backwards in time as far as our records reach. What men were doing was relevant to men, was written by men, about men for men" (Smith, 1978:281).

Social scientists have omitted women from their studies in the same way that humans ignore the animal world around them in their descriptions of "life" (Epstein, 1974b). If female scholars were also overlooking the study of women, it may have been because such studies were unfashionable in mainstream social science, and female sociologists were warned that the study of women was not the route to professional success. Correspondingly, it was often difficult to get research on women funded or to interest Ph.D. supervisors in these topics (Epstein, 1974b).

As a result, a male bias has pervaded the methods, conceptual schemes, and theories of social science, so that the social reality described has been a "male universe" in which women are outsiders or deviants (see this argument in Hesse et al., 1979; Millman and Kanter, 1975; Smith, 1974; Snyder, 1979). Studies have centered on male groups, settings, and concerns; women have been "fuzzy, shadowy, background figures framing the male at the center stage" (Lofland, 1975 : 145). Lofland has pointed out that classic urban sociology is dominated by portrayals of a male world of "corner boys and college boys" (Whyte, 1955), black "streetcorner men" (Liebow, 1967), and men's social codes and communities (Whyte, 1943; Suttles, 1968).

When women were not ignored altogether, they have been regarded simply as the deviants or exceptions to the male case. Thus, in the sociology of work specifically, generalizations about sex differences in commitment and attachment to occupation have been biased by reliance on a male professional prototype, which is then misapplied to women at large (Hesselbart, 1980). Likewise, the vast sex differences reported in the literature on organizational and psychological experiences of business managers are distorted by comparison of women with the "successful male myth" (Harlan and Weiss, 1980).

Reliance on a male model—based on the idealized or, for that matter, the average male experience—results in the postulate that the work attitudes and behavior of men are "normal" and those of women are, by implication, "deviant" and "abnormal" (Acker, 1976, 1978). Hence, if women's work commitment, job continuity, and career aspirations are different from men's, these behaviors have been attributed to women's sex role and socialization for that role. With this focus on sex and socialization, social scientists have overlooked structural factors such as access to power, opportunity, and advancement, which explain the work behavior and attitudes of both males and females (Kanter, 1977a; Laws, 1976). In like manner, social scientists have regarded women's depressed position and status in work as an individual rather than an organizational problem, and the onus is placed on women's own styles and preferences, rather than on the disadvantaged jobs, settings, and institutions to which they have been restricted (see, for example, Hennig and Jardim, 1976, as discussed in Chapter 6, and the economic arguments discussed in Chapter 4).

Beyond the issue of blaming the victims or the institutions for women's depressed occupational position, a more fundamental bias and oversight has been social science's long-standing failure to even analyze the issue of sex stratification, or the inequalities in men's and women's social and economic rankings (see Acker, 1973). If women's income or prestige were, indeed, equivalent to that of men with the same social background, sexual inequality would ñot be distinct from social stratification in general, and sex stratification might then be overlooked. But even when women's social background (race, religion, ethnicity) and work background (education, experience) are comparable to men's, their rewards are not (Fox, 1978:2–3). For example, considerable discrepancies remain in the wages of men compared to women, even after controlling for their qualifications and abilities and for their types of work and occupation (Treiman and Roos, 1980; Treiman and Terrell, 1975; U.S. Department of Labor, Bureau of Labor Statistics, 1979). These data suggest, then, that rewards are determined partly by sex itself and that men and women occupy different structural positions in the socioeconomic system.

Yet until recently the inequalities pertaining to women in particular were overlooked, and the issue of stratification by sex was sidestepped. This oversight is rooted in a traditional theoretical perspective on men, women, and the family.[3] Fundamental to this perspective is a model of the family as one "equivalent unit," with the status of all family members, including adult women, determined by the social and economic position of the male "head of household." In a classic formulation of this perspective, Talcott Parsons states,

> The most fundamental basis of the family's status is the occupational status of the husband and father. The woman's fundamental status is that of her husband's wife, the mother of his children, and traditionally the person responsible for a complex of activities in the management of household, care of children, etc. (Parsons, 1942)

Because women are regarded as daughters, wives, and mothers without independent social status, any position they hold in the labor force becomes inconsequential and superfluous in the study of work and society. And for those women working within the home, there has been no attempt to measure their social or economic rank and position as housewives (Eichler, 1980).

This practice and perspective of assigning the husband's status to his wife and children have been defended and justified as a source of "solidarity" and "stability" for the family. Shared status is said to reduce competition and jealousy and to increase the clarity of roles for family members, especially for the spouses. Likewise, traditional sex roles are thought to be efficient and complementary divisions for carrying out different kinds of activities: Men perform a task-oriented, public and visible role; women, a socioemotional, private, and invisible role. Correspondingly, the activities of men are prominent and emphasized; women's activities are secondary and auxiliary.

These divisions have been offered not simply as a social description, but rather as a prescription for the way in which the sexes *ought* to behave (Snyder, 1979). Because wife and mother are the prescribed female roles, activities other than domestic ones are viewed as potential causes of stress and conflict for women. Studies in this tradition have regarded female employment as a social "problem" that creates role strain for women and detrimental consequences for their homes and families. These studies reinforce the notions of women and the family as internal units and of men and the economy as external units. In fact, the classic statement of the perspective (Parsons and Bales, 1955) offers these divisions as a universal social pattern.

Studies in this theoretical perspective have given us an incomplete and distorted view of social reality. By separating male and female sex-role divisions into artificial categories, they overlook the instrumental (task-oriented) and expressive (socioemotional) functions of both family and economy. Furthermore, the assumptions run counter to the actual experience of the American family.

The patriarchal model of full-time working husband and full-time homemaking wife represents a minority experience. In 1979, over half of all wives, and almost half of all married women with children, were employed. Active labor-force roles are, then, a fact of life for the majority of American women. Furthermore, in the home women perform major instrumental roles as representatives of the family to outside institutions, including church, school, and retail businesses (Hesselbart, 1980). In contrast, except for economic support, men's family roles tend to center not on instrumental but rather on expressive functions such as recreation and playing with (rather than caring for) children (Hesselbart, 1980). In addition, survey data indicate that, for men, the family rather than work ranks as the greatest source of satisfaction (Hesselbart, 1978, 1980). These findings do not suggest egalitarian sex and family roles: Women continue, for example, to bear the burden of housework even when they are employed, and the routine care of children almost invariably falls on wives. Still, family roles are much less insulated and differentiated than the functionalist model indicates.

Furthermore, along with structure, family functions are also changing, so that the female reproductive role implicit in the functionalist perspective is no longer so predominant among American women. In the 1970s, the birthrate reached all-time lows of 14.8 births per 1,000 people, or an average of 1.9 children per family. The rates of childlessness have also increased, so that over 14 percent of all women with at least one year's college education claim that they never expect to bear children (Moore and Hofferth, 1979).

With these changes, the competition presumed to result from the independent status of family members is a questionable assumption. In fact, it has been argued recently that women's employment makes a positive, not competitive, contribution to the family's position (Oppenheimer, 1977). And with high rates of inflation, households with only one employed worker are increasingly disadvantaged, economically. Such factors have finally begun to shake social science out of its traditional biases, and after years of oversight women's labor-force work is gaining due research attention.

A STUDY OF WOMEN AT WORK: AIMS, OBJECTIVES, AND PERSPECTIVE

With the growing research and writing on the topic of women and work, interested students, teachers, and scholars are now confronted with the difficult task of sorting through a barrage of literature from a variety of sources and approaches. In spite of the proliferation of literature on women and work, there is no one book that draws together and analyzes this growing body of knowledge for the student and scholar. This volume is a response to the need for such a book. Correspondingly, our aim is to provide an overview of the most important dimensions regarding American women at work. To fulfill this aim, our task is threefold: (1) to provide an analysis of the central employment patterns of American women—their participation, location, and rewards; (2) to explain women's pattern of high participation but low status in the work force; and (3) to identify the constraints on women's working lives and suggest ways in which these constraints might be resolved.

In order to understand the female pattern of high employment participation but low status, we employ an interinstitutional and a structural perspective. From the interinstitutional perspective, work does not exist in a vacuum, and employment is not an isolated segment of women's lives. Rather, women's status and experience at work reflect and connect with their position and plight in other organizations, institutions, and settings. Thus, we maintain that, to understand women's position in the labor force, one needs to look at the linkages between work and society's other institutions—the family, the schools, and the government, as well as the economic system.

In this way, we observe that women's family demands place onerous burdens so that employed women have dual—home and market—work roles. The domestic responsibilities, and their drain on women's time and resources, can make women less competitive at work, especially in jobs that demand heavy commitment and single-minded pursuit. Reciprocally, women's limited opportunities on the job restrict their aspirations for promotion and advancement and hence, by default, increase their investment at home.

Similarly, various arrangements and processes of the educational system—including the imagery of texts and books, the schools' structure of power and authority, and the tracking of male and female students—influence the occupational destinies of men and women. As we shall see, they do so indirectly by restricting patterns of achievement, aspiration, and esteem, and more directly by limiting access to education and training.

The female occupational position also reflects both (1) economic arrangements that discriminate against women and (2) a legal and political structure that tolerates and often encourages discrimination. Thus, we must understand the employment practices discriminating against women, the nine-to-five schedule and its consequences for female occupational position, and modern industry's promotion of and profit from a cheap, temporary—but skilled and educated—female labor force. Along with these economic factors, we examine also the legal system's reluctance to combat sex discrimination, and its slowness to pass equal employment laws and to enforce affirmative-action statutes.

Thus, with our interinstitutional perspective, we focus on the ways in which various social arrangements and processes—in family, education, government, and economy—operate together to explain women's plight and position in the labor force. Likewise, in proposing strategies for improvement in women's labor-force position, we stress that improvement will involve alterations in the behavior and operations of each of society's basic institutions—its family, schools and colleges, employers, laws and legal institutions. Moreover, we emphasize that there is no single institution on which women and men can exert pressure and expect the others to follow suit. It does little good, for example, to increase access to education if discriminatory employment practices continue to operate. Likewise, it does little good to develop affirmative-action plans for employment if the legal system fails to monitor and enforce equity for the sexes. And each of these changes is worth little if women continue to be burdened by the demands of a traditional family structure, which assumes the presence of a full-time working husband and a full-time homemaking wife.

Our perspective is also that of feminist social scientists. This means that, first, we are critical of social structures as they disadvantage women. Furthermore, we are alert to the ways in which social science has ignored women and has biased and distorted women's role in work and society. This concern about sexism in social science is not simply a consideration for those interested in feminism or women's studies (see Morgan, 1981). Rather, a concern about bias in social science and concern about the inclusion of women in the study of work and society is a "scholarly requisite" for all those who seek knowledge about, and explanation of, the world about them.

Finally, as feminist social scientists, we are vigilant in looking beyond sex as a causal variable, and look, instead, to social structure as it explains men's and women's status in work and society. This does not mean that we overlook individual characteristics of women—their motivations, aspirations, and orientations, or their credentials, qualifications, and abilities. In the chapter on socialization (Chapter 3), specifically, we examine in some detail patterns of women's development, aspirations, and esteem as they are acquired in family and schools and as they help account for women's eventual location in traditional, female sex-typed jobs. We maintain, however, that to fully understand women's status in the labor force we must look beyond the individual characteristics of the gender group and examine certain structural and organizational factors—the characteristics of the settings in which women work, the jobs they hold, and the particular tasks they perform, among other factors in family and education as well as in employment and economy.

Thus, in our analysis of blue-collar work (Chapter 5), we look beyond individual motivations and preferences to structural factors, such as trade-union and industrial organization, in order to understand women's absence from skilled trades and their presence, disproportionately, in unskilled and service work. Likewise, in our analysis of women in the professions and management (Chapter 6), we maintain that women are constrained not simply by their own attitudes and aspirations, or even by their credentials and achievements, but rather by certain employment practices, organizational patterns, and networks of interaction, support, and communication from which they are excluded.

To put it another way, we maintain that, even if women assumed "male" attitudes, aspirations, and behaviors, they would still be encumbered by biased practices in recruitment, hiring, and promotion, by exclusionary patterns of informal interaction in work and occupation, and by social arrangements and processes of the other, nonemployment institutions (family, education, polity). Strategies that emphasize alterations in attitudes and behavior of individual women—their conceptions of work, their patterns of commitment, styles of interaction, or levels of assertiveness—may be of some use. But these individual-level alterations will effect little basic change in women's labor-force position unless we eradicate the external barriers that have restricted women's opportunities for performance in promising positions, settings, and organizations. Thus, in the chapters ahead (and in Chapters 4, 6, and 8 especially), we examine the limitations of the "individual-level" model and the greater possibilities of the "structural" model for understanding and explaining as well as improving women's status in the labor force.

CHAPTER PLAN

In the next chapter of this book, we document and discuss the historical and contemporary employment patterns of women—their participation, location, and rewards. In the two chapters that follow, we put the interinstitutional perspective to work and analyze the particular social processes and arrangements in family and educational systems (Chapter 3), and in economic, political, and legal institutions (Chapter 4), as they help to explain the labor-force position of women.

Having analyzed and explained these general patterns, we turn to detailed analyses of women in particular occupations and situations. Chapter 5 focuses on women in clerical, sales, pink- and blue-collar work; Chapter 6, on women in professional and managerial work. In both of these chapters, we analyze the labor-force status of the women, provide explanations for their occupational position and plight, and propose certain strategies for relieving institutional and organizational constraints and improving their occupational status. Chapter 7 then analyzes the particular problems and position of minority women—the dual burdens of racism and sexism that beset these women and the myths that prevail about their status in work and society.

The last chapters focus on strategies to lift institutional constraints and improve women's status at work. Chapter 8 analyzes the particular conflicts of work and family and proposes ways to reduce these strains. Chapter 9 reviews and summarizes the ways in which the four major institutions—family, education, economy, and polity—disadvantage women in the labor force, and we propose specific ways in which each of the institutions can alter to improve women's opportunities in work and society. The earlier chapters offer strategies for improving women's employment status in particular occupations and situations; the final chapter points to strategies to redress the disadvantaged status of women both within and between occupational classifications.

2 • Women in the Work Force: Past and Present

We are only beginning to understand the determinants and consequences of women's entrance into the work force. For decades, women were "invisible" workers whose labor and skills were considered insignificant compared to those of men. The traditional social-science approach has perpetuated this illusion by treating the topic of labor-force participation as though it involved only men, as we discussed in Chapter 1. Furthermore, as late as the 1960s and even into the early 1970s, most people disapproved of women working outside the home (Axelson, 1963; Oppenheimer, 1970). These attitudes are changing, however. In a recent nationwide poll, men and women were asked what kind of lifestyle would give them the most satisfaction and interest. A majority of women chose a married life with husband and wife sharing responsibilities—both working and sharing homemaking and child-care responsibilities. Nearly half the men also chose this lifestyle (Roper, 1980). And the majority of American women (51 percent in 1980) are now working in the labor force (see Figure 2.1).

In order to understand women's current participation and status in the labor force, one must look to social, economic, and demographic factors that have shaped women's labor-force patterns throughout history. Social upheavals such as war, economic depression, and technological revolution have had a profound impact (Chafe, 1977; Greenwald, 1980; Anderson, 1981).

The advantage of a historical overview is that it lets "us know where we

F i g u r e   2 . 1 / *Percentage of Women in the Paid Labor Force, 1890–1980*

Note: Pre-1945 data include women 14 years of age and over; other years include women 16 years of age and over.

SOURCE: Prepared from data in U.S. Department of Labor, Bureau of Labor Statistics, *Women in the Labor Force: Some New Data Series* (Washington, D.C.: U.S. Government Printing Office, 1979), p. 1; and U.S. Department of Labor, Bureau of Labor Statistics, *Perspectives on Working Women: A Databook*, Bulletin 2080 (Washington, D.C.: U.S. Government Printing Office, October 1980), p. 8.

have been, so that we will know where we are going" (Cott and Pleck, 1979:9). Yet until recently there has been little historical research on women workers, or on women in general. Historians have tended to limit the scope of women's history to three types of research: (1) institutional histories of women's organizations and movements; (2) biographies of important suffragists and "token women" (first ladies, isolated nineteenth-century professional women); and (3) "prescriptive history," or discussions of class or societal ideals rather than actual cultural practices; for example, content analyses of child-rearing practices found in books or magazines (Gordon, Buhle, and Schrom, 1971). In general, there have been few studies on what women have done as workers—either inside or outside their homes. In recent decades, however, women have become the subject of wider historical interest (see, for example, Baker, 1964; Smuts, 1971; Baxandall, Gordon, and Reverby, 1976; Wertheimer, 1977; Cott and Pleck, 1979; Hesse, 1979; Scott and Tilly, 1980; Anderson, 1981).

We now know enough about the past that we can begin to identify the contributions of women workers. We now know better who they are, why they work, in which occupations and industries they work, and what problems they have encountered. A historical overview enriches our understanding of the interplay of social, economic, and political factors that have influenced and shaped women's relationship to the paid labor force throughout this country's development. Knowing more about "where women have been" helps us understand "where women are" now and "where they are going" in the future. The analysis in this chapter focuses on the white woman worker. The institution of slavery in the southern colonies created conditions for black women that were so distinct from those for white women that we focus on the black women's experience in a separate chapter, along with the experiences of other minority women.

WOMEN WORKERS: PREINDUSTRIAL AMERICA

In the preindustrial economy of the American colonial period, work was closely identified with home and family life; the family was the primary economic unit, and family members were dependent on one another for basic sustenance. Men performed the agricultural work, while women's work was done chiefly in the home, where the women manufactured nearly all articles used in daily life. The American colonial home was a center of production. In addition to cooking, cleaning, and caring for children, women engaged in such work as spinning and weaving, making lace, soap, candles, and shoes (Flexner, 1959). Women's work was highly valued, and the colonies relied on the production of these "cottage industries."

Although most colonial women worked primarily in the home, some also worked outside the home—as innkeepers, shopkeepers, crafts workers, nurses, printers, teachers, and landholders (Dexter, 1924). In the city of Boston during 1690, for example, approximately 40 percent of all taverns were run by women. During that year city officials also granted more than thirty women the right to saw lumber and manufacture potash (Chafe, 1977:19). Women acted as physicians and midwives in all the early settlements, producing medicines, salves, and ointments. Many of the women who worked outside their homes were widows with dependent children, who took their husbands' places in family enterprises. Colonial women engaged in a great range of occupations, and as old documents are discovered and new histories of women's work are written, that range appears greater still. It seems that at one time or another, colonial women engaged in many of the occupations practiced by men (Leonard, Drinker, and Holden, 1962).

The foregoing account of life in the colonies is interpreted by some historians to mean that the colonial period was a "golden age of equality" for women, by pointing out, as we have noted, that women occupied "mas-

culine fields": they were merchants, tavern owners, and shopkeepers. However, this view is not without historical controversy. Other historians argue
for an alternative interpetation. They argue that these jobs were the "exceptions to a rule which excluded women from any common activities with
men" (Matthaei, 1982:29). Furthermore, "they claim Colonial times were
characterized by a strict and simple division of labor between men and
women which assigned them to fields and house, or to the public and private
spheres, respectively" (Matthaei, 1982:29; see also Abbott, 1910; Smuts,
1971).

Some historians also claim that this range of activity for women did not
imply, however, a disappearance of the dominant ideology: that a woman's
place was at home, raising children. Although the daily activities of most
women's lives may appear to indicate otherwise, people also held idealized
beliefs about the appropriate social roles for the sexes (Chafe, 1977:20).
Norton's (1980) research on 450 eighteenth-century families indicates that
people held "very definite ideas of which tasks were properly 'feminine' and
which were not, and of what functions 'the sex' was expected to perform.
Moreover, both men and women continually indicated by subtle forms that
they believed women to be inferior to men" (Norton, 1980:xiv). Let us
comment, however, that some indications of women's inferior position were
anything but subtle. Wife-beating, for example, was a fairly common and
socially sanctioned husband's right or a way to maintain discipline.

The traditional norms might not have precluded the day-to-day sharing
of labor between the sexes, but they did dictate the forms that official recognition would take on ritual occasions. For example, Ann Catherine Green,
an eighteenth-century citizen of Maryland,

> married and bore fourteen children, eight of whom died before maturity. When
> her husband died also, she took over his printing business, assuming responsi-
> bility as editor of the Maryland Gazette and official printer of the colony. For
> eight years she carried on the business, performing the same work and receiving
> the same payment from the government as had her husband. Yet upon her
> death, the obituary read: "she was of a mild and benevolent disposition, and
> for conjugal affection and parental tenderness, an example of her sex." (Chafe,
> 1977:21)

A sharp disparity existed between the reality of women's lives and the cultural myths that defined women primarily in terms of biological and nurturing roles.

INDUSTRIALIZATION AND
WOMEN'S WORK

The transformation of society from an agrarian rural economy to an urban industrial society ushered in a new era in roles and definitions of wom-

en's work. With the advent of industrialization, many of the products women made at home—cloth, shoes, candles—gradually moved out of the home and into the factory. At first, women still performed the work at home. Merchants would contract for work to be done, supplying women with the raw materials that were made into finished articles. The most common of these manufacturing trades for women was sewing for the newly emerging clothing industry. Since women had always sewn for their families, this work was considered an extension of women's traditional role, and therefore a respectable activity.

As the demand for goods increased, however, home production declined and gave way to the factory system, which was more efficient in meeting emerging needs (although sweatshops have continued to survive, especially in the garment industry). The rise of factory production truly separated the home from the work place. With the decline of the household unit as the center of industrial and economic activity, the importance of women's economic role also declined. Although women continued to perform important tasks inside and outside their homes, male and female spheres of activity became more separated, as did the definition of men's and women's roles. Man's role continued to be primarily that of worker and provider; woman's role became primarily supportive. She was to maintain a smooth and orderly household, to be cheerful and warm, and to thus provide the husband with the support and services he needed to continue his work life (Kessler-Harris, 1981:35). Biological and social arguments often justified women's exclusion from the labor force. (The biological perspective is discussed in Chapter 3.) Women were seen as too weak and delicate to participate in the rough work world of men. It was believed that women lacked strength and stamina, that their brains were small, that the feminine perspective and sensitivity were liabilities in the marketplace. Such arguments rationalized the roles of homemaker and mother that people accepted as the industrial revolution spread across the country (Kessler-Harris, 1981:14).

The Entrance of Women into the Work Force

Women were not entirely excluded from participation in the industrialization process, however. Because men were primarily occupied with agricultural work and were unavailable or unwilling to enter the early factories, male laborers were in short supply. American industry depended, then, on a steady supply of women workers. Yet how could society tolerate women's working in the factories, given the dominant ideology of the times, which dictated that a woman's place was at home? Single white women provided the answer. Their employment was viewed as a fulfillment of their family responsibilities—their work outside the home was an interlude before marriage and family life. *Interval*

The employment of single women in the early Lowell (Massachusetts)

mills is a prime example of the reconciliation of ideology with the needs of industry. Francis Cabot Lowell devised a route to respectability through employment for young single women. Recruiting the daughters of farm families to work in his mill, which opened in 1821 in Lowell, he provided supervised boardinghouses, salaries sufficient to allow the young women to offer financial aid to their families or to save for their own trousseaux, and assurances to their families that the hard work and discipline of the mill would help prepare them for marriage and motherhood (Kessler-Harris, 1975).

While single white women of established early immigrations and both single and married women of later immigrations played a crucial role in the development of the textile industry, the first important manufacturing industry in America, women also found employment in many other occupations during the process of industrialization. As railroads and other business enterprises expanded and consolidated, women's work began to encompass these industries as well. In fact, the U.S. Labor Commissioner, C. D. Wright, reported that by 1890 only 9 out of 360 general groups to which the country's industries had been assigned did not employ women (Baker, 1964).

By 1900, more than five million, or about one in every five, of the female population 10 years old and over had become a paid employee (Baker, 1964). The largest proportion (40 percent) remained close to home in domestic and personal service, but domestic service was on the decline for white working-class women at the turn of the century. About 25 percent (1.3 million) of employed women worked in the manufacturing industries: in cotton mills, in the manufacture of woolen and worsted goods, silk goods, hosiery, and knit wear. The third largest group of employed women (over 18 percent) were working on farms. Women in the trade and transportation industries (about 10 percent) worked as saleswomen, telegraph and telephone operators, stenographers, clerks, copyists, accountants, and bookkeepers. Women in the professions (about 9 percent) were employed primarily in elementary and secondary teaching. The fastest growing of these occupational groups were manufacturing, trade, and transportation. In the last thirty years of the nineteenth century, the number of women working in trade and transportation rose from 19,000 to over 0.5 million (Baker, 1964).

Class Divisions and the Working Woman

By the late 1830s, immigration began to supply a strongly competitive permanent work force willing to be employed for low wages in the factories, under increasingly mechanized and hazardous conditions. By the late 1850s most of the better-educated single native-born women had left the mills, leaving newly immigrated women and men to fill these positions. Black women, on the other hand, were denied entrance to the factories and faced discriminatory hiring practices that closed off opportunities in the newly expanded office and sales jobs. Many of these black women entered domestic service, which offered one of the few alternative means of employment. (The labor-force trends and patterns of black and other minority women are discussed in Chapter 7.)

What of the majority of upper- and middle-class women? Most of the better-educated women had left the mills to marry, to become teachers, or to obtain employment in white-collar occupations. By the turn of the century, a sharp break occurred between working-class women and women of the middle and upper classes. During this time, social-class distinctions were beginning to become more prominent in American society, and traditional role expectations were defined more sharply along racial and class lines. Increasing affluence among the population as a whole—as a result of the industrial revolution and steady supply of immigrant labor—lessened the influx of single native-born white women workers into industry.

As families began to achieve some social and economic status, employment opportunities for their daughters diminished. Young women could not be allowed to degrade the family by working at unskilled jobs in factory conditions or by associating with the immigrant laborers who were employed there. Since there were few other opportunities for paid employment, the middle- and upper-class prejudice against women working was reinforced (Smuts, 1971:4).

The Cult of True Womanhood

The industrial revolution created a set of social and economic conditions in which the basic lifestyle of white middle-class women more nearly approached society's expectations concerning woman's role. More and more middle-class women could now aspire to that position formerly reserved for the upper classes—the status of "lady" (Chafe, 1977). The nineteenth-century concept of a lady was that of a fragile, idle, pure creature, submissive and subservient to her husband and to domestic needs. Her worth was based on her decorative value, a quality that embraced her beauty, her character, and her temperament. She was certainly not a paid employee. This ideal—later referred to as the "cult of true womanhood" because of its rigid, almost religious standards—demanded uncompromising virtue and compliance to its image (Gordon et al., 1971:28).

Despite this cult, some middle-class women were active in the feminist movement and were involved in social reform, volunteer activities, and employment outside the home in professions such as teaching or nursing. The typical professional woman was young, educated, and single, of native-born parentage. By the mid-nineteenth and early twentieth centuries, nursing and teaching at the primary and secondary levels drew the majority of educated working women. Other professions—law, medicine, business, college teaching—did not employ large numbers of people and tended to exclude women. Women who engaged in trade and transportation were young, single native-born Americans; immigrants and minority women were excluded from these white-collar positions (Smuts, 1971).

Few married women (with the exception of black women) worked away from their homes during this time. They continued to be heavily involved in childbearing and child rearing and in the heavy responsibility for the domestic work within the family unit. Even fewer middle-class wives worked; those who did work were divorced, widowed, or supporting disabled or unemployed husbands (Pleck, 1979:367). Among many immigrant groups, cultural traditions of male authority effectively prohibited married women from working, even when the husband was unemployed and the family's economic situation was precarious (see Yans-McLaughlin's 1977 study of Italian immigrant families in Buffalo from 1890 to 1900). However, the demand for female labor was not great during this period, and a large proportion of women were mothers of young children (Tilly, 1974). The occupations available to women were easily filled by single women.

Working Conditions During
Early Industrialization

In the early industrial era, working conditions were arduous and hours were long. Working-class women were increasingly devalued by their continued participation in activities men had taken over (such as factory work) because these activities were regarded as lacking in the Victorian virtue and purity intrinsic to the "cult of womanhood." Male working-class immigrants whose wages rose sufficiently saw their wives withdraw from the marketplace "to pursue the goal, often elusive, of equipping their children to join the middle class" (Brownlee and Brownlee, 1976:31).

Although at least some working-class men were becoming successes in large enterprises and the professions, working-class women were limited to low-paying jobs and unskilled jobs that carried little if any promise of advancement. The single white woman worker was not fully integrated into the work force, either. The young single woman who was employed was assumed to be working only temporarily—until she married. Women who complained of low wages were often asked "but haven't you a male friend that helps support you?" (Baker, 1964). Older single women workers were considered "spinsters"—women who had been unsuccessful in getting a husband and who had substituted work for family life (Grossman, 1975).

In addition, sexual harassment was a growing "occupational hazard" affecting women in almost every occupation (Bularzik, 1978). In 1908, *Harper's Bazaar* printed a series of letters in which working women wrote of these difficulties. The following letter from a woman seeking a job as a stenographer describes such an experience:

I purchased several papers, and plodded faithfully through their multitude of "ads." I took the addresses of some I intended to call upon. . . . The first "ad" I answered the second day was that of a doctor who desired a stenographer at once, good wages paid. It sounded rather well, I thought, and felt that this time I would meet a gentleman. The doctor was very kind and seemed to like my appearance and references; as to salary, he offered me $15 a week, with a speedy prospect of more. As I was leaving his office, feeling that at last I was launched safely upon the road to a good living, he said casually, "I have an auto; and as my wife doesn't care for that sort of thing, I shall expect you to accompany me frequently on pleasure trips." That settled the doctor; I never appeared. After that experience I was ill for two weeks. (*Harper's Bazaar*, 1908, quoted in Bularzik, 1978:25)

Women's working conditions were also aggravated by women's exclusion from the organized labor movements of the day, which were steadily improving conditions for men. For the first half of the nineteenth century, unions—which were primarily for craft and skilled workers—did not accept female members (Wertheimer, 1977:341). By 1920, only 7 percent of women workers belonged to trade unions, compared with 25 percent of male workers (Baxandall et al., 1976:255). In a number of industries, women formed their own unions, but these affected only a small minority of employed women. The Working Girl's Societies, the Women's Trade Union League, and other such groups tried to little avail to change the widely held beliefs that women were temporary workers whose motivation was to earn pocket money, or who, if they had other goals, were selfish creatures ignoring family responsibilities. Such attitudes have persisted well into the twentieth century and still persist (Gordon et al., 1971:43).

By the turn of the century, the labor market had become clearly divided according to gender and class. Fewer manufacturing jobs were being defined as suitable for women, especially with the rising dominance of heavy industry—employment for which female workers were considered too delicate. White women's occupations shifted from primarily domestic service (which became increasingly identified as "black women's work"; see Katzman, 1978) and from light manufacturing to the rapidly growing opportunities in office and sales work. These jobs were also considered more appropriate to feminine roles as defined by the "cult of true womanhood" (Brownlee and Brownlee, 1976). Black women did not share in this occupational transformation, as we will see in Chapter 7.

WORLD WAR I AND THE DEPRESSION

World War I accelerated the entry of women into new fields of industry. The pressure of war production and the shortage of male industrial workers

F i g u r e   2 . 2 / *Increase and Decrease in the Number of Women Employed in the Principal Nonagricultural Occupations, 1910–1920*

SOURCE: Adapted from Joseph A. Hill, *Women in Gainful Occupations, 1870–1920* U.S. Department of Commerce, Bureau of the Census, Census Monograph no. 9 (Washington, D.C.: U.S. Government Printing Office, 1929), p. 34.

necessitated the introduction of women into what had been male-dominated occupations. Women replaced men at jobs in factories and business offices, and in general, they kept the nation working, fed, and clothed (Havener, 1940:394). For the most part, the wartime work-force pattern represented a reshuffling of the existing female work force (see Figure 2.2), rather than an increase in the numbers of women employed (Greenwald, 1980:13). Al-

Instead of change in numbers of women work force change in the types of work

though the popular myth is that homemakers abandoned their kitchens for the toolroom or airplane hangar (Greenwald, 1980:12), only about 5 percent of women workers were *new* to the labor force during the war years (Chafe, 1972:52).

The wartime labor shortage *did* create new job opportunities for woman workers, and at higher wages than they had previously earned. (This was not necessarily the case for black women, however. Although the range of job opportunities did increase for black women, that range was limited to the least desirable occupations, which had already been rejected by white women.) Figure 2.2 shows that there was a significant decrease in the number of white women employed in domestic occupations (cleaners, laundresses, dressmakers, seamstresses, and servants) and a sharp increase in the number of female office workers, laborers in manufacturing, saleswomen in stores, schoolteachers, telephone operators, trained nurses, and waitresses. (Obviously, the women who were no longer employed as domestics did not become the secretaries.) The mechanization and routinization of industry during this period enabled women to quickly master the various new skills in a short period of time (Greenwald, 1980:13).

World War I produced no substantial or lasting change in women's participation in the labor force. The employment rate of women in 1920 was actually a bit lower (20.4 percent) than in 1910 (20.9 percent). The labor unions, the government, and the society at large were not ready to accept a permanent shift in women's economic role. Instead, women filled an urgent need during the wartime years and were relegated to their former positions as soon as peace returned. As the reformer Mary Von Kleeck wrote, "When the immediate dangers . . . were passed, the prejudices came to life once more" (Chafe, 1972:54).

When the men returned from the war, they were given priority in hiring, and although a number of women left the labor force voluntarily, many were forced out by layoffs. Those women who did not leave the labor force remained employed in the low-paying, unskilled positions they had always occupied and in those occupations that had become accepted as women's domain. For example, although during the war some women had worked in nontraditional occupations (such as machinists) in the railroads, after the war the railroads employed women only as typists, card punchers, accountants, receptionists, and file clerks. Women also continued to be employed in railroad yards, shops, and offices as janitresses and laundresses and railroad matrons (Greenwald, 1980:13–137). Many women resented having been encouraged to enter a nontraditional occupation only to be fired at the war's end. One woman wrote to the director general of the railroad administration in hopes of restoring such jobs (she had been employed as a laborer in a machine shop during the war):

We are women that needed the work very much one woman gave her only support to the army one has her aged Father another has a small son and I support
my disabled Sister. . . . We never took a soldier's place, a soldier would not do
the work we did . . . such as sweeping, picking up waste and paper and hauling
steel shavings. . . . We are . . . respectable but poor women and were liked and
respected by all who knew us. . . . Womens work is so very hard to find that
time of year and expences are so high with Liberty bonds and insurance to pay
and home expenses it is hard to get by. We like our job very much and I hope
you will do for us whatever you can and place us back at the shop. (quoted in
Greenwald, 1980:135)

After the 1920s, most female workers continued to be poorly paid, and
most continued to be confined to occupations that were defined as "wom-
en's work." The common image of women workers, even in business and
the professions, was still that they were "temporary" employees (Chafe,
1972:65).

The Great Depression of the 1930s that followed threw millions out of
work. The severe employment problems during this period intensified the
general attitude that a woman with a job was taking that job away from a
male breadwinner (Smuts, 1971). Yet during the 1930s an increasing number of women went to work for the first time. The increase was most marked
among younger married women, who worked at least until the first child,
and among older married women, who reentered the marketplace because
of dire economic need or in response to changing patterns of consumer demand (Scharf, 1980:158). Most jobs held by women were part-time, seasonal, and marginal. Women's labor-force participation increased slowly
throughout this period and into the early 1940s (see Figure 2.1), except in
the professions, including feminized professions such as elementary teaching, nursing, librarianship, and social work (Scharf, 1980:86). The proportion of women in all professions declined from 14.2 percent to 12.3 percent
during the Depression decade (Scharf, 1980:86).[1]

WORLD WAR II

The ordeal of World War II disrupted traditional roles for everyone and
produced a tremendous change in the numbers and occupational distribution of working women. The mounting pressures of war production and
the shortage of male workers who had gone off to fight the war brought
women into the work force and influenced a corresponding shift in attitudes
about women's aptitudes and proper roles (Trey, 1972:40). Women entered
the munitions factories and other heavy industries to support the war effort.
The War Manpower Commission instituted a massive advertising campaign
to attract women to the war industries. Patriotic appeals were common:

Women, let it be understood, have a double stake in the winning of this war. Citizens of the United States of America, and partners in the United Nations, they are in and a part of the common struggle to crush Fascism—the acknowledged Number One foe of the progress of women. No women are supernumerary. All must fight with their fathers, their husbands, their brothers, their sweethearts, to make certain that never again will dictators and aggressors such as Hitler, Mussolini, and Hirohito have the freedom to rise and persecute and enslave and murder first their own people, and then peoples of other nations. The essence of Fascism is bullying individuals and whole races of people—and women and men alike must destroy this monstrous organism of fear and cruelty once and for all. (Anthony, 1943:3)

During World War II, women had access to skilled, higher-paying industrial jobs. Many women in industrial positions had worked before, but only at lower-paying unskilled service jobs. Women now became switchmen, precision-tool makers, overhead-crane operators, lumberjacks, drill-press operators, and stevedores (Baxandall et al., 1976). Women in these jobs had to "toughen up." Augusta Clawson, a federal employee working in an Oregon shipyard, described her job as a welder:

And it isn't only your muscles that must harden. It's your nerve too. I admit quite frankly that I was scared pink when I had to climb on top deck today. It's as if you had to climb from the edge of a fifth story to the sixth of a house whose outside walls have not been put on. Even the scaffolding around the side is not very reassuring, for there are gaps between, where you are sure you'll fall through. The men know their muscles are strong enough to pull them up if they get a firm grip on a bar above. But we women do not yet trust our strength, and some of us do not like heights. But one does what one has to. And it's surprising what one can do when it's necessary. (Clawson, 1975:134)

Equal work did not mean equal pay for the women in these varied wartime occupations. Some readers may see in the Augusta Clawson quote something that they believe to be evidence against the equal-pay-for-equal-work argument; that is, her remarks about the difficulties of unaccustomed demands on women's strength, fear of heights, and the like. The relative strength of men and women, and so forth, does not provide such evidence and is not the issue. The issue remains that for equal work people should receive equal pay. Augusta Clawson was performing the same work that had been performed by men, and was being paid less. Although the National War Labor Board issued a directive to industries that stipulated equal pay for equal work, the order was unclear and subject to interpretation; most employers continued to pay women at a lower rate (Chafe, 1976:19). Furthermore, women had little opportunity to advance in their new occupations (Baxandall et al., 1976).

According to Anderson (1981), World War II marked an important turning point. The social prohibition concerning married women working gave way under wartime pressure, and women wartime workers demonstrated that it was possible for women to maintain their households while covering their husbands' responsibilities with outside employment. The experience was the beginning of learning to accommodate the simultaneous demands of family and work, and "pointed the way to a greater degree of choice for American women" (Anderson, 1981:174).

However, at the war's end, with the return of men to civilian life, there was a tremendous pressure on women to return to their former positions in the home. During this time, a new social ideology began to emerge; Betty Friedan later called it "the feminine mystique" (Friedan, 1963). This ideology drew in social workers, educators, journalists, and psychologists, who all tried to convince women that their place was again in the home. It was not unlike the "cult of true womanhood" advanced in the late 1800s to differentiate middle-class women from working-class women. Friedan notes that in the fifteen years following World War II, the image of "women at home" rather than "at work" became a cherished and self-perpetuating core of contemporary American culture. The war brought up a generation of young people to glory in the values of the home and family, and woman's role was defined as the domestic center around which all else revolved. Women were supposed to live like Norman Rockwell *Saturday Evening Post* illustrations. The idealized image was of smiling mothers baking cookies for their wholesome children, driving their station wagons loaded with freckled youngsters to an endless round of lessons and activities, returning with groceries and other consumer goods to the identical ranch houses they cared for with such pride. Women were supposed to revel in these roles and gladly leave the running of the world to men (Friedan, 1963:14).

This image was nourished by the new psychological and child-development theories of the time. Psychoanalytic theory held that "Biology is destiny" and that "Woman's identity is defined by the inescapable fact of her sex." The argument followed that a woman's needs are best fulfilled by meeting the needs of her family. These "new experts" maintained that women's employment during the war years had fostered certain individual neuroses and social maladjustments—which could be corrected only by women's return to a domestic (and subordinate and dependent) status (see Anderson, 1981). In this way, "'Rosie the Riveter' was transformed with dizzying speed from a wartime heroine to a neurotic, castrating victim of penis envy" (Anderson, 1981:176).

Along with these ideological arguments to bring women back to the home were important economic considerations. The traditional notion of women's place in the home became, after the war, integrally linked with the housewife's function as primary consumer of goods. The war had wound up the economy with massive production, inflation, growth, and low rates of unemployment. With the reduction in military spending, the country could not support full employment or continued industrial profits without an increase in a major market such as household goods. Both Federal Housing Administration-guaranteed loans and government-subsidized construction of commuter highways encouraged a general migration to the suburbs, where families would buy more household goods. Women were the key to this market—and homemaking was encouraged as a necessary stimulant to the postwar industrial economy (Baxandall et al., 1976:282–283).

Yet, unlike the post–World War I period, after World War II women did not go back to the kitchens. Instead, women's labor-force participation continued to increase throughout the post-World War II decades, so that by 1980 over half of American women were in the labor force. Who were the women most likely to be part of this "new majority" of women at work?

AFTER WORLD WAR II: THE RISE OF THE MARRIED WOMAN WORKER

Up until the beginning of World War II, young, single women had dominated the labor force. Between 1890 and the beginning of World War II, single women comprised at least half the female labor force (Grossman, 1979:46). (The others were married black, immigrant, and working-class women.)

The decade of the 1940s saw a change in the type of women worker, as increasing numbers of married women went out to work (see Figure 2.3). Although single women continued to have the highest labor-force participation rates among women, during the 1940s the percentage of married women in the work force grew more rapidly than any other category. Between 1940 and 1950, single women workers were in short supply because of low birthrates in the 1930s. Furthermore, those single women available for work were marrying at younger ages and leaving the labor market to raise their families. On the other hand, an ample supply of older married women was available, and these women (who had married younger, had had fewer children, and were living longer) were eager for paid employment.

In 1940, about 15 percent of married women were employed; by 1950, married women workers had increased to 24 percent. This increase has continued: by 1960, the proportion of married women workers was 31 percent; in 1970, over 40 percent; by 1978, reached 48 percent (U.S. Department of Labor, Bureau of Labor Statistics, 1980:27).

The entrance of married women into the work force occurred in several stages. During the 1940s, 1950s, and 1960s, the largest proportion of married women entering the work force was older married women. In 1957, for example, the labor-force participation rate among women aged forty-five to forty-nine years exceeded the rate for twenty- to twenty-four-year-old women (Oppenheimer, 1970:15). During the 1960s, a second type of mar-

F i g u r e   2 . 3 / *Women's Labor-Force Participation Rates by Marital Status, 1890–1976*

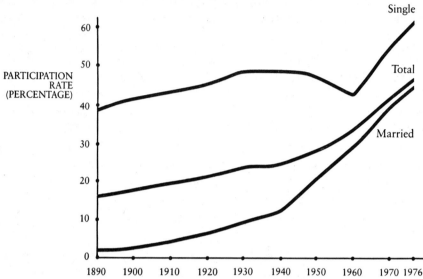

SOURCE: Prepared from data in Claudia Goldin, "Female Labor Force Participation: The Origins of Black and White Differences, 1870 and 1880," *Journal of Economic History* 37 (March 1977): 88.

ried women began to enter the work force—the young married mother who had preschool- or school-age children. By 1980, almost two-thirds of women with children between six and eighteen years of age were employed, and, most significantly, half of those women with children under the age of six were in the labor force (see Table 2.1).

Still, never-married and divorced women have historically had the highest rates of participation in the labor force—a pattern that continues into the 1980s. Despite the growth in the number of never-married and divorced women in the labor force in the 1970s, the majority of women employed (in absolute numbers) are married women. In 1978, about 23 million (or 56 percent) of the 41 million female workers were married women who were living with their husbands.

Furthermore, the most dramatic increase in participation rates for women has occurred among women aged twenty-five to thirty-four. Many women of this age group, who in previous decades had stopped working when they married and had children, are no longer staying home but instead are remaining in the work force.

T a b l e 2 . 1 / *U.S. Women's Labor-Force Participation, by Marital Status and Presence and Age of Children, March 1980*

Marital Status	Total	With No Children Under 18	With Children Under Age 18		With Children Under Age 6	
			Total	Ages 6–17 Only	Total	Under Age 3
Total	51.1	48.0	56.6	64.4	46.6	41.7
Never married	61.2	61.8	51.5	67.3	43.4	41.1
Married, husband present	50.2	46.1	54.2	61.8	45.0	41.1
Married, husband absent	59.4	58.7	59.9	66.4	51.8	42.0
Widowed	22.5	19.9	58.8	61.1	45.6	ᵃ
Divorced	74.5	71.4	78.1	82.3	68.0	56.5

SOURCE: Linda J. Waite, "U.S. Women at Work," *Population Bulletin*, vol. 36, no. 2 (Washington, D.C.: Population Reference Bureau, 1981), p. 22.
NOTE: All figures refer to women aged 16 and over.
ᵃRate not shown because base is less than 75,000 women.

WHY WOMEN WORK

Kreps (1971) points out that asking the question "Why do women work?" implies tacit acceptance of the traditional role of woman's place "at home." It also implies the contrasting cultural norm for men: that men work throughout their lives. Hence, studies of men's labor-force participation focus on significant *absences*. However, because it is assumed that women are primarily running households and raising families, women catch our attention by their *presence* in the marketplace. Indeed, studies generally focus on the "unusual" factors that influence women's participation, such as being single, childless, or divorced, having low income, high education, or grown children. No one asks why women *don't* work—or why men *do*.

Bearing this in mind, the evidence indicates several factors that account for women's participation in the labor force. These factors range from economic necessity to changes in women's traditional values.

Economic Reasons for Working

Despite the negative social attitudes toward women's employment outside the home after World War II, many women did not return to their former way of life, even though they were for the most part displaced from heavy industry by men. Important changes in the economy and growing economic necessity encouraged a further break with traditional roles and

F i g u r e   2 . 4 /   *Women's Reasons for Working, 1980*

QUESTION: Are you working primarily to support yourself, to support your family, to bring in extra money, or for something interesting to do?

ANSWERS:

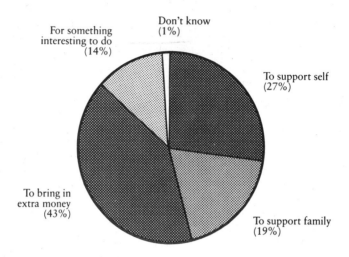

Don't know (1%)

For something interesting to do (14%)

To support self (27%)

To bring in extra money (43%)

To support family (19%)

Note: Percentages sum to more than 100 because of rounding.

SOURCE: Adapted from Roper Organization, *The 1980 Virginia Slims American Women's Opinion Poll: A Survey of Contemporary Attitudes* (Storrs, Conn.: The Roper Center, University of Connecticut, 1980), p. 37.

facilitated the entrance of more married women into the work force. After World War II, the demand for female workers continued, especially in those industries that had traditionally employed women—education, health care, and other occupations in the service sector. This increased demand for women workers was complemented by a growing economic need for women to obtain employment. The prevalent myth that women were working only for "pin money" distorts the truth about why women work:

> I hear on all sides that I should go back to the kitchen. . . . Do they think I'm working just for fun or pin money? They should know that it's no easy task for a woman to take care of her husband and her young children and at the same time keep a job. I am fearful with all these cutbacks that because I am a woman I will be among the first to go. (Young and Shouse, 1945:274–275)

Economic necessity is a powerful motive that accounts for the continued participation of women in the work force over time. A recent poll that asked women why they worked found that 43 percent were working to bring in money to supplement the family income, 27 percent were working to support themselves, and 19 percent were working to support their families (Roper Organization, 1980). Only a small minority of women, 14 percent, were working because they wanted something interesting to do. (See Figure 2.4.) Economic necessity also accounts for the increase in the number of women who hold more than one job. Since 1970, the proportion of women among "moonlighters" has risen from 16 to 27 percent (Brown, 1978:28).

It is important to note that "working because of economic need" can be interpreted as an extension of "serving the family," which thus provides a socially accepted motive for entering the work force. Such needs are of course relative—families do redefine their economic goals once basic sustenance is attained, and even those women who work because of "need" usually say they would continue even if their incomes were not essential.

The median contribution to the family by working wives in 1974 was more than one-fourth of total family income; among those who worked full time and year round, it was nearly two-fifths. About 2.5 million wives, or 12 percent of all wives who worked, contribute half or more of the family income. This contribution is crucial, especially where family income has been raised from low to middle levels by wives' employment (U.S. Department of Labor, Employment and Training Administration, 1976).

Life-Cycle Factors

A number of other factors also combined to encourage women's entrance into the labor force. Most dramatic among these is the changing life cycle of women. Today the years devoted to childbearing and child rearing are decreasing, while the average life span is increasing. The time between the birth of the first child and the last has declined to about 7 years (Glick, 1977). At the turn of the century, the average number of children born to a couple was six; by the early 1950s, the average was three. Today, the number has declined to two or fewer, with many couples deciding to remain childless (Veevers, 1973). With increasing longevity, a couple can also now expect to spend 13 years together after their last child has left home (Neugarten and Brown-Rezanka, 1978:26). Consequently, women are finding that they have more years to engage in activities beyond bearing and rearing children, and this makes active participation in the labor force more appealing.

Other changes are also occurring in the life-cycle status of women, as divorce rates continue to rise, especially among younger married women with children. Divorced or separated mothers with young children are finding it economically necessary to either enter or remain in the work force. It is estimated that approximately 40 percent of first marriages of women now aged twenty-five to thirty-five will end in divorce (Neugarten and Brown-Rezanka, 1978:30).

Changing Attitudes

Attitudinal factors also play an important role in the increased participation of women in the labor force. Rising levels of education are important in determining women's attitudes concerning work, especially their attitudes about a career. In a recent survey of working women, 45 percent reported planning to make their jobs full-time careers. Among women with college degrees, the proportion was even higher: 56 percent planned to pursue full-time careers (Roper Organization, 1980:36). The higher the educational level, the higher the participation rate in the work force. In 1978, for example, the lowest labor-force participation rates for women were for individuals who failed to graduate high school (32 percent, for women), whereas the highest rates (66 percent) were among women with four or more years of college (U.S. Department of Commerce, Bureau of the Census, 1980:42). This positive relationship between education and labor-force participation may be related to the greater benefit (that is, earning power) of employment derived by women with higher education (Bednarzik and Klein, 1977).

In addition, husbands' attitudes can be an important factor influencing whether married women work. The results of a national longitudinal survey of working women (aged thirty-five to thirty-nine in 1972) reveal that a married woman is more likely to work if she perceives her husband's attitude as favorable (U.S. Department of Labor, Employment and Training Administration, 1976:14). It is equally plausible, however, that the husband's more favorable attitude follows rather than precedes his wife's decision to work. Oppenheimer (1970) found that attitudes toward a working wife changed more slowly than the actual increase in a wife's labor-force participation. It may be, then, that it is the tremendous increase in married women workers that is influencing society's, and more specifically husbands', attitudes about married women working.

Political Factors

The influence of the women's movement in the late 1960s and 1970s has been a major factor in changing attitudes of men and women about their traditional roles. This movement has heightened social consciousness by questioning the assumptions, values, and images concerning a woman's "place." The key to the success of the women's movement is seen in its broad-based approach to issues. Rather than aligning support simply from special-interest groups or focusing on single issues—as earlier movements had done—the modern movement has relied on grass-roots development and organization in the community. Those sympathetic to such change have been drawn together rather than splintered by disparate or distant goals. Women have been able to direct their concerns to those causes within the broad movement that most appealed to them (Chafe, 1976:23). Many of these women's groups have helped reject the idea that women do not want better jobs or that they prefer to remain at home. The National Organization for Women's "Do-It-Now" slogan asserted the rights of women in the labor force. The Coalition of Labor Union Women has also fought to place women in leadership positions and to raise women's issues at the collective bargaining table, and professional women have organized caucuses to argue that public policies affirming women's home roles engender a series of self-images and behavior that reinforce women's inferior position in the work world (Kessler-Harris, 1981 : 148).

Interplay of Social, Political, and Economic Factors

After World War II, these various social, economic, and political factors coalesced over time to transform women's place in the economy and society. Each factor has reinforced the continued participation of women in the labor force and has encouraged the entrance of different types of women workers. The overwhelming change in attitudes toward women at work is reflected in a recent survey in which men and women were asked to speculate on their futures. In the survey, 72 percent of women and 74 percent of men reported that they foresaw considerable changes in the status of women, changes that would alter traditional attitudes. More than half the women surveyed believed that by the end of the century nearly all women who can, will be working—"some as presidents of corporations, others as draftees in army combat units" (Roper Organization, 1980 : 10).

WOMEN'S ECONOMIC AND SOCIAL PARTICIPATION IN THE LABOR FORCE

We have seen an historical upswing of women in the labor force—more women are moving from the domestic sphere into the paid labor force—and we have seen the growing heterogeneity of women workers. But, while the number and types of women who work have changed dramatically, numerous other aspects of women's work have remained impervious to change: the clustering of women into sex-typed jobs, the disproportionate number of women in low-ranking positions and their comparatively low earnings relative to men, as well as the overall underutilization (unemployment and underemployment) of women workers. Although the women's movement and recent legislation have produced pressure for changes, there is still resistance to the enforcement of laws that run counter to deeply held attitudes and institutionalized practices concerning the differential treatment of the sexes. Equal opportunity and equal pay have not yet been established.

Sex Segregation of Occupations

Women are still clustered in occupations in which they have been dominant throughout this country's history. Although women are represented in all occupational groups, they remain *concentrated* in the clerical and service occupations—a situation that has not changed over the most recent decades. Specifically, one-fourth of all women in the labor force are in just five jobs—the jobs of secretary, household worker, bookkeeper, elementary-school teacher, and waitress. These five jobs, plus those of typist, cashier, nurse, and seamstress, claim fully 40 percent of all female workers (Blau, 1978). (A more detailed analysis of the sex segregation of the labor force appears in Chapter 4.)

Lapidus (1976) notes that this occupational segregation results in the domination of certain sectors or occupations by women and others by men, out of all proportion to their overall participation in the work force (see Figure 2.5). As a result, occupations become "sex typed" as either male or female jobs. Women are overrepresented in clerical, service, sales, and private household work, and underrepresented as managers, skilled crafts workers, nonretail sales workers, and in the operative and professional categories. Clerical work, perhaps more than any other paid occupation, has come to dominate the definition of "women's work." In 1880 the proportion of women in the clerical work force was 4 percent; by 1920 the proportion had risen to 50 percent; by 1960, to 72 percent; and by the mid-1970s, to 80 percent (Davies, 1975).

In recent years, there has been some limited movement of women into male-dominated employment categories, including the male-dominated professions. The most notable increases have been in the fields of law, pharmacy, and medicine (U.S. Department of Labor, Employment Standards Administration, Women's Bureau, 1975). Women have entered other male-dominated occupations as well. Between 1972 and 1978 there were some increases in the proportion of women employed as managers and administrators, crafts workers, and laborers. However, these increases have not been large: in 1978, there were 6 female crafts workers and 12 female laborers for every 100 males employed in each of these occupational groups; among managers and administrators, there were 30 women for every 100 men (U.S. Department of Commerce, Bureau of the Census, 1980a:60).

In addition to occupational sex typing, there is hierarchical or vertical segregation *within* given occupations, so that the proportion of women declines at successively higher levels of job skill, status, responsibility, and income (Lapidus, 1976). Moreover, many traditional "female" jobs have limited career ladders. These female-typed jobs provide few promotional opportunities and provide little or no on-the-job training. Clerical work, as we shall see in Chapter 5, is a prime example. The field is surrounded by "dead space"; it lacks linkages to other areas in most employing organiza-

Figure 2.5 / *Occupational Distribution of Employed Men and Women, 1979*

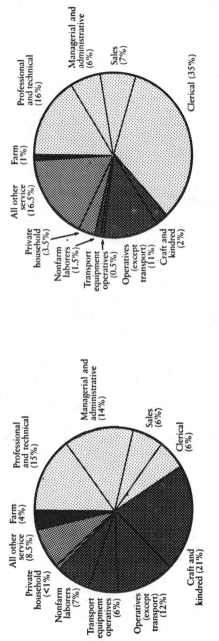

MEN

Total number of employed men = 56,500,000 (58.3% of work force)

Professional and technical (15%)

Managerial and administrative (14%)

Sales (6%)

Clerical (6%)

Farm (4%)

All other service (8.5%)

Private household (<1%)

Nonfarm laborers (7%)

Transport equipment operatives (6%)

Operatives (except transport) (12%)

Craft and kindred (21%)

White-collar occupations (41%)

Farm (4%)

Service occupations (9%)

Blue-collar occupations (46%)

WOMEN

Total number of employed women = 40,446,000 (41.7% of work force)

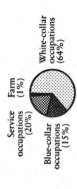

Managerial and administrative (6%)

Professional and technical (16%)

Sales (7%)

Clerical (35%)

Farm (1%)

All other service (16.5%)

Private household (3.5%)

Nonfarm laborers (1.5%)

Transport equipment operatives (0.5%)

Operatives (except transport) (11%)

Craft and kindred (2%)

White-collar occupations (64%)

Farm (1%)

Service occupations (20%)

Blue-collar occupations (15%)

Note: Data include persons 16 years of age and over; data do not include unpaid housework and volunteer work.

SOURCE: Adapted from U.S. Department of Labor, Bureau of Labor Statistics, *Employment and Unemployment During 1979: An Analysis* (Washington, D.C.: U.S. Government Printing Office, 1980), Table 21, p. A-20.

F i g u r e   2 . 6 / *Annual Earnings by Men and Women, 1956–1978 (Year-Round, Full-Time Workers)*

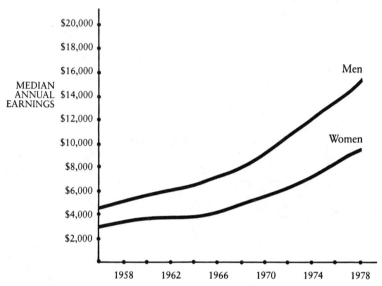

SOURCE: Prepared from data in U.S. Department of Labor, Bureau of Labor Statistics, *Perspectives on Working Women: A Databook*, Bulletin 2080 (Washington, D.C.: U.S. Government Printing Office, October 1980), p. 52.

tions. Nonclerical jobs are more likely given to outsiders, who usually receive on-the-job training; the clerical worker within the organization is rarely considered for promotion to these higher-level positions (Seidman, 1978:77).

Even when women are in occupations with more extensive career opportunities, they are likely to receive fewer promotions than their male counterparts. For example, in the field of higher education, the career mobility of women is more restricted than that of men. Fewer women are at the professorial ranks—positions that carry higher prestige and job security; women are concentrated instead within the instructor, adjunct, and lower-level teaching or staff ranks—in positions with less security and less opportunity for career advancement.

The Male/Female Earnings Gap

According to the biblical book of Leviticus, God said to Moses that a man was worth fifty shekels of silver; a woman, thirty. This is about the earnings gap that prevails today. Furthermore, the earnings gap is increasing. In 1956 women's average annual earnings for full-time year-round

T a b l e   2 . 2 / *Median Usual Weekly Earnings of Full-Time Wage and Salary Workers, by Sex and Occupational Group, Second Quarter 1979 (Preliminary)*

Occupational Group	Women	Men	Women's Earnings as a Percentage of Men's
Total	$183	$295	62
Professional and technical workers	261	375	70
Managers and administrators, except farm	232	386	60
Sales workers	154	297	52
Clerical workers	180	287	63
Craft and kindred workers	189	305	62
Operatives, except transport	156	257	61
Transport equipment operatives	194	277	70
Nonfarm laborers	166	220	75
Service workers	138	203	68
Farm workers	125	153	82

SOURCE: U.S. Department of Labor, Bureau of Labor Statistics, *Women in the Labor Force: Some New Data Series*, (Washington, D.C.: U.S. Government Printing Office, 1979), p. 7.
NOTE: All figures refer to workers aged 16 and over.

work was 64 percent of what comparable men earned; in 1978, women's earnings were only 59 percent of men's (see Figure 2.6).

Even within the same major occupational groups, women's earnings are lower than men's (see Table 2.2). The average weekly earnings in 1979 of full-time women workers in all occupations, from sales work to the professions, ranged from 52 to 82 percent of men's earnings. In sales work, women's earnings were 52 percent that of men; in clerical occupations, 63 percent. Even when women enter "male-dominated" occupations, they typically earn less than men. In the professions, for example, women's earnings were 70 percent of men's.

In addition to receiving less pay, women are often excluded from important fringe benefits. Women in executive positions are a case in point. Stock options, membership fees in exclusive executive clubs, sponsorship at professional seminars, and executive insurance are often available only to men, or only rarely offered to women. And, because professional contacts are as important as the informal business conducted within male-dominated enclaves, the exclusion or restriction of women interferes with their profes-

sional advancement and status as well as diminishes their income by denying them perquisites (Wallace, 1973). (These and other practices that disadvantage professional and managerial women are discussed at length in
Chapter 6).

The continued presence and widening of the earnings gap is an important
issue for working women, because most women work because of economic
need and have assumed an important role in the economic support of their
families. In many cases, women's earnings help to keep their families above
the poverty level. The earnings gap is particularly devastating for female-
headed families. Almost two-fifths of all families headed by women are below the poverty level (U.S. Department of Labor, Bureau of Labor Statistics,
1980:7).

There are many obstacles to women's work equality. Throughout this
book, we identify numerous barriers and constraints, including discriminatory recruitment, hiring, and promotion practices; inflexible work hours;
and women's unequal burden of paid work together with child-care and
household responsibilities. In Chapter 3, we look specifically at barriers
produced by discrimination in sex-role stereotyping of life skills—through
differences in child rearing and educational instruction at home and in
school. Attitudes and basic assumptions of men and women regarding their
specific economic roles are ingrained early and have persistent effects. As we
shall see, certain family practices and educational arrangements operate to
prepare women for traditional sex roles. Many of these experiences limit
women's aspirations and opportunities in work and society.

SUMMARY

From colonial times to the present, women have been increasingly employed in the labor force. Colonial women held a critical economic position,
carrying on the production of food, goods, and services, as well as having
responsibility for bearing and rearing children. Many colonial women were
engaged in a variety of occupations outside the home, but the predominant
pattern was that of women working at home.

The transformation of society from an agrarian rural economy to an urban industrial one ushered in a new era of roles and definitions of women's
work. At first women's work at home expanded to include production of
goods and services for market sale. This cottage-industry system, however,
became obsolete with the entry of single women into the textile factories.
Demographic and economic changes served to propel the shift. Labor, especially that of males, was in short supply. Men were needed in the fields to
tend to the demands of a still largely agrarian society. Young, single, white
women filled industrial positions, viewing their work as a temporary interlude before mariage. As the economy expanded, more and more jobs

opened up to women, so that by the turn of the century women were employed in a variety of occupations.

The turn of the century saw a dramatic change in the composition of the female work force, as new waves of immigrants increasingly replaced earlier, assimilated-immigrant women in factories. As the economy expanded and prosperity came to more and more middle-class families, middle-class women could "become ladies," a rank formerly reserved for upper-class women. Once again, a "woman's place" was defined as at home. If these women did work outside the home, the appropriate occupation was a white-collar job (sales, clerical, and professional occupations). Middle- and working-class employment became more distinct; factory work was now considered undesirable.

Although women did go out to work and make substantial inroads in a variety of occupations, their work was still largely confined to a few occupations, where they held unskilled, low-paying jobs (even when "white-collar"). World War I accelerated the entry of women into new fields of industry; the Depression reversed this pattern. World War II brought a tremendous increase in women's labor-force participation, one that continued to accelerate after the war. The composition of the work force also changed dramatically as more and more older married women, and then married women in their twenties and thirties with young children, entered the labor force.

Women's place in today's labor market is one of higher visibility, and women's employment is expected to continue to increase in the future. Estimates are that, by 1990, at least 55 percent of the female population aged sixteen and over will be working. Other labor analysts' estimates are even higher.

In spite of these high and growing rates of participation in the labor force, women continue to face tremendous occupational barriers. Their work capacity is still funneled into a few sex-typed jobs in which their pay is low, their influence is limited, and their mobility and options are restricted. Even though social norms and values are changing, and even though the women's movement has helped set the pace for further changes, the labor-force status of women continues to be depressed. Much remains to be done if women are to enjoy a fuller range of work opportunities and a greater share of work rewards.

3 • Family and Educational Context: Socialization for Work

Even at a tender age, females have restricted occupational aspirations and narrow options. By the time they enter grade school, one-half to three-quarters of the girls have narrowed their aspirations to three occupations—teacher, nurse, and secretary (Looft, 1971; O'Hara, 1962; Siegel, 1973). Moreover, these limited choices are independent of girls' race and class. At the same age, boys' choices cover a much broader range of possibilities, and a significant minority of boys indulge themselves in choices of pure fantasy, while fanciful choices are negligible among girls (O'Hara, 1962).

These early aspirations are actually consistent with the reality of occupational outcomes for women compared to men. As Chapter 2 documents, women are concentrated in many fewer occupations than are men. And women's rank, recognition, and rewards in work are much lower than men's. This depressed labor-force position reflects the constraints of discriminatory economic and of political and legal practices, as discussed in Chapter 4. But, in other, though lesser ways, women's occupational position is restricted also by certain patterns of compliance, dependence, and self-doubt, which are acquired in a process called *socialization.*

Socialization is a process of learning the expectations appropriate for the various social positions we occupy and the groups to which we belong. This process includes learning both attitudes and behaviors, and the rights as well as the duties associated with our social positions—as friends and neighbors, workers and citizens, customers and clients, and so forth. But socialization isn't simply a process of coming to know and conform with certain expectations and assumptions. Rather, successful socialization means becoming committed to, or internalizing, rather than just complying with, those expectations. Once values and norms are internalized, one responds to the expectations of *self* just as one might react to others.

Because we occupy social positions and belong to groups at all ages, socialization is a lifelong process. Throughout life, we acquire certain behaviors and attitudes, and then modify and adjust them as our social environment and conditions change. Of all the groups with which we come into contact and which train and condition us for social participation, two of the most important are the family and the school. Consequently, in our discussion of the socialization process and its occupational consequences for males and females, we focus on the family and educational institutions. The first part of the chapter analyzes sex-role socialization through family; the second section, socialization through education; and the last section, the consequences of both of these socialization processes as they operate together to influence the occupational outcomes of females compared to males. Because of the book's focus on American women at work, the socialization processes discussed refer to those in American society. Socialization practices vary by culture and subculture.

EARLY INFLUENCES: SEX-ROLE SOCIALIZATION AND THE FAMILY

Certain features of the family group make it a most critical agent of socialization. First, the family represents one's initial social contact—at a stage in which all of life is new and everything is yet to be learned. Furthermore, as a socialization agent, the family reigns when the child's resources are minimal and his or her alternatives are nearly nil. Hence the family permeates a child's existence and constitutes nearly the whole of experience. Finally, the family is an enduring influence. A child lives with his or her family for many years, and even after the child leaves home the family influence continues.

As the family begins to identify and evaluate its new offspring, probably the first trait noticed is the child's particular sex. Even before its actual birth, parents and relatives speculate on the baby's sex and are anxious to identify the child as boy or girl nearly as soon as he or she is born. Furthermore, in announcing the child's birth, both informally in phone calls and formally in written notices, parents invariably indicate, along with birthdate and name, the child's sex. And of course the name by which the child is called will vary with sex; so that in agonizing over choices and alternatives, parents classify into male and female categories their preferences for names.

In this way, a baby's sex is a central feature in the family's labeling of the child to themselves and to their friends, relatives, and community. Thus, from the start, our sex represents a central and important feature in determining who we are, how others think of us, and, indeed, how we will come to think of ourselves—in occupation, as in other behaviors and attitudes. The whole complex of social expectations and assumptions about males versus females constitutes what we call the "sex role." As an indication of the salience of this social role, we find that people are anxious and uncomfortable interacting with someone if they are unable to label quickly that person's sex. Even when interacting with an infant, people are uneasy if they do not know whether the baby is a boy or girl (Seavey, Katz, and Zalk, 1975).

Thus, almost immediately after birth, parents not only identify the sex of the child but also begin assigning sex-role expectations to their newborn. These expectations are manifest in the different descriptions parents give for boy and girl babies and are aptly illustrated in a study of parents whose children were only twenty-four hours old (Rubin, Provenzano, and Luria, 1974). For this study, the researchers had hospital personnel select a group of baby girls and baby boys who were matched, or comparable to each other, in their weight, size, skeletal frame, and even muscle response. Parents were then asked to describe their own child, and comparisons were made between descriptions for sons versus daughters. The results show that parents of girls rated their children as softer, smaller, finer featured, prettier, and more attentive. In comparison, parents of boys were already rating, and hence regarding, their children as stronger, bolder, larger featured, and better coordinated. Accordingly, parents tend to select different colors, clothing, and decors to fit their expectations for sons and daughters (Rheingold and Cook, 1975). To accompany the softness and prettiness of baby girls, they tend to choose delicate fabrics, pastel colors, and floral designs; for the perceived boldness of baby boys, they select primary colors, coarser fabrics, and bright animal motifs.

It is important to note that these sex-role expectations are apparent even among parents who insist that they do not differentiate between boys and girls and that they treat boys and girls alike. For example, one study reports that parents say they expect similar behavior from sons and daughters— that they expect them to be equally neat, helpful around the house, considerate, and able to control their anger as well as their crying. Yet, when asked "in what ways do you think boys and girls are different," these same parents responded that the boys are naturally messier, noisier, and more aggressive, while the girls are neater, quieter and more helpful and considerate (Maccoby and Jacklin, 1974). So from an early age, parents believe that female children display the characteristics appropriate for nurturant and supportive roles and that males display the characteristics for more assertive and dominant roles.

Determining the *actual* behavioral differences between male and female children, however, is not an easy task. Reliable sex differences are difficult to establish, because observed differences may be specific to certain age periods and subject to subtle features of the social setting in which the differences were observed (Emmerich, 1975). In the most extensive search for conclusive sex differences, Maccoby and Jacklin (1974) surveyed 1,600 studies published on the subject between 1966 and 1973. They organized the studies into eight broad topics and further classified them by particular psychological dimensions, which included perception, learning, intellectual abilities, social behavior, and achievement motivation. They then constructed eighty-three tables presenting the studies' findings of, and statistical significance for, the between-sex differences. From this survey and evaluation, Maccoby and Jacklin conclude that there are few "well-established" sex differences. The two notable exceptions are females' greater verbal skills and males' higher level of aggressiveness.

An evaluation of the empirical literature on sex differences is a controversial endeavor. The task is subject to arbitrary and complicated decisions about what literature to include and how to organize and interpret that literature. For this reason, critics have charged that, by broadly redefining concepts such as sociability, Maccoby and Jacklin have underestimated sex differences in such areas as social and affiliative interests and in assessment of performance and anxiety (Block, 1976; Stockard and Johnson, 1980). Still, while some critics maintain that reliable sex differences are manifest in additional areas, researchers do not disagree about the two items, namely that girls are more verbal, and boys more aggressive.

By age two, boys are more likely to shout, shove, and hit with the intent of hurting another (Maccoby and Jacklin, 1974:227), and as the children grow older the sex/aggression difference increases. It is not necessarily that boys increase their volatility, but rather that the response diminishes much more rapidly in females than in males. Maccoby and Jacklin suggest that these sex differences are related to males' versus females' *willingness* to behave hostilely. Thus, when children are presented with films or tapes showing aggressive behavior, boys are much more likely than girls to imitate this behavior. However, when the children are actually offered rewards for the imitation, the sex differences decrease.

In verbal precociousness, the sex differences are somewhat less consistent. Girls do begin to talk at an earlier age, and as toddlers and preschoolers they also speak more frequently. Furthermore, while Maccoby and Jacklin do not concur, other researchers report that girls are also somewhat more interested in people, personalities, and social experiences. For example, when two- to five-year-olds are given a paper and pencil and asked to make a drawing, over half the girls draw pictures of people—family, friends, children, and babies. Yet only 15 percent of the boys draw such figures. Rather, boys draw things, such as cars, trains, or rocks (Pitcher, 1974). Similarly, when 350 preschoolers were asked to "tell a story," a disproportionate number of girls gave accounts involving people, particularly their parents. In contrast, boys' stories centered around vehicles, machines, and inanimate objects such as rockets, parachutes, and dump trucks (Pitcher, 1974). Inferences from such findings on early sex differences in "sociability" are probably more suggestive than conclusive. Yet some people maintain that these early sex differences demonstrate the "natural inclinations" of females for more person-centered occupations, and of males for more task-oriented occupations.

Origins of Sex-Role Acquisition

Thus, the existence of certain sex differences in traits and behaviors brings us to the long-debated argument over their origin: How do these differences emerge and persist, and more specifically, how much of the difference is due to (1) nature and biology, compared to (2) nurturance and experience? This question of origin is critical to interpreting occupational outcomes of men and women. Some contend that the occupational differences of men and women simply reflect their natural "tendencies and dispositions"; others maintain that the occupational "choices" of men and women are socially conditioned. Thus, in the study of men, women, and work, it is important to analyze the major perspectives on origins of sex-role differences.

The biological perspective

Of the two perspectives, the biological argument is the oldest and is reflected in philosophies from Plato through Spinoza, which maintain that sex differentiation is both natural and necessary. The contemporary biological argument contends that sex-linked attitudes, temperaments, and behaviors are rooted in innate characteristics, which are essentially fixed at conception when the X chromosome is joined by a Y to form a male, or another X to form a female. The fundamental assumption is that male and female hormones influence the development not only of primary and secondary reproductive characteristics but also of psychological and social differences in occupational as well as other spheres.

In establishing a link between hormones and sex-typed behavior, the biological theory draws evidence from observations and experiments with nonhumans as well as with humans (Lewis and Weinraub, 1979). The experiments with nonhumans tend to involve the manipulation of male and female hormone levels in order to determine the effect on mating, maternal, play, and other behaviors. For example, male hormones have been administered to pregnant rhesus monkeys, whose female offspring are then compared with the female offspring of untreated mothers for differences in aggressive, rough, and threat behavior (Goy, 1970).

By underlining differences that characterize the male and female of each species, the biological perspective emphasizes the pervasiveness of sex differentiation. In like manner, this perspective emphasizes, among humans, the universality of certain male and female traits and behaviors, such as male dominance in hunting and warfare activities. If certain sex differences are found across cultures, despite various environments and conditions, then from this perspective it may be more aptly argued that the differences reflect basic biological or innate factors (Frieze, Parsons, Johnson, Ruble, and Zellman, 1978). Finally, the biological perspective stresses male/female differences, such as mechanical versus verbal skills, which appear in early childhood and persist through adulthood. Obviously, if sex differences are innate, they should remain stable. Thus, sex differences that are pervasive, universal, and stable are highlighted, in support of the contention that they are determined by nature rather than environment.

Social and environmental perspectives

A major weakness of the biological perspective is implicit in our earlier discussion that very few sex differences, except for aggressiveness (male) and verbal precociousness (female), are strong and invariable enough to suggest a biological basis for the tendencies (Frieze et al., 1978). Furthermore, although males and females differ physiologically in the proportions of each hormone they secrete, both sexes have the same hormone *types* in their bloodstreams (Richardson, 1981). Moreover, current research indicates that the social setting in which men and women interact greatly affects the particular secretion level of their hormones, and in turn, changes the effect of these hormones on their behavior (see Richardson, 1981:179).

Thus, sex-typed behaviors are highly susceptible to social cues and conditions and suggest that the differences represent acquired rather than innate traits. This then turns us toward the social and environmental perspectives on sex differences. The common focus of these perspectives is that sex roles are learned or acquired. They differ, however, in their various emphases on *how* the learning occurs and how importantly biological factors figure in that process.

One viewpoint is rooted in classic psychoanalytic theory and maintains that *identification* is the root of sex-role acquisition. The Freudian concept of identification refers to a process whereby one incorporates into one's self various aspects of another's personality. In terms of sex-role identification, specifically, the child takes on or acquires the behaviors, attitudes, and traits of the same-sex parent. This process, in turn, fosters permanent and global personality differences between males and females (Frieze et al., 1978). Freud maintained that identification with the parent of the same sex is biologically based. Boys identify with their fathers, and girls with their mothers, because the children share and perceive anatomical similarity with that parent. In its classical statement, the theory allocates a large part of the identification process to biological factors.

The second social and environmental perspective rejects identification as a root of sex-role acquisition and focuses, instead, on the principle of *reinforcement*. From this viewpoint, children develop the culturally, sex-appropriate responses because they receive rewards and avoid punishments by behaving in ways that resemble their parents' notions about what is appropriate for girls or boys (Mischel, 1966).

Advocates of this perspective also employ the principle of modeling (Bandura, 1969; Bandura and Walters, 1963; Mischel, 1966). In short, they claim that children acquire sex-appropriate behavior by observing and imitating the characteristic behaviors of the same-sex parent. Little girls then imitate nurturant but dependent behavior of their mothers, and boys the more self-reliant and autonomous behavior of their fathers. A major difference between modeling and the psychoanalytic identification principle is that a strong emotional bond between parent and child is necessary for identification, while imitation can occur without such a relationship.

From this reinforcement perspective, children's sex-role development is highly dependent on their parents' expectations—the behavior parents exhibit, and the rewards and punishments they give to girl and to boy children. There is, indeed, evidence to be found of different messages and behaviors applied to sons and daughters. For example, from children's earliest age—within the first weeks of life—mothers consistently look at and talk to baby daughters more than to sons (Lewis, 1972a; Lewis and Cherry, 1977; Moss, 1967). Furthermore, studies of parents and their one- to two-year-old toddlers reveal that parents remain in more proximal, or closer, contact with their daughters. For example, compared to boys, little girls are less likely to have their attention diverted from their mothers, to be physically turned away from their parents, or to have a parent throw a ball far away in a game of catch (Lewis, 1972a). These patterns may begin to encourage more autonomy and independence in male children and more dependence and passivity in female children—traits that can later have consequences for attitudes and behaviors and for occupational choice and participation. Thus,

> When one compares the life of the young girl to that of the young boy, a critical difference emerges: She is treated more protectively and she is subjected to more restrictions and controls; he receives greater achievement demands and higher expectations. Failing to receive sufficient "independence and mastery training" throughout the infant and early childhood years, girls are allowed and at times

even encouraged to exhibit dependency, passivity, and conformity. In contrast, parents more often and consistently disapprove of passivity and docility in their sons, and they encourage active display of his aggression. (Frazier and Sadker, 1973:84)

Although reinforcement mechanisms are certainly involved in the acquisition of sex roles, the extent of parents' differential reinforcement and the consequences for children's sex-typed behavior and occupational conceptions are open to question and controversy (Block, 1976; Frieze et al., 1978; Maccoby and Jacklin, 1974). Specifically, many researchers maintain that reinforcement is too simplistic to account for the complexity of sex-role behavior (Frieze et al., 1978; Katz, 1979) and that parents do not necessarily reinforce boys and girls for different, rather than similar, behavior (Maccoby and Jacklin, 1974). Yet these researchers tend to concede that parental reinforcement nonetheless clarifies and emphasizes certain sex differences. Moreover, especially in the area of toys and activities, parents' sex-typed choices of these items set for the child a precedent "which demonstrates that rewards can be obtained by conforming to sex-appropriate standards" (Lewis and Weinraub, 1979:142).

Researchers who have rejected the reinforcement theory offer a third perspective—*cognitive development*. This perspective contends that, in learning the sex role, children are not necessarily passive and inert products of their parents' imprinting. Rather, the child may actively participate in and influence sex-role development by seeking information and reacting to his or her environment (Kohlberg, 1966; Lewis and Brooks, 1975). This position is called the cognitive-development theory because it assumes the importance of the child's own knowledge or cognition—of self, others, and the relationship between self and others (Katz, 1979; Lewis and Weinraub, 1979).

In the first stage of this development, the child recognizes the self as a boy or girl. After recognition and self-labeling, the child places a certain value on the objects, activities, and other behaviors associated with his or her sex. From here, sex-role development progresses by self-reinforcement as the child actively strives to adopt same-sex characteristics and summarily begins to have positive feelings when behaving in "sex-appropriate" ways.

This cognitive perspective does not deny the importance of parents in the child's environment. Clearly, parents provide models that the child observes and imitates. Furthermore, parents' rewards and punishments for sex-appropriate and sex-inappropriate behavior act as powerful determinants of sex-role development of female compared to male children. But the cognitive view maintains that the child plays an active part in his or her own development by selecting, organizing, and acting on the parent's messages. Thus, despite what parents say and do to encourage or discourage traditional or nontraditional sex role behavior, children still actively use the messages that their larger culture presents. In the development of their gender identity, children act on messages such as the different hair styles, clothing, and occupational locations of men and women in the community at large. In doing so, for example, girls cognitively rehearse roles as nurse and mother, and boys rehearse roles as fireman and father (Richardson, 1981:44).

Summary Interpretation of Sex-Role Acquisition in the Family

Sex-role acquisition is a complex process involving each of the factors—observation, imitation, identification, and reinforcement—emphasized by the various social and environmental theories discussed. Because the cognitive perspective integrates a number of these factors, including the behavior of those people in children's social world as well as the interpretation and responses of the children themselves, the perspective is gaining support as a thorough framework for analyzing sex-role acquisition and occupational outcomes (Frieze et al., 1978).

The social and environmental perspective on sex-role acquisition does not necessarily preclude consideration of biological factors. From the environmental viewpoint, however, biological factors are only one variable—just a starting point—in the development of sex-role differences. For example, there may be some biological sex differences in auditory alertness; compared to boys, female infants tend to show more attention to complex auditory signals (Lewis, 1972a; Maccoby and Jacklin, 1974; Watson, 1969). Girls' greater auditory sensitivity may be a reason why, compared with boys, they are spoken to by parents more frequently and at younger ages. Yet, by speaking with girls, parents in turn may encourage their verbal precociousness and hence their proclivity for people-oriented activities and occupations. Similarly, males' tendency toward aggressiveness may be biologically founded. But it is also socially fostered as parents respond to, and encourage, their sons' attempts to dominate others.

Therefore, sex differences reflect different biological tendencies and orientations of girls and boys, as well as the different expectations and responses of their parents and others. In other words, biology may influence certain temperaments, senses, and attentions of the sexes, but these differences are steadily reinforced and strengthened by the responses of the developing child and by other people in the child's environment.

The fostering of competitiveness and assertiveness for boys compared to girls may be especially consequential for the sex's differential readiness for and adjustment to certain occupations—particularly the executive, managerial, and supervisory jobs for which these aggressive traits are characteristic. However, it is not simply that males are better socialized for the *requirements* of these jobs; it is also that these occupations reflect the male attributes of their incumbents. Thus, given the early family socialization of women plus the fact that occupational structures are shaped by men and their values, females start out "handicapped" for the competitiveness and assertiveness of occupational roles (Marciano, 1981). The term *handicap* does not denote an inherently negative quality to the socialization content of girls compared to boys. Rather, it denotes the negative *effects* on women of socialization in values that are different from, or antithetical to, those of the work place (Marciano, 1981).

Still, parents' socialization of sons and daughters is not constant, but rather varies with the families' social characteristics, including (1) maternal employment status and (2) race of the family. In families with employed mothers, children are provided with somewhat less traditional models of male and female behavior. In addition, because of the demands on employed mothers' time and resources, both their daughters and sons assume more independence and responsibilities for themselves than do children of nonemployed mothers. Both the maternal model and the responsibilities influence the children's perceptions of occupational and sex roles. And these influences are particularly marked for daughters.

Among daughters as young as kindergarten age and as old as college age, the girls with employed mothers report less traditional views of marital and sex roles (Miller, 1975; Stein, 1973). Furthermore, daughters with employed versus nonemployed mothers seem to regard women as more competent (Broverman, Vogel, Broverman, Clarkson, and Rosenkrantz, 1972) and to perceive female accomplishments more positively (Baruch, 1972). In turn, young women, whose mothers have been employed, are more likely to plan on employment as well as family for themselves. These plans are especially strong for those daughters who perceive their mothers as having enjoyed their jobs (Angrist and Almquist, 1975).

Daughters' socialization patterns and employment outcomes also vary with race. Black women are much more likely than whites to have been reared by a mother who was a provider as well as a parent. Among blacks, the mother-provider figure appears not necessarily in the absence, but rather alongside of, a father. The majority of black families are intact, with both husband and wife present (Epstein, 1973). Yet, because of economic need, black wives are more likely to be employed than are white wives. Moreover, interviews with black daughters, particularly those who have made it into high-status occupations, reveal that the model of work, activity, and energy shown by their mothers is something that they cherish and value (Epstein, 1973). Epstein suggests that, because of economic circumstances, black mothers may cancel for their daughters part of the traditional feminine model, and offer, instead, an alternative model of adult womanhood. (For an extended discussion of this study, as well as for conflicting research on the subject, see Chapter 7 on minority women at work.)

LATER INFLUENCES: SEX-ROLE
SOCIALIZATION THROUGH EDUCATION

Although the family is an early influence in children's sex-role development, the schools soon join, and in certain ways intensify and take over, the process of socializing boys and girls. For a number of reasons, the schools are particularly important for socialization in general and for the occupational outcomes of the sexes in particular. And it is for these same reasons that we devote the major proportion of this chapter's discussion to the school and its influence on occupation.

First, simply by virtue of the time spent in attendance, the school has tremendous impact on the child (Stacey et al., 1974; Walum, 1977). From the age of 5, children spend up to six hours per day in the classroom. School, then, claims from the child more hours than any other activity except sleep. As the adult's time is structured by a schedule of work, so the days, weeks, and seasons of a child's life are governed by an academic schedule. Hence, the school bell determines the time of a child's arising, leaving home, lunching, and returning, as well as the time available for Cub Scouts, Brownies, music lessons, and other recreational activities.

Second, the school's socializing influence is heightened because it is society's official socializing agent (Stacey et al., 1974). By law, children are subject to school, as to their parents. And during the classroom hours, the school assumes parental authority over the child's actions and behavior.

Third, compared to the family, school socialization more directly channels children toward occupational outcomes. One reason is that, in certain ways, the role of a student represents and resembles an occupational role—especially an occupation that has a strong intellectual component (Slocum, 1966). As with many other workers, students are given assignments that must be completed by specified deadlines, are evaluated according to oral and written performance, and are rewarded or punished on the basis of that performance. In addition, many of the satisfactions, as well as the problems, of children's work at their studies parallel those of employees at their occupation. For example, certain rewards of employment, such as social contact, esteem, and identity, are also rewards of schoolwork. Likewise, the worker's problems of alienation, boredom, and tedium plague students as well. It makes sense that young people, when filling out forms that request occupation, write into the blank "student."

Finally, schools are an important root of occupational choice and performance, because they take vocational and occupational preparation as one of their primary functions. In fact, young people who emerge from school without any job aspirations or prospects are often considered failures of the educational system.

But as an institution that socializes the young for future occupational roles, the school trains and prepares its male and female students in a very different manner. The ways and means by which the school determines the different occupational destinies of the sexes may be found in the very structure or arrangements, and processes or operations, of that institution. Of the arrangements, one of the most important is the segregation, tracking, and funneling of male and female students.

Direct Sex-Role Socialization:
Segregation and Tracking

As the labor force divides men and women into different jobs and industries, so too the schools formally segregate males and females in classes and curriculum, and informally in their play and activities. Classifications of people and groups according to some criterion such as light and dark skin, native and foreign born, tall and short—or in this case, male and female— do not in themselves constitute inequality. But when groups are classified according to characteristics, they may be ranked and differentially evaluated—and this does create social inequality.

Sex stratification is a fact of social life in the society at large. But the schools reflect and reinforce that stratification by instructing very young and malleable children that males and females are expected to lead different lives. Sex-segregating practices suggest to children that, for education and other social groupings, sex is a more important consideration than individual interests, aspirations, or abilities. Ultimately, such practices imply that sex is an acceptable basis for discrimination.

Even in preschool nurseries and kindergartens, at a stage at which adults concede there are fewest sex differences, the sexes may be nonetheless divided. The little boys and girls may have their separate classroom toys, chores, lineups, and even enrollment lists (Joffe, 1974). Similarly, in elementary school, playgrounds are organized quite frequently into male and female territories; for example, the boys dominate the tetherball equipment, and the girls rule the sidewalk converted into a hop-scotch grid. In this way, children's play space divides into separate domains—in which the same-sex prevails and the opposite-sex only intrudes.

However, this segregation is not "symmetric." As in occupational segregation, males are more welcome in feminine activities than vice versa. In both schools and occupations, as indeed throughout the society, the male is esteemed as the higher-status figure and, as such, is believed to "upgrade" the prestige of a previously all-female group (Fox, 1981b). In practice, however, women are more likely to participate in predominately male groups and activities than men in females' activities. Thus, within occupations, we are more likely to find women in the male roles of dentist, doctor, or school principal than men in positions as dental hygienist, nurse, or kindergarten teacher. Likewise, among children, girls are more likely to play in predominately male games than boys in girls' games (Lever, 1976). And accordingly, a larger proportion of girls than boys indicate a preference for the role of the opposite sex (Lynn, 1966). Again, these patterns in school and occupations probably reflect the presumption that women stand to gain, but men to lose, from participation in groups of the opposite sex.

The sex-segregating practices within the schools do not reflect inherent dispositions and tendencies of the child. Rather, they are learned practices, which are encouraged, endorsed, and even instigated by teachers and school administrators, who hold cultural stereotypes about the sexes and condone segregation as a means of maintaining order and discipline in the schools.

If the sex segregation were a matter of "separate but equal," the issues would be different, and the segregation might be defensible and desirable. But separate hasn't been equal. Consider, for example, the separate athletic programs for boys and girls in the secondary schools. Before the recent cases of compliance with Federal Title IX, which was enacted in 1972, more funds, faculty, and resources were allotted to the male than to the female athletic programs. The boys had scheduling priority on the soccer field, the swimming pool, and the basketball courts; and the girls made do with the remainders. Furthermore, boys' athletic uniforms and traveling expenses came out of schools' operating funds; girls' out of their own pockets. Male coaching staffs tended to be substantial; females', in comparison, rather paltry. These differences in the quality and quantity of the male and female programs took their toll in the abilities and aspirations developed, and the opportunities created in athletics among male compared to female students. (A discussion of Title IX and its consequences can be found in Chapter 9.)

Yet, even before enactment and enforcement of Title IX, there was some pretense of parallelism in athletic programs for the boys and girls. In other educational programs, however, the male and female sectors have constituted "tracks" that overtly diverge, rather than parallel, each other. This divergence is particularly apparent in vocational education. Although there have been some changes in vocational education, these programs continue to train girls for low-paying, already overcrowded jobs in homemaking, retailing, and health fields and to train boys for more highly skilled and better-paying jobs in agribusiness, technical fields, and industrial trades (see Table 3.1). The consequences in occupational outcomes are apparent—and consistent with the labor-force position of women in jobs with low pay, power, and prestige.

Dividing and tracking of male and female students is not confined to special programs and options such as athletics and vocational education.

T a b l e   3 . 1 / *Vocational Education Enrollments, by Sex (1969 and 1979)*

Program Area	1969 Enrollments		1979 Enrollments	
	Percentage Male	Percentage Female	Percentage Male	Percentage Female
Agriculture	98	2	81	19
Health	8	92	16	84
Consumer and homemaking	4	96	21	79
Technical	91	9	80	20
Trade and industry	89	11	83	17

SOURCE: Mary Abrams, "Title IX—A Modest Success," *Graduate Woman* 76 (January–February 1982): 23–25. Reprinted with permission of *Graduate Woman*, the magazine of the American Association of University Women.

Rather, it pervades the basic academic and college-preparatory programs. In the preparatory program, the most critical and ultimately consequential male/female tracking is in the scientific and mathematical sequences.

Mathematics has been typed as a male skill. Girls are not expected to do very well in the subject, and those who do show ability are not particularly encouraged. Soon girls come to believe that they are less able than boys in handling numbers, logic, and problem-solving tasks (Tobias, 1978). By the time the seventh- and eighth-grade standardized achievement tests are administered, girls, not surprisingly, are earning lower scores.

Later, when the female high-school student encounters difficulty with her now-optional math courses, she often decides, with the advice and approval of teachers, counselors, and parents, to forgo further study. So, at the tender age of fifteen, hordes of tenth-grade girls, struggling with elementary geometry, terminate their math sequence. Some research indicates that girls become discouraged earlier, in junior high (Meece, Parsons, Kaczala, Goff, and Futterman, 1982). But it is after elementary geometry that even college-bound girls actually drop out of the mathematics sequence. Consequently, even those girls who attend highly competitive colleges have relatively poor math backgrounds. For example, among the 1973 entering class at Berkeley, only 8 percent of the females, compared to 57 percent of the males, had studied four years of high-school math (Sell, 1974).

It is often only years later that the young woman discovers that in forgoing mathematics she has, by default, severely restricted her educational and occupational possibilities. In formal education, the study of mathematics is more structured than other areas of study, and it forms a true sequence of learning: One masters a given unit and progresses to the next; completes a given course and advances to the following. Once out of sequence and track, it is very difficult to acquire the prerequisites and somehow catch up. Most women never do. As a result, they are then disqualified from subsequent education in 75 percent of the possible college and university majors, including the business, medical, scientific, and technical programs, all of which require mathematical prerequisites and sequences.

Furthermore, in the job world mathematical skills are required for upward mobility in three out of every four well-paying occupations. For management-level positions in almost every field, one must be familiar with quantitative comparisons, contrasts, ratios, proportions, and the like. Indeed, as Sheila Tobias points out, mathematics has become the universal language of business, government, and the social sciences. Even when managers are not speaking of mathematics per se, they tend, because of math's power and precision, to use quantitative concepts such as "exponential" growth, sales "increments," or "marginal" costs. And they expect their employees to understand those terms (Tobias, 1978).

Indirect Sex-Role Socialization:
School Texts, Teachers, and Staff

The tracking and routing of male and female students represent some of the more direct ways in which schools socialize the sexes for different occupational positions and spheres. But the school accomplishes the same outcomes more indirectly through (1) implicit messages of the texts and instructional materials, (2) the modeling or examples the teachers and counselors provide, and (3) the ways in which these personnel interact with female compared to male students. These implicit messages constitute a "hidden curriculum" in the schools:

> There is no course in the official curriculum called "Male Sex Role Development" or "Learning How to be a Girl," but such learning takes place incidentally, and a variety of signals—some obvious, some hidden—insure that sex-typing will be reinforced. (Frazier and Sadker, 1973:85)

In children's texts and readers, the sex-role stereotyping is pervasive. One of the most thorough studies of this sex typing is the investigation conducted by Women on Words and Images (1972), a task force of the National Organization for Women (NOW). In reviewing 134 children's readers, this group found sex stereotyping throughout the materials. First of all, males are omnipresent in the stories; in comparison, females are virtually absent. Males are three times more likely to be the main story character, and six times more likely to be the figure of a biography. In animal stories, too, males outnumber females two to one. And even in personifications of inanimate objects such as autos, boats, trains, and machines, the figures are almost invariably male (Fisher, 1974).

Furthermore, the behavior and activities of the female characters are highly restricted. Women and girls are passive, fearful, and fretful characters, who frequently get themselves into snags and muddles from which they must be rescued. In contrast, boys and males make and do things, and go places, overcoming obstacles and solving their own problems with courage and ingenuity. Throughout the stories, men's range of options are broader, and their possibilities greater. Adult males are both fathers and jobholders, while women are either jobholders or mothers, and usually only the latter. When women do work, they do so primarily in traditionally female areas, as nurses, teachers, or librarians. Significantly, male characters work in six times more occupations than do females.

Publishers and editors have defended these books and have maintained that the imagery of the sexes simply parallels and reflects the reality of men and women, in society at large. Yet even cursory examination shows that these books fall short of reality. For while in actuality 50 percent of American women are in the labor force, the books infrequently show women outside the home. And while most men, in fact, follow humdrum daily routines in factories, offices, and businesses, children's books picture males as impossibly strong, brave, and heroic figures.

Moreover, while women's roles did change between the 1960s and 1970s, children's literature did not, indicating that the books lag behind, rather than keep up with, social change (Wirtenberg and Nakamura, 1976). A recent update and review (1975) by the Women on Words and Images group shows that the sex biasing in children's literature has not declined materially. Among the books published after 1972, the proportion of male-centered biographies had decreased, but the overall ratio of boy-centered to girl-centered stories had actually increased. The most recently published texts have begun to eliminate sex stereotyping. But many schools, particularly those which are financially pressed, continue to use older materials.

Authors, editors, and publishers have not joined in an overt conspiracy to exclude females from their books. Rather, they are motivated in part by marketing considerations. If a book centers around a male figure, it is thought acceptable reading for both boys and girls; but if it centers around a female, it is assumed to appeal to girls alone (because as we discussed earlier, it is presumed that men stand to lose and women to gain from participation in groups and activities of the opposite sex). Some of the male bias in children's literature may, then, represent an effort to maximize the audience for a book.

If it were inconsequential, the stereotyping might be overlooked. But it *is* consequential. Through these media, children form images of their worth, the expectations they will assume, and roles they will hold (Fisher, 1974). Social psychological research shows that, on hearing and reading these stories, children symbolically rehearse the episodes, playing out the morals and models of the accounts (Walum, 1977:59). Furthermore, these books come at a critical stage in children's lives—during their first experience with reading, at a time when learning to read is among the most salient activities in their lives (Wirtenberg and Nakamura, 1976).

Sex-biased content is not limited to readers. It pervades texts throughout the schools' curriculum. Mathematics texts, for example, depict boys in story problems working at physical activities, building things, earning money, and going places; meanwhile, the girls are close to home, measuring ingredients, cutting fabrics, and shopping for food and sewing supplies (Federbush, 1974; Frazier and Sadker, 1973). Recent mathematics texts have story problems, with more active girls competing at sports and traveling—but the boys still aren't sewing or cleaning, and males continue to be the more spry and enterprising figures.

Along with the curriculum materials, the school staff—its faculty, counselors, and administrators—also play an important part in socializing children into traditional sex roles. Indeed, the school's very structure of authority conveys a strong social message: "The higher the rank, the fewer the women." Women constitute 84 percent of all elementary-school teachers, but only 20 percent of the principals. In the secondary schools, women are more absent, and constitute 49 percent of the teachers, and a mere 6 percent of the principals. And in the top position, that of school superintendent, women are almost totally absent (Parelius and Parelius, 1978). In this gender-biased authority structure, the school is no different from the law office, corporate firm, medical facility, or indeed any other organization employing both men and women. For socialization, however, the school's particular structure is more important, because it is a central institution in children's lives, claiming a large proportion of their wakeful hours. And here students may readily learn about the subordinate position of women simply by virtue of exposure and observation. To illustrate:

> Joanne is in the sixth grade at Barnes Elementary School. She has gone there all her life, and all her teachers have been women. Joanne has seen that sometimes students get fresh and hard to handle, and then the teacher sends these students to the principal's office. She has also noted that whenever the teacher doesn't know the answer to a question about school rules and regulations, the teacher says that she will find out the answer from the principal. All her teachers have taken their orders from the principal and have gone to him when they need help. And the principal is a man. (Frazier and Sadker, 1973:97)

Students are subject to other staff attitudes and behavior that foster and maintain traditional sex roles. To begin with, boys are more highly regarded by their teachers. When asked which sex they prefer to teach, teachers who do express a preference say that they prefer to teach boys (Ricks and Pike,

1973). Boys, they claim, are more outspoken, active, open, and willing to exchange ideas. The only reason given for a female preference is that girls are easier to discipline.

In like manner, compared to girls, boys receive more of their teachers' attention—both negative and positive. Consistent with popular lore, studies show that boys do receive more punishment and reprimands in the classroom (Good, Sikes, and Brophy, 1973; Sears and Feldman, 1974; Willis and Brophy, 1974). But these same studies demonstrate that boys are also more likely to receive positive responses—approval, instruction, and careful listening.

These results suggest that in the course of being disapproved, yet praised and listened to, boys are taught more actively than girls and are provided with more opportunities to participate in the classroom (Good et al., 1973; Sears and Feldman, 1974). This active instruction may explain why boys seem to initiate more questions, call out more responses, and make guesses at questions more frequently than do girls (Good et al., 1973).

Together with the teachers, school psychologists and counselors also contribute to students' socialization into traditional sex roles. These guidance personnel are probably no more or less sexist in their attitudes than the population at large. However, as counselors they occupy influential positions for the outcomes of their students.

By high school, students are in a quandary about choices for course work, college options, and career alternatives. Many converge on the school guidance office as the logical source of information and direction. What they tend to receive is strong reinforcement for traditionally feminine or masculine occupational goals. First, evidence suggests that, at the college level particularly, counselors regard female clients less seriously, dismissing their problems as "socioemotional" rather than "vocational-educational" (Collins and Selacke, 1972). Furthermore, counselors tend to respond more positively to the female client if she holds traditionally feminine career goals (Abromowitz, Weitz, Schwartz, Amira, Gomes, and Abromowitz, 1975).

No less biased are the standardized vocational-interest tests, administered by the counselors. With the presumption that vocational behavior is strongly related to sex (Harmon, 1975), these tests have employed separate forms, separate scales, and separate norms for male and female students. And because the methodology of these tests is a correlational technique, they tend to promote a stable and conservative socialization process (Tittle, 1974). For example, these tests measure the association between the likes and dislikes of people within a given occupation. If a respondent has interests and preferences similar to those of certain occupational incumbents, it is then presumed that he or she is likely to be satisfied in that occupation. But this presumption rests on a static and stable model about occupations and their incumbents; descriptions of the interests and preferences among current occupation holders become prescriptions for future incumbents. In this way, the tests have promoted conservative tendencies, including traditional sex typing of occupations.

The format of the widely used Strong Vocational Test has now been revised. As late as 1975, however, this test classified occupations into male and female categories. The other widely used test, the Kuder Occupational Interest Survey, continues to be sex biased. On this test, females can learn their aptitude for prestigious occupations, such as law, business, finance, and medicine, only if they leave the sex item blank on the test (see Richardson, 1981:83).

Sex-Role Socialization and Higher Education

Until very recently, males were more likely than females to go on to college after high school. Parents and counselors were more apt to encourage and finance the education of sons, and admission standards were more favorable for boys. Even as late as 1971, a study of 240 colleges across the country revealed that, among students of comparable credentials, the males were more likely to be admitted (Frazier and Sadker, 1973). Or to put it another way: in order to be admitted to college, the females had to have higher credentials.

Over the past three decades, the proportion of males going on to college has remained about the same. But for women, the proportions have been increasing, so that by 1978 women represented 50 percent of all college students (Heyns and Bird, 1982). And about half of the bachelor's degrees awarded in this country now go to women.

However, for our attempt to explain the position of American women at work, the data on baccalaureate education are misleading or, at the least, incomplete. First, it is important to note that the majority of currently employed women were products of an educational system before the advent of these recent trends. Furthermore, for a study of women and work such as this one, the data on proportions obtaining baccalaureate degrees contain limited information. We need to look beyond these data and examine men's and women's fields of study, their patterns of postbaccalaureate (professional and graduate school) education, and their particular experiences within higher education.

Although the sex differences are not as great as they used to be, men and women still concentrate in separate fields of study. Men are twice as likely as women to specialize in business and in the physical sciences, and they are nearly seven times more likely to concentrate in the engineering fields. Women, on the other hand, cluster in the humanities, in certain health sciences, and especially in education (see Table 3.2). Hence, women tend to study the fields aligned with the poorer-paying, lower-status occupations in

T a b l e   3 . 2 / *Field of Study Among College Students, Ages 14–34,*
Percentage Distribution by Sex, 1966 and 1974

Major Fields	1966		1974	
	Women	Men	Women	Men
Agriculture and forestry	0.1	1.9	0.4	1.8
Biological sciences and health	11.7	9.0	16.6	9.7
Business and commerce	8.9	18.4	11.2	19.1
Education	33.2	9.7	21.6	6.5
Engineering	0.4	14.1	0.7	7.8
Humanities	13.8	8.2	9.0	6.4
Math and statistics	3.8	4.0	1.9	1.9
Physical sciences	1.1	5.4	.9	2.0
Social sciences	10.6	10.8	8.8	8.7
Other	5.5	9.0	17.7	25.0
"Don't know" and not reported	11.0	9.4	11.3	11.0
Total	99.9	100.1	100.1	99.9

SOURCE: Barbara Heyns and Joyce Adair Bird, "Recent Trends in the Higher Education of
Women," in Pamela Perun, ed., *The Undergraduate Woman: Issues in Educational Equity*
(Lexington, Mass.: Heath, 1982), Ch. 3, Table 2.

health, education, and the services; and men pursue fields aligned with
better-paying, more powerful positions of business, science, and technology.
   Moreover, the sex distributions in education beyond the baccalaureate
are especially important, because this education is a prelude to, and prerequisite for, entry into high-status positions in the professions and, increasingly, within government and business as well. In postbaccalaureate
education, we find that women have made gains over the past decade. Fifteen years ago, women earned less than 5 percent of the professional degrees; that proportion rose to 12 percent in 1975, and to 19 percent by
1977. In doctoral degrees, too, the proportion earned by women rose from
11 percent in 1965 to 21 percent in 1975. And by 1977 almost 25 percent of
the nation's doctorates were being awarded to women (see Table 3.3). Still,
although women's educational edge is improving, their proportion in graduate programs is far below men's. Moreover, the experiences and socialization processes of male and female graduate students are very different, and
these differences have important consequences for the practice of their
training, and ultimately, for their position in the business and professional
world.
   The heart of men's and women's different graduate-school experiences
lies in the quality and quantity of their relationships with the faculty. Compared to men, women see their faculty and research advisors much less fre-

T a b l e 3 . 3 / *Percentage of Bachelor's and Higher Degrees Earned by*
Women, 1964–65, 1969–70, and 1974–77

School Year	Bachelor's Degree	Master's Degree	Doctor's Degree	First Professional
1964–65	42.4	33.8	10.8	3.5
1969–70	43.1	39.7	13.3	5.0
1974–75	45.3	44.8	21.3	12.4
1975–76	45.5	46.3	22.9	14.0
1976–77	46.1	47.1	24.3	18.6

SOURCE: Barbara Heyns and Joyce Adair Bird, "Recent Trends in the Higher Education of Women," in Pamela Perun, ed., *The Undergraduate Woman: Issues in Educational Equity* (Lexington, Mass.: Heath, 1982), Ch. 3, Table 4.

quently, especially outside of the formal classroom or office context (Holmstrom and Holmstrom, 1974; Kjerulff and Blood, 1973). Women have more limited patterns of communication with faculty, and compared to men they are less relaxed, jocular, and egalitarian in their interactions with advisors (Kjerulff and Blood, 1973). Women regard themselves as "students" rather than as colleagues of their teachers, and they report problems in being taken "seriously."

In order to comprehend the implications of these sex differences, we must understand that (1) professional socialization is a central aspect of graduate school education and (2) that this education is largely a function of informal interaction and alliance with faculty. It is through faculty relationships that students' progress is eased and facilitated. For favored students, faculty provide laboratory and office space, and research training and experience. They also support preferred students in the allocation of scarce departmental resources, such as fellowships and stipends, and they take a stand for them in the perennial disputes surrounding qualifying and certifying examinations. Faculty give their protegés exposure at professional meetings and conventions, and help them to develop the skills necessary for presenting and publishing their research. And, perhaps most importantly, they find for their students the best available jobs and thus place them on the path of career mobility.

It is not that it's impossible for students to accomplish these things for themselves—to compete for fellowships, pass qualifying examinations, locate research topics, acquire professional skills, and find a job. It's just that doing it on one's own is a long and arduous battle, which is subject to obstacle, discouragement, and failure.

The limited interaction and communication that women have with faculty indicates how female students are more likely to be among those trying to make it through graduate school and into professional life on their own.

The irony is that, although women are less likely to have professional mentors, they are actually more in need of alliances with influential and powerful sponsors (Kanter, 1977a). Women are missing these alliances not because they are reluctant or simply because faculty object to female assistants. Rather, women are excluded primarily because the graduate school and professional world is a "male milieu." The male members have grown up together, learned, and competed together. Women are outsiders who do not share the male traditions and settings—in the bar, committee room, and squash court. Moreover, the men who dominate are unable to see a reflection, or heirship, of themselves in a student who is female.[1] In the following statement about the consequences of this "male milieu," Korda is referring to the business corporation, but the principle applies aptly to academic organizations as well:

> Nothing contributes more to the psychology of serfdom of women than the subtle notion that the corporation [or organization] is not 'it' but 'him.' Women know that behind each man is a door leading to a more powerful man, each step up the ladder moving nearer to the magic inner circle that is essentially masculine. The process of rewards above a certain level remains in the hands of men, and most men . . . are unable to see the mechanism of success except in masculine terms. (Korda, 1972:68–69)

OUTCOMES OF SEX-ROLE SOCIALIZATION

These differences in the training, conditioning, and preparation of males compared to females take their toll in the expectations, aspirations, and behaviors of men and women within the school, the family, and later in the occupational world.

Patterns of Dependence

We have observed that, compared to males, female children are more likely to be kept in close physical contact with their parents. One example given was that as toddlers, girls are less likely to have their attention diverted from their parents, to have a ball thrown far away in a game of catch, or to be encouraged to run and play some distance from parents. And as children grow older, dependency that is seen as normal for young children of both sexes comes to be regarded as a more exclusively feminine trait. Thus, timidity among older boys is disdained, but is more expected for older girls. As a consequence, girls continue to depend on their families as a source of support and affection for a much longer period of time. In doing so, they may be less likely to develop internal controls and an independent sense of self (Bardwick, 1970). Rather, their selfhood becomes more contingent on the responses, reactions, and appraisals of others. Compared with males, females may then develop a greater need for the approval of others, and a higher fear of rejection.

In fact, Kegan (1964) has noted that our cultural definition of femininity—as nurturant, giving, caring—*requires* responses from others. In order to affirm these characteristics, one is forced to depend directly on, and react to, the responses of others. This dependent and self-doubting behavior may be suited to certain family roles and occupational roles in female-typed jobs. But it is at odds with many other occupations—particularly jobs that are characterized by independent judgment, management, and decision making, and that, in turn, provide higher rewards in pay, power, and prestige. In this way, women's learned capacity to anticipate and respond to the needs and wishes of others can contribute to their subordinate status at work (Marciano, 1981). Furthermore, because female-centered values such as civility, humanism, and deference have not been incorporated into the work place, it is the women who are compelled to learn the male values through such programs as "assertiveness training." Men, however, are exempt from any parallel program in "humanism" or "civility" that might equip them with female-centered values and skills (Marciano, 1981:24).

Intellectual Development

Within the schools themselves, the sex-differential outcomes form a subtle and confounding pattern. First, girls are "good students." In grade school, through high school, and into college, females outrank males in the grades they attain. And parents and teachers, alike, report that girls seem better adjusted and adapted to school rules and routines. This isn't surprising. In elementary school, particularly, the classroom values of silence, neatness, and politeness are, in some sense, a stylized version of feminine, ladylike virtues in the society at large (Bruner, 1966; Frazier and Sadker, 1973). Thus, the roles "girl" and "student" are mutually reinforcing, and being "good" at the one role reinforces the other.

Yet this picture of female success and adjustment to the school is a real irony, because these "good" female students quickly lose academic potential. The passive classroom qualities for which girls are reinforced have no positive relationship with intellectual or cognitive endeavor. In contrast to the acquiescent classroom model, the intellectual enterprise is actually an active process—of inquiry, solution, and mastery. And for this enterprise one needs vigor, confidence, and—perhaps above all—courage. In order to address questions and solve problems, one must have the courage to take risks, make mistakes, and tolerate error.

However, "the good student," overly anxious to please the teacher and win approval, has a high aversion to risk. In a study of grade-school children, Silberman (1971) found that those students who are most responsive to extrinsic rewards (such as grades, praise, prizes) are the least willing to reveal error and mistakes and to take chances with more difficult material. Other studies reveal that, compared with boys, girls are more likely to hide weakness and avoid risk, and they show more concern with losing rather than with further success and approval. For example, given a chance to repeat a puzzle they had already solved or to try a new one, girls were much more likely to avoid the challenge and opt for the safe alternative (Crandall and Robson, 1960). In doing so, these good and conforming students may curb not only their intellectual development but also their occupational capacities.

Patterns of Achievement, Aspiration, and Esteem

Another irony of girls' classroom success is that although, as a group, their performance is relatively high, their expectations and esteem are low. Compared to males, females tend to underestimate their ability and performance and to exaggerate their liabilities. When they fail, they attribute the failure to their own shortcomings. Yet when they succeed, they dismiss the success as chance, luck, or hard work and effort—and they still expect to do poorly next time. So if females fail, they take the blame; if they succeed, they don't take the credit. And hence, compared with men, women tend to attribute their successes to unstable and external factors over which they have no control, and conversely, their failures to fixed factors within themselves (Frieze et al., 1978).

This particular attribution pattern clearly perpetuates low expectations and low self-esteem. And it may explain, in part, why women's achievements translate into aspirations at a level lower than that of males (Fox and Faver, 1981). Throughout the educational life cycle, we find that, relative to their current achievements, women underestimate their future possibilities. In elementary school, girls are less likely than their male counterparts to believe themselves able to do college work (Wylie, 1963). In high school, academic achievements have a much weaker effect on girls', compared to boys', occupational aspirations (Marini and Greenberger, 1978). Among college students, men who had only C+ grades believed that they were perfectly capable of attaining Ph.D.'s, yet women with B+ averages doubted that they were this capable (Baird, 1973). At some of the country's most prestigious undergraduate schools (including Brown, Wellesley, Barnard, Dartmouth, and Princeton) the women are "more likely to worry about grades, underestimate their academic ability . . . , and underestimate their career goals" (Monteiro, 1978). Finally, among graduate students with comparable credentials, the female students have been likely to aspire for only a junior-college teaching career, versus the more prestigious university career (Feldman, 1974).

The origins of these patterns of achievement, aspiration, and esteem are the subject of debate, as, indeed, are the sources of other sex differences. Yet we do know that, along with the family, the school is a central and powerful agent in socializing the American child and that a number of these sex-differential patterns can be traced to the educational arrangements and process discussed earlier, including the direct practices of tracking and segregation and the indirect messages of teachers, counselors, and texts.

Conflicts and Consequences: Conclusions

At the cultural root of women's socialization is a basic conflict between the definitions, expectations, and demands of (1) their gender and family roles and (2) their occupational and extrafamilial roles. This conflict has provided the theme for art and literature across the ages. However, even if the conflict is proverbial, it is no less real. Traditionally, women's socialization has been directed more toward virtue and acceptance in femininity than toward competition and accomplishment in worldly occupation (Barnett and Baruch, 1978). Yet society rewards with pay, power, and prestige those who accomplish and compete, and it gives only testimonials to those who are noble, nurturant, and loved. Consequently, women who devote themselves to feeding, nourishing, and nurturing gain few extrinsic rewards. In spite of rhetoric to the contrary, our culture holds childbearing and child rearing in low esteem and gives little compensation to those who do this work (Lott, 1974). At the same time, the women who do seek power and prestige often lose in virtue and acceptance (Barnett and Baruch, 1978). This no-win predicament contains the classic conditions for a "double-bind" (no-win) situation.

Moreover, the central importance of women's family role imposes onerous household demands. These demands, in turn, place constraints on their occupational activities. Despite women's rapid increase in labor-force participation, the family's allocation of household responsibilities has, in comparison, changed very little (see Hofferth and Moore, 1979). Consequently, when women become employed, they don't relinquish housework for market work; rather, they add one work role to the other. The addition of an occupational, to a domestic, role then creates dual work—house and market—for women. (These dual work roles for women are the focus of discussion in Chapter 8.)

Partly in response to these conflicts—in values, demands, and expectations—between their family and occupational roles, women frequently limit their aspirations and modify their occupational "choices" in favor of socially realistic and more easily attained options. And these options are represented by the traditional, feminine sex-typed jobs.

As we shall see in Chapter 4, three-quarters of all employed women are working at jobs in which the majority of their fellow workers are female.

The major concomitants of these feminine sex-typed occupations are poor pay and low prestige (Stevenson, 1975b; Weisskoff, 1972). Since most women do work in these jobs, their occupational location then helps to explain their low, average occupational rewards.[2]

Even highly educated women have channeled occupational achievement into areas such as teaching or nursing, which integrate and consolidate, rather than divide, her gender and occupational roles and demands. Or else women work very hard, but without public recognition and reward, within secondary and invisible roles as lab assistant rather than director, nurse rather than doctor, dental hygienist instead of dentist, or research assistant but not professor. And in this way, the same family and educational process that makes little girls anxious to please their teachers and receive good grades also puts women into jobs at which they assume secondary roles supporting and pleasing their superiors.

Women respond to the pressures, conflicts, and constraints of their socialization not only by employment in these sex-typed jobs, but also through part-time work. In 1975, just over 40 percent of all employed women, and only 10 percent of all employed married women, were working full time, year round (Kreps and Leaper, 1976; U.S. Department of Labor, 1976). The rest of the working women had part-time employment for either the whole or part of the year, or they worked part time for some fraction of the year. This part-time employment allows women to adjust to both family and occupational demands. But, as with employment in feminine sex-typed occupations, part-time work puts women in places and positions where the pay is low and the benefits are few.

The sex differences in these choices for part-time or feminine-typed jobs reflect, in part, conditioned "preferences," learned in the course of family and educational socialization as we have discussed. But they also reflect responses to the *opportunities available*—in a world in which options are not equally possible or accessible for men and women alike. Females' occupational activities are subject to the constraints of their family demands and of their educational and occupational possibilities. And hence, as with the cars we drive, the clothes we buy, and the houses we rent, what one chooses does not necessarily represent what one favors. Looking beyond the female tokens in a few conspicuous places, women find the reality that the higher the rank, the fewer the women. And from this, they can ultimately deduce their own occupational probabilities. The restricted female opportunities, in turn, reflect (1) economic practices and arrangements discriminating against women and (2) a political and legal structure that tolerates and in some cases promotes this discrimination. We turn toward those economic and legal factors in the next chapter.

SUMMARY

Women's depressed position in the labor force is partly a function of "socialization"—a process whereby we learn the expectations appropriate to the positions we occupy and the groups to which we belong.

Of all the groups that socialize the sexes for different roles, two of the most important institutions are the family and the school. Almost immediately after birth, parents sex-type their children and respond differently to boys and girls. They regard daughters as softer, quieter, and more delicate, and sons as stronger, bolder, and more active.

Although parents and others clearly characterize girls and boys in different ways, it is more difficult to determine the *actual* behavioral differences between male and female children, because differences can be specific to certain age periods and subject to the social context in which they occur. Researchers agree on only two items about early sex differences: girls are more verbal, and boys are more aggressive. Some persons would take this a step further and argue that these differences indicate early female inclinations toward people-oriented occupations and male inclinations toward more task-oriented occupations.

This brings us then to the long-debated argument over origin of sex differences as a function of (1) nature and biology or (2) nurture and experience. From our examination of these major perspectives, we conclude that biological differences between the sexes are just a starting point in the development of sex-role differences and their occupational consequences. Biology may influence certain tendencies, but these differences are strengthened by the social environment of the child. In addition, the "cognitive perspective" on development stresses that the children, themselves, play an active part in their development by selecting, organizing, and acting on the messages they receive about sex-appropriate and sex-inappropriate behavior and occupational roles.

The family is the earliest socializing influence. But the schools soon join in and, in certain ways, intensify the process of socializing males and females and influencing their occupational outcomes. The schools influence the destinies of females compared to males through a variety of social arrangements and processes, including

1. The segregation, tracking, and funneling of boys and girls into different groups, activities, classes and courses
2. The imagery of books, texts, and readers depicting boys and men as the doers, goers, and makers of ideas, places, and things, and women and girls as spiritless observers

3. The schools' structure of power and authority in which children see males in superordinate and females in subordinate positions
4. The teachers' preference for male students in spite of girls' good behavior; and teachers' more active interaction with boys, not just in reprimands, but also in instruction, careful listening, and opportunities for response
5. The guidance staff's covert and overt reinforcement of traditional, cultural definitions of masculinity and femininity

Each of these educational processes and arrangements operate toward the following final outcomes. First, they lower women's esteem and depress confidence so that as they progress through school, girls become less confident about their accomplishments and the adequacy of their whole gender group. Second, they form self-defeating attributions of success and failure. Third, they inhibit the development of growth and potential so that between adolescence and adulthood, when men's I.Q.'s are still rising, women are making few gains. Fourth, they restrict development, particularly, of the mathematical, technical, and scientific skills on which are based 75 percent of majors in higher education, and 75 percent of all well-paying jobs.

These socialization processes in family and school account, in part, for women's location in traditional, feminine-typed jobs with low pay and low power. However, beyond conditioned "preferences" of the socialization process, women's occupational location is a response to the limited opportunities available to them. These restricted opportunities reflect, in turn, the constraints of economic and of political and legal institutions, discussed in the next chapter.

4 • Working Women: Economic and Legal Context

American society puts a high premium on achievement, particularly in its economic life. Rewards such as earnings, status, occupational opportunities are said to be based on merit and performance, rather than on incidental or ascribed characteristics such as gender and race. Presumably, then, people who are equally qualified for a given job should have equal chances of obtaining it; having obtained it, they should receive equal compensation.

The economy is structured so that some jobs bring greater rewards than do other jobs. Certain occupations and activities are considered more important than others in responsibilities, degree of power, and the range of social and economic areas affected by the decisions of those who hold such positions. These high-level jobs require high levels of ability, training, and expertise; their rewards, in terms of status and compensation, are correspondingly high.[1] Society rewards its chiefs of state, its business executives, its medicine men well. Positions of less responsibility—requiring less experience, expertise, and training—have correspondingly lower levels of status and compensation. Housekeepers earn less than lawyers, waitresses less than scientists, and nurses less than doctors.

However, the American occupational structure has another pervasive characteristic—one that runs counter to its achievement ideology: the higher-level, better-paying jobs tend to be held by the members of one dominant group (white males) and the lower-level, poorer-paying jobs tend to be held by all others (women and minority-group members). Some believe that this arrangement reflects differences in abilities and qualifications, differences in interests, talents, preferences. Others argue that the arrangement results from exclusionary practices that reflect discriminatory attitudes. Most observers assume that the situation results from a combination of these and other, related factors.

In this chapter, we focus on the major explanations and rationales that have been offered to account for the pervasiveness of sex segregation and inequity in our society's work force. As we emphasized in Chapter 2, one of the most enduring characteristics of women workers is their high degree of concentration in female-dominated jobs. This occupational segregation by sex is still as pervasive today as it was at the turn of this century. In 1980, as in 1900, the great majority of working women were concentrated in female-typed occupations. In 1900, 60 percent of all women workers were in occupations in which at least 50 percent of their fellow workers were women. This female concentration has actually increased over time so that by 1980, 75 percent of all working women were in occupations where women are the majority. In salary as well, women employed full time, year round, average only $0.60 for every $1.00 men earn. This earnings gap has not changed over the last three decades (Waite, 1981).

How is this occupational segregation by sex to be explained? How can we account for the differences between men and women's earnings? To what extent are discriminatory practices to blame? To what extent does the disparity reflect differences in individual characteristics, such as women's training, credentials, their particular interests, innate abilities, preferences, and socialization? To what extent, on the other hand, does the disparity reflect structural features of the society—in particular, its economic and legal institutions?

THE ECONOMIC CONTEXT

Economists have only recently begun to analyze gender differences in the economic status of workers. Individual approaches to explaining economic factors emphasize specific characteristics attributed to women and differences in men and women's levels of productivity.

The Individual Approach

The underlying assumption of the individual approach is that inequalities in the labor force reflect differences in the individual workers—differences in ability, training, and the like. For example, women workers are viewed as lacking the essential qualities to "make it" in an economic setting. These deficiencies range from women's lack of specific job-related credentials (such as education, training, relevant work experience) to a variety of presumed personality deficits (such as women's "fear of success" [see Horner, 1968, 1972] or characteristic submissiveness). The typical solution to the woman's dilemma lies in changing the woman—by appropriate career counseling and by helping her to offset "personality deficits" (for example, through assertiveness training and a variety of related self-help techniques). A good example of this approach is provided by the recent book *Wising Up* (Foxworth, 1980). The author describes the most common "mistakes" women make on the job; it is these mistakes that purportedly hamper women's progress. The implication is that if women would only "wise up," they would be able to get ahead.

> Why don't more of these underpaid, undervalued women move on to better things? Anne Hyde, President of Management Woman, an executive recruitment firm specializing in placement of women ($30,000-a-year minimum), says it can be summed up in one bleak, bad word, "Fear." Asked for more words, Hyde explains: "Time and time again, I've seen very superior women walk away from spectacular opportunity when all systems were 'Go.' They've come to us brimming with confidence and determination, ready to move up the executive ladder to the positions their backgrounds have prepared them to command. We have matched their credentials up with corporations actively seeking gifted women for their executive staffs—only to have the whole thing come a cropper at the last minute!" . . . At the moment of truth, she panics. Panics! The confidence and determination collapse. She says she's sorry but she's afraid she wouldn't be right for the job. (Foxworth, 1980:92–93)

It is important to recognize that such individual-level explanations imply that women's poor economic position stems from choices made by women and from their lack of qualifications for the better jobs that bring higher salaries. In either case, the explanations point to the individual woman worker: they suggest she does not have the motivation, qualifications, or personal attributes necessary for the pursuit of higher-status and higher-paid employment. But these explanations are not surprising, because the socialization process emphasizes different roles, norms, and values for men and women.

Sex-role socialization and women's "choices"

As discussed in Chapter 3, men and women are brought up to behave in particular, culturally prescribed ways. Their respective social responsibilities constitute a division of labor whereby women assume the role of wife and mother and men the role of provider (Parsons and Bales, 1956; Weisskoff, 1972). The sex segregation of the labor market reflects this broader division of labor. The occupations held predominantly by women (such as waitressing, child care, secretarial work, nursing, elementary-school teaching) are those that reflect the traditional female nurturing and supportive roles. The more task-oriented and intellectually demanding jobs—such as doctor, lawyer, executive, crafts worker—belong to men.[2]

Furthermore, women are believed to seek employment that allows them the flexibility to spend time with their families; these choices prevent their obtaining the training and other credentials they would need to compete more effectively in the job market. In other words, women end up concentrated in "women's jobs" *partly* because they choose to do so. A recent survey of 5,000 young women between the ages of twenty-one and thirty-one lends some support to this belief: the majority aspired to "traditionally" female occupations, even though they rejected the role of full-time homemaker (Barrett, 1979a : 53).

The essence of the individual model is that women's preferences—for traditionally female-typed jobs, and thus the types of work for which they apply, the types of training they receive, and the occupations they wind up in—are the *primary* determinants of women's labor-force position. Furthermore, the individual model assumes women's freedom of choice in the selection of a given occupation.

But many observers question whether a woman's choice is so free. They point to the constraints imposed by society (for example, employer discrimination) that serve to limit a woman's ability to choose freely (Blau and Jusenius, 1976 : 187). Critics also note that explanations emphasizing female choice rely on "an elusive factor termed tastes to explain why women 'chose' to enter a given occupation or to have a given preference for nonmarket work, without providing an underlying theory that explains the choice. Moreover, it is not clear why *only* women should have such tastes, nor is it clear why a large proportion of women should exhibit the same set of tastes—as demonstrated by their occupational distribution" (Blau and Jusenius, 1976 : 188). A related argument, one that shifts the focus only slightly, comes from "human-capital theory."

Human-capital theory

As a result of socialized attitudes and values, women are said to invest less in their own "human capital." That is, they do not invest in those qualities—education, training, or job-related experience—that lead to a "return on investment" in the labor market. Men *do* invest in their own human capital; they are therefore able to make a greater economic contribution to society. Their occupational opportunities and their rewards are correspondingly greater. Men's and women's positions in the labor market are said to reflect these differences in human-capital investment.

Human-capital theory derives from a neoclassical view of economics, which suggests that workers are in an ideal competitive labor market where the economic rewards received by workers and the occupations they obtain are determined entirely by their investments in human capital (see Becker,

1964, 1975; Polachek, 1976, 1978, 1979). These human investments are similar to investments an employer makes in physical capital—a factory, or machinery—because they ensure high productivity and earnings (see Becker, 1975). The term *human capital* refers to those dimensions that affect one's ability to produce on the job—such things as educational level attained, number of years worked, job training, absenteeism, and turnover. Because men and women make unequal investments in human capital, they have unequal productive skills; the result is unequal occupational attainments and differences in wages (Mincer, 1962).

Human capital theory has both conceptual and empirical problems. The conceptual problems result partly from the theory's attempt to focus exclusively on individual factors and partly from the unavoidable tangle of individual and structural factors. This tangle produces difficulties when human capital researchers attempt to translate the theory into empirical terms for research.

To measure wage inequities that result from differences in qualifications, human-capital theorists have compared wage differences with differences in economic contributions. Any remaining wage differences are attributed to discrimination. Treiman and Hartmann's (1981) review of human-capital studies indicates, however, that only two of the seven studies examined— Corcoran and Duncan (1979) and Mincer and Polachek (1974)—explain a fair percentage of the gap in wages between men and women. (See Table 4.1.) We will briefly describe Corcoran and Duncan's (1979) study, as it is perhaps the more detailed of the two. Corcoran and Duncan obtained a detailed history of the educational attainment, on-the-job training, work history, and degree of labor-force commitment for a national sample of husbands and their spouses in the labor force in 1975. These factors accounted for approximately 44 percent of the differences in men's and women's wages. The largest single factor was differences in work history. Women had less work experience in terms of general on-the-job training. (On-the-job training cannot properly be considered part of a worker's "investment" in his or her human capital, as it is typically under the employer's [rather than the employee's] control.)

Treiman and Hartmann (1981) pointed out that although the returns on investment (work experience) are generally lower for women than for men, women's lesser experience does not completely account for the earnings differential. Furthermore, they argue that women's lesser job experience needs a fuller explanation than the conventional interpretation that women voluntarily limit their labor-force experience because of family demands. Women's limited job-related experience may reflect discriminatory restriction of occupational opportunities:

> Employers may be reluctant to hire or to train women because they assume that women will leave the labor force to bear or raise children (Sawhill, 1973). Or

Table 4.1 / *Summary of Studies Accounting for Sex Differences in Earnings on the Basis of Worker Characteristics Only*

Author	Data Source and Population Studied	Measure of Earnings	Statistical Method and Explanatory Variables[a]	Women's Earnings as a Percentage of Men's[b]		Percentage of Gap Explained[d]
				Observed	Adjusted[c]	
		REPRESENTATIVE NATIONAL SAMPLES				
Blinder	SID:[e] White employed household heads, age 25+, and employed spouses	1969 mean hourly earnings	R, S: 2, 9, 11, 12, 13, 14	56	56	0
Corcoran and Duncan	SID:[e] White employed household heads and employed spouses, age 18–64	1975 hourly earnings	R, S: 1, 5, 6, 9, 11, 12, 13, 14, 17	74	85	44
Gwartney and Stroup	Census: U.S. population, age 25+	Median annual income 1959	F, R: 1, 2	33	39	9
		Median annual income 1969	F, R: 1, 2	32	40	12
	Full-time, year-round workers	Mean annual income 1959	F, R: 1, 2	56	58	4
Oaxaca[f]	SEO:[g] Urban employees, age 16+	1967 hourly earnings	R, S: 1, 3, 7–10, 12, 13			
	White			65	72	20
	Black			67	69	6
Sawhill	CPS:[h] Wage and salary workers	1966 annual earnings	R: 1, 3, 10, 13	46	56	18
		NATIONAL SAMPLES, RESTRICTED AGE				
Kohen and Roderick	NLS:[i] Nonstudent, full-time wage and salary workers, age 18–25	1968–1969 hourly earnings	R, S: 1, 3, 4, 7–9, 13–15			
	White				78	8
	Black				81	−6
Mincer and Polachek	NLS;[i] SEO:[g] Married white wage and salary workers, age 30–44	1967 hourly earnings	R, S: 1, 6, 11	66	80	41

SOURCE: Donald Treiman and Heidi Hartmann, *Women, Work, and Wages: Equal Pay for Jobs of Equal Value* (Washington, D.C.: National Academy Press, 1981), pp. 20–21. Samples: Alan S. Blinder, "Wage Discrimination: Reduced Form and Structural Estimates," *Journal of Human Resources* 8(4), (1973): 436–455; Mary Corcoran and Gregory Duncan, "Work History, Labor-Force Attachment, and Earnings: Differences Between the Races and Sexes," *Journal of Human Resources* 14 (Winter 1979):3–20; James D. Gwartney and Richard Stroup, "Measurement of Employment Discrimination According to Sex," *Southern Economic Journal* 39(4), (1975):575–587; Arly Ashenfelter and Albert Rees (eds.), *Discrimination in Labor Markets* (Princeton, N.J.: Princeton University Press, 1973); Isabel V. Sawhill, "The Economics of Discrimination Against Women: Some New Findings," *Journal of Human Earnings* 8(3), (Summer 1973):383–396; Andrew I. Kohen and Roger D. Roderick, "The Effects of Race and Sex Discrimination on Early-Career Earnings," mimeo, Center for Human Resource Research, College of Administrative Science, Ohio State University, 1975; Jacob Mincer and Solomon Polachek, "Family Investments in Human Capital: Earnings of Women," *Journal of Political Economy* 82(2,2, Part II), (March–April, 1974):S76–S108.

[a] Statistical methods: F = frequency distribution or tabular standardization, R = regression analysis, S = separate equations for males and females. Explanatory variables:

1. Education
2. Age
3. Race
4. Mental ability (intelligence)
5. Formal training
6. Actual labor market experience
7. Proxy for labor market experience
8. Marital status
9. Health
10. Hours of work (annual, weekly, full time/part time)
11. Tenure (length of service with current employer)
12. Size of city of residence
13. Region of residence
14. Socioeconomic background (parental education, occupation, income, number of siblings, migration history, ethnicity, etc.)
15. Quality of schooling
16. Record of absenteeism
17. Dual burden (number of children, limits on hours or location, plans to stop work for reasons other than training, etc.)

[b] Average female earnings expressed as a percentage of average male earnings.

[c] Adjusted earnings indicate the ratio of female to male earnings if the two sexes had the same average levels (or composition) on the explanatory variables. When several adjustments are presented in the original study their average is shown here.

[d] This is given by (expected − observed)/(100 − observed).

[e] SID = Panel Study of Income Dynamics

[f] Oaxaca also conducted some investigations using job characteristics as well as worker characteristics.

[g] SEO = Survey of Economic Opportunity

[h] CPS = Current Population Survey

[i] NLS = National Longitudinal Surveys (Parnes)

the difference in the amount of on-the-job training between men and women may be largely the result of institutional practices that tend to exclude women (Duncan and Hoffman, 1978). (Treiman and Hartmann, 1981:23–24)

Human-capital studies have other shortcomings. Some researchers argue that research from the human-capital perspective is problematic because of difficulties in measuring differences in productivity among jobs. Such things as education, training, and work experience are taken as indirect measures; these variables do not easily translate into measures of productivity. Thus, "Even those who accept the idea that education enhances productivity do not necessarily accept years of school completed as a good indicator of the quality and extent of job-specific skills learned in school" (Treiman and Hartmann, 1981:19).

Other research on human-capital theory (see Suter and Miller, 1973; Treiman and Terrell, 1975; Featherman and Hauser, 1976) indicates that even if women equaled men in human-capital investment and achievement, their earnings would still be markedly lower. For example, Suter and Miller (1973) reported that even when male and female differences in education, year-round full-time employment, occupational status, and lifetime work experience are accounted for, a wage gap of 38 percent remains unexplained.

In a recent detailed test of human-capital theory as set forth by Polachek (1976, 1978, 1979), England (1982) analyzed data from the 1967 National Longitudinal Survey (NLS) of a sample of women between the ages of thirty and forty-four. England concluded that human-capital theory fails to explain occupational sex segregation. More specifically, England notes that women whose employment is more continuous are not more apt to choose male occupations. She also concludes that women are not penalized less for time spent out of the labor force if they choose a female occupation. On the contrary, she notes that women have higher wages if they are employed in occupations containing more males (holding schooling, home time, and experience constant).

Human-capital theory does not adequately explain the wage differences between men and women; the sizable earnings gap between the sexes cannot be explained simply by differences in the characteristics of the workers such as their educational level and their job experience. Beyond this, human-capital theory remains descriptive. The theory fails to provide an adequate account of the underlying mechanisms of discrimination because it relies solely on characteristics of individuals to explain the group's inferior economic position. This exclusive focus on individual factors limits the theory's usefulness.

Limitations of the individual approach

This individual approach to explaining women's inferior economic position implies that the solution to the problem lies within the individual: the individual is the locus of the problem and is therefore the target of change. The Foxworth quotation (page 71) is typical of this approach. Clearly, efforts to provide women with better information, increased access to job training, and help for their various "personality deficits" would be useful in improving their labor-force status. Yet this approach amounts to "blaming the victim" (Ryan, 1971), and it fails to consider the problem within the wider context.

Ryan (1971) describes the process of "blaming the victim" as follows:

> [Victim blamers] must learn how to demonstrate that the poor, the black, the ill, the jobless, the slum tenants, are different and strange. They must learn to conduct or interpret the research that shows how "these people" think in different forms, act in different patterns, cling to different values, seek different goals, and learn different truths. Which is to say that they are strangers, barbarians, savages. This is how the distressed and disinherited are redefined in order to make it possible for us to look at society's problems and to attribute their causation to the individuals affected. (Ryan, 1971:10)

It has not escaped notice that scholars in any society have vested interests in making the status quo appear chosen—and our society is no exception. To suggest that women's inferior economic situation results from their choice of inferior positions (in order to avoid gender-role conflict) is to make women into "victims by choice." The following account by Coser and Rokoff, made in the early 1970s, is typical of individual-level explanations for women's lower economic standing:

> If women were to press for admission to medical schools and law schools and academic disciplines . . . they would crash the gates. They do not. . . . This is because they accept the cultural mandate in defining their own priorities as belonging to the family. The reason for this lies in the most familiar of all facts: that almost every woman is married or hopes to be married to a man. The family is the locus of consensus regarding the cultural mandate. (Coser and Rokoff, 1971:540)

Moreover, the individual perspective is inherently conservative. By concentrating solely on individual deficits and by focusing on changing the individual—that is, locating causes within individuals, perceiving their characteristics and deficiencies as causes—the structural factors influencing women's disadvantaged economic situation are overlooked. Overlooking the structural factors precludes consideration of structural changes that are necessary to improve women's labor-market position.

Human-capital theory argues for a noninterventionist approach. This argument follows from its underlying assumption that women's status reflects their preferences. In other words, it assumes that women freely choose to obtain certain jobs, to acquire less formal education than men, to enter into lower-paying work, and to be underemployed. As one critic has pointed out,

> Neoclassical theory abstracts economics from power by assuming that individuals exercise freedom of choice. This is not an unreasonable assumption in a world populated by atomistic individuals with roughly equal endowments of material and human capital. But in a world in which men and women, and workers and capitalists, have unequal wealth and power, their abilities to exercise freedom of choice differ. In such a world, all women may be subject to discrimination. All may be saddled with child-rearing responsibilities. Working-class wives may have little choice about whether or not to work. The working class as a whole has no choice at all. If this is the kind of world which one believes to exist, then the neoclassical assumption of freedom of choice yields no insights into the realities of women's problems. It mystifies them. (Amsden, 1980:32)

The Structural Approach

Many observers argue that structural rather than individual characteristics are most critical in determining women's labor-force position (see Edwards, Reich, and Gordon, 1975; Bibb and Form, 1977; Beck, Horan, and Tolbert, 1978). The structural approach focuses on basic societal institutions—the economy, the legal institution, the family, their policies and practices—that operate to confine women to particular jobs characterized by low wages, little mobility, and limited prestige. This approach blames the structure instead of the victim and suggests a different strategy for improving women's labor force status. Even at the level of specific jobs, for example, we may find that the characteristics of the job are more important than the characteristics of the individual who occupies the job:

> It is often said that women "have higher turnover rates," as though this were a property of women and not of the jobs which they occupy. Of course, it may be true to say that women, as a group, are more likely to want to leave jobs more frequently than men, but this should not be confused with the existence of higher *involuntary* turnover rates for women (a property of the job), nor should we ignore the possibility that higher *voluntary* turnover rates can also reflect properties of the job—like low pay and poor work conditions. A failure to unravel the different strands of "individual" and "structural" causation can lead to a crude reification of individual characteristics and an unwanted emphasis upon these characteristics as causes. (Barron and Norris, 1976:50)

Economic studies reviewed by Sawhill (1973) indicate that male/female differences in absenteeism and turnover rates are actually quite small and are a function of the job's status rather than of the worker's gender.

From a structural perspective, it appears that even if women were to increase their "human capital" they would meet with resistance—resistance unrelated to qualifications, but tied instead to women's structural position in the labor market. Individuals work within a setting that determines educational and occupational attainment. The structure of the labor market (its hierarchy, its hiring and firing practices) largely determines women's status in the labor force.

Dual labor markets

In contrast to the assumptions of human-capital theory, Piore (1975) argues that there is no single competitive labor market in the economy. He contends that the labor market consists of two distinct sectors. The primary sector consists of professional and managerial-administrative jobs with relatively high wages and status, good working conditions, opportunity for advancement, equity, and due process in the administration of work rules, and employment stability. The secondary sector is the mirror image of the first: jobs are characterized by low wages, poor working conditions, little chance for advancement, lack of stability, and highly personalized employer/employee relations, which are conducive to arbitrary and capricious work discipline. Secondary-sector jobs include semiskilled, operative, nonfarm labor, and service work. Generally, the two sectors of the labor market are mutually exclusive; workers rarely move from the secondary to the primary sector (Doeringer and Piore, 1971; Piore, 1975).

The sectors are further divided into tiers. In the primary sector, the upper tier consists of professional, managerial-administrative, and technical jobs with high pay and status. Formal education is an absolute prerequisite for entry into the upper tier, where the jobs allow for individual creativity and initiative and provide greater economic security. The jobs in the lower tier are primarily white-collar and clerical positions, sales jobs, and positions for skilled workers. In many ways, the difference between the upper and lower tiers is as great as the difference between the primary and secondary sector.

In this dual labor market, women are concentrated in a few occupations, primarily in the lower tier of primary-sector jobs (for example, white-collar clerical jobs). In 1979, 22 percent of employed women were in the upper tier of the primary sector, and 44 percent were in the lower tier; the remaining 34 percent are in the secondary sector, in service and support jobs and blue-collar occupations. (See Table 4.2.) Gender appears to be an important criteria for placement in primary- and secondary-sector jobs.

Furthermore, the dual labor market reinforces the differences in earnings between men and women through what is called the "crowding" effect (Edgeworth, 1922; Bergmann, 1971; Stevenson, 1975b). Women's crowding in lower-tier primary sector and in secondary-sector jobs inflates the

T a b l e 4 . 2 / *Male and Female Workers in the Primary and Secondary Labor Markets, 1979*

	Percentage in occupation	
	Males	Females
Primary sector	62	66
Upper tier	29	22
Professional/technical workers	15	16
Managers and administrators	14	6
Lower tier	33	44
Salespersons	6	7
Clerical workers	6	35
Skilled workers (craftspersons)	21	2
Secondary sector	38	34
Semiskilled workers	29	14
Operators (except transport)	12	11
Transport equipment operators	6	0.5
Laborers (farm and nonfarm)	11	2.5
Service workers	9	20
Total	100	100
Total number (thousands)	56,500	40,446

SOURCE: U.S. Department of Labor, Bureau of Labor Statistics, *Employment and Unemployment During 1979: An Analysis* (Washington, D.C.: U.S. Government Printing Office, 1980), Table 21, p. A-20.

NOTE: The classification of occupational categories in primary and secondary sections is from Piore, 1972.

supply of labor, thus reducing their level of earnings (for these jobs) below what one might anticipate in a truly competitive market (Bergmann, 1971). Men (especially white men) are concentrated, on the other hand, in primary-sector occupations; there is thus little competition from women. This situation operates to men's advantage, since the labor supply in the primary sector is "artificially reduced and male earnings are thereby inflated" (Stevenson, 1975b:175).

In keeping with assumptions of the dual labor-market theory, Blau's (1977) research on pay differentials and the occupational distribution of male and female office workers found that differences in earnings of men and women within occupations are largely attributed to pay differences *between* firms rather than *within* a given firm. For example, a male clerk and female clerk will earn more nearly the same wage if they work in the same firm than if they work in different firms (even in the same industrial sector). Blau also found that the higher the wages a firm pays across occupations, the smaller the proportion of women employed in the firm—a finding consistent with dual labor-market theories. Because women are concentrated in lower-wage firms, they earn less than men (even in the same occupations—clerk, bookkeeper, janitor) in the higher-wage firms in which men are concentrated (Blau, 1977).

Yet the dual labor-market theory, like human-capital theory, remains descriptive. Both theories describe the results—that is, women's inferior economic position—but neither addresses the issue of how these patterns emerge. There has as yet been little empirical testing of the dual labor-market theory. As one economist has noted, "a great deal of additional refinement is required to facilitate further empirical testing. Even such a fundamental matter as distinguishing the primary sector from the secondary sector empirically still has received no definitive resolution" (Rima, 1981:234). (For a critique of the dual labor-market approach, see Wachter [1974] and Cain [1976].) However, although the mechanisms are only incompletely understood, it appears that discriminatory practices of one sort or another are involved.

Discriminatory practices

Exclusionary practices by employees are one mechanism that can help explain the presence of a dual labor market. Male employees, especially those employed in primary-sector jobs, wish to protect their current economic advantages (see Bergmann, 1971; Bonacich, 1972) by reducing competition and increasing wages in male-dominated occupations. There are some grounds for the fear that if women enter a particular occupation, wages will fall (see Hodge and Hodge, 1965): men employed in industries and occupations that exclude women are reported to have higher earnings than men in less sex-segregated industries and occupations (Fuchs, 1971:14; Blau, 1977).

However, some controversy exists concerning the causal relationship between income level and the sex composition of occupations. Snyder and Hudis (1976) found some empirical support for the wage-competition argument that the entrance of women and minorities depresses occupational income. But they concluded that neither "the overall pattern of results nor the magnitude of effects provide compelling support for female or black male wage competition with white men in this decade" (Snyder and Hudis, 1976:232). They suggested that the explanation for the differences in occupational income or compensation lies in a more careful historical analysis and understanding of mechanisms of occupational segregation (Snyder and Hudis, 1976).

Burris and Wharton (1981) also point out that male workers have traditionally used a variety of mechanisms to control the sex composition of their occupations. Craft unions, for example, have frequently excluded female workers (Hartmann, 1976; Milkman, 1980). Although it may be argued that such practices are not directed toward women in particular but toward unskilled workers in general (Beechey, 1977:55), it must be acknowledged that craft-union policies have contributed to the underrepresentation of women in the skilled trades. Similarly, male-dominated professional associations have restricted female entry into medicine (Walsh, 1977), law, and the other higher professions (Burris and Wharton, 1981: 9–10).

Another important mechanism for explaining the dual labor market lies in employers' "tastes" for discrimination. Just as women choose certain jobs that fit the traditional image of appropriate work for women, employers are influenced by these cultural images. Thus, employers may choose male or female workers because they seek traits believed to be masculine or feminine, regardless of whether specific women or men possess such traits. To this extent, women's labor-market situation is a result of employers' "irrational preferences" (Becker, 1957). Deckard has pointed out some disadvantages to business of holding these preferences. When equally qualified male and female workers are available, and an employer's "tastes" are such that he or she prefers to hire only males, the employer is paying higher wages because, owing to discrimination, women can be hired more cheaply. The irrational exclusion of women is thus expensive to the business world, and therefore to the consumer (Deckard, 1979:107).

An illustration of the attitudes that produce irrational preferences is given in a recent study of women in management (Hennig and Jardim, 1977):

> In our professional work, we have often spent many hours convincing a man in management that it was important for him to try to understand the differences which women were bringing to the organizational setting. He would respond to our argument by repeating again and again that he agreed that men and women are different but that he thanked God that they are. He would agree that women are less successful in management careers but say thank God that is so . . . (Finally) we would say to him . . . "If you had known on the day your daughter was born that starting at the age of twenty she would have to work continuously to survive, would you have . . . done anything differently with her than you have done up until now?" . . . One corporate senior vice-president . . . said, "I feel sick to my stomach. If she has to work, then I have done it all wrong." (Hennig and Jardim, 1977:203–204)

A variation on "irrational preferences" is "statistical discrimination" (Phelps, 1972; Treiman and Hartmann, 1981). This form of discrimination operates in the following way: Employers screen potential workers according to certain guidelines. To minimize training and turnover costs, employers try to select those workers who have the best cost/benefit potential. Believing that women and minorities have higher turnover rates, employers prefer not to hire them. This practice is intended as good (cost-effective) business procedure, but it produces sexual and racial discrimination. On the basis of statistical information of group characteristics, employers can eliminate those candidates least likely to be productive workers. Employers acknowledge that the system is not foolproof, but they assume that it is fairly reliable. Workers excluded from such jobs will be hired in occupations for which turnover rates are less important or for which wages are sufficiently low that employers are compensated for their expected higher costs (Treiman and Hartmann, 1981:64).

Whether these practices are considered to be unfair sexual discrimination or whether they are viewed as standard "sound" business practice, the effect is the same: women remain concentrated in lower-tier primary-sector jobs and in secondary-sector jobs. It may be that these practices actually hurt employers—for example, if the costs of screening statistically undesirable workers are greater than the costs of hiring the excluded workers (see Treiman and Hartmann, 1981:64). Opinions vary along conservative/radical lines. Conservative economists argue that in the long run employers lose financially because female labor is cheaper (Becker, 1957) and that therefore discrimination is not in the interests of employers. More radical economists argue that employers do benefit from discrimination (Edwards et al., 1975) because it protects their economic interests by dividing the interests of workers and prevents workers from gaining firmer control of their economic situation (Gordon, 1972; Edwards, 1979). Employers may also benefit by the segregation of women in the secondary sector of the dual labor market, because this concentration permits employers to pay women less and thereby to maximize profits.

Given the formidable structural limits on women's access to better labor opportunities, one may ask whether women should even bother to change characteristics that the individual approach identifies as problematic, such as lack of aggressiveness. Such improvements are probably worthwhile, nevertheless, in that they could help solve those work problems that result from factors within the individual's control. And ideally, of course, if women were to solve all such individual problems, the remaining constraints on women's economic advancement would be unequivocally identifiable as structural.

Structural problems, or problems considered from a structural perspective, require a different course of action, however. Just as the individual approach implies individual change, the structural approach implies structural change. Structural change is often effected through legal means, but legal institutions and practices also *reflect* the prevailing social and economic structure. If we assume that we can have reliable recourse to the law to make amends, we may find instead that the law more often supports the status quo.

THE LEGAL CONTEXT

When Susan B. Anthony stood on trial in June 1873 for having voted the previous November, she accused the judge of having convicted her using "forms of law all made by men, interpreted by men, administered by men, in favor of men, and against women" (Anthony, 1873, quoted by Sachs and Wilson, 1978:92). Unfortunately, Anthony's words describe, to a large extent, the legal history of women in America until almost the present day. While Anthony was struggling with the legal question of whether she was a person, and therefore a citizen entitled to vote, still other women were seeing their property and contractual rights narrowed and their status in the work place constricted by paternalistic protective legislation. Even with the achievement of the right to vote in 1920, the legal status of women was little improved, with most of the crucial issues lying dormant until the coming of the women's movement in the 1960s. The Equal Rights Amendment, which would at long last grant full legal rights to all citizens regardless of sex, is (at this writing, in 1983) completely stalled. Throughout the history of women in the United States, the law has done little more than sanction discriminatory practices that have served to perpetuate occupational segregation and earnings differentials between men and women.

A Short History: The Colonial Period

The law during our early colonial period was based on English common-law tradition, characterized by rigid notions about the role of women (Lee, 1980). Under the law, when a woman married, she lost all control over her property, she lost the right to contract or sue, and she was legally obligated to perform domestic services for her husband. However, according to Sachs and Wilson (1978), colonial times may have been more liberal for the status of women than were later periods, as local customs often took precedence over established law. The married woman's (*feme couverte*) legal status was lower than that of a single woman (*feme sole*), as it was in English common law. But in commercial areas of the colonies, some married women were declared "*feme-sole* traders," giving them the right to sue, to enter into contracts, to sell property, and to have the power of attorney in the absence of their husbands, rights that unmarried women enjoyed.

Similarly, because of a general labor shortage, common-law restrictions on female activities were often ignored. Because of the wide range of occupations in which females participated, it seems that the job market was not as sex segregated during the colonial period as it was to become later (see Chapter 2). For example, in Philadelphia, women were employed as silversmiths, barbers, bakers, brewers, tanners, lumberjacks, gunsmiths, butchers, harness makers, printers, morticians, woodworkers, tailors, and in many other crafts. In other areas of the colonies as well, women worked as artisans, merchants, blacksmiths, teachers, nurses, and midwives, and in taverns and coffeehouses (Foner, 1978). In many cases, a widow inherited her husband's trade, often keeping it going under her own name, even if she remarried. The social or economic code of colonial America did not exclude a woman from working outside her home. At that stage in American history, social mores favoring women's participation in the labor force superseded the existing common-law restrictions. Not surprisingly, however, women's wages in this period were significantly lower than those of men (Foner, 1978).

For poor women, there were other incentives to work outside the home. Local poor laws encouraged single poor women to work rather than to become recipients of relief. The choice of jobs was much more limited, and many poor women became laundresses, house servants, or cooks. Again, however, female laborers were paid approximately 30 percent less than the lowest-paid unskilled free white male workers and 20 percent less than hired-out male slaves.

Things began to change at the end of the eighteenth century and in the early nineteenth century, "as increased mercantile specialization demanded greater economic stability and hence a closer application of the more conservative aspects of English common law" (Sachs and Wilson, 1978:71). Widows had previously been granted "dower rights" by the court, which in fact overruled the common-law provision prohibiting them from inheriting property, and had often been named executrices of their husbands' estates. However, by 1800 dower rights had been renounced, and 85 percent of wills named sons as executors. Further codification of law throughout the nineteenth century contributed to the regression in the legal status of women. The Married Women Property Acts, passed by nine states before the Civil War, were designed to protect (rather than liberate) women. In fact, they ended up protecting the common-law property rights of fathers who were afraid their sons-in-law would squander their daughters' dowries. These acts also "strictly adhered to the traditional ideas of patriarchy by denying women the right to sell, sue, or contract without their husbands' or other male relatives' approval" (Sachs and Wilson, 1978:78). Obviously, such legislation served to exclude women from the many businesses and trades to which they had had access in the pre-Revolutionary times, and led the way to the "cult of true womanhood" that characterized the nineteenth century (see Chapter 2).

Women, the Factory System, and
Protective Legislation

With the coming of the Industrial Revolution, women's place in the work force underwent major changes. By the 1820s and 1830s, the New England textile mills had recruited thousands of young women (Foner, 1978). As described in Chapter 2, the "Boston system" of factories, pioneered by Francis Cabot Lowell, consisted of young women (rather than whole families) working in the mills and living in company-owned boardinghouses with house mothers and strict rules and regulations. Within the factories, men held the supervisory and the skilled-labor positions, while women tended spinning machines and looms. Men's wages were established by negotiations; women were paid on a piecework basis. "Wages were set at a level that was high enough to induce young women to leave the farms and stay away from competing employment such as household manufacture and domestic service, but low enough to offer the owners an advantage in employing women rather than men" (Foner, 1978:25).

As a result of the long tedious hours, the work speedups, and the low wages, strikes broke out in the 1830s and 1840s and women formed organizations such as the Female Labor Reform Association in 1844. The Association's founder, Sarah Bagley, the first woman labor leader in American history, spoke out against the falsely glamorous image of factory life fostered by the owners and joined with other factory girls to work for the ten-hour workday and for improvements in sanitary and lighting conditions in the textile factories. (The typical workday was fourteen hours, from 5 A.M. to 7 P.M., with two half-hour breaks, for breakfast and dinner.)

The battle for the ten-hour day was a key issue for women workers in the nineteenth century. Foner (1978) speaks of this issue as uniting working men and women of the 1840s. However, while it is true that mill workers, male and female, struggled for reduced hours, other (male) occupations had long since achieved these hours. "Male workers had frequently won by the 1840s, 50s and 60s the hours limitations which legislation began to win for women in the 70s, 80s and 90s" (Baer, 1978:16). For example, in the 1840s the building trades, dominated by men, had achieved a sixty-hour, six-day workweek.

Clearly, legislation was needed to regulate women's hours and working conditions, which were considerably worse than those of men. Improvements in women's industries lagged behind men's "partly because of their [women's] particular suitability for such work, and partly because usually only the least fortunate women were permanent workers" (Baer, 1978:23). In addition, women lacked strong labor organizations. Working conditions for women differed greatly from those of men in the nineteenth century, creating a need for special legislation pertaining to women in the workforce. (This was particularly true in the mid- to late nineteenth century as recently immigrated women, destined to spend a lifetime in the mills, replaced the New England farm girls, who usually spent only a few years there.) However, the vast body of "protective legislation" that grew out of these conditions did more than remedy the real problems; these laws often went on to place unnecessary constraints on women who sought a better and larger role in the labor force.

Protective legislation

Baer (1978) explores the physical, social, economic, and political factors that have been used to promote and justify protective legislation. Most arguments for such legislation have their basis in "two phenomena which are common only to some men or to some women: physical strength and child-bearing" (Baer, 1978:23). Needless to say, such arguments are simplistic, since some women may be stronger than some men and not all women bear children; even those who do are not doing so constantly. More important, it seems that the real differences between men and women are the social expectations that surround their roles. The greater responsibility of women for housework and child care has been used by "reformers" as a rationalization for special legislation. A more insidious factor contributing to protective legislation is the economic one. Florence Kelley (cited in Baer, 1978), a reformer in women's legislation, claimed that men whose own occupations were threatened by competition from women workers demanded restrictions on women's hours of work, thus making women less desirable as employees. Men also managed to obtain reduced hours for themselves by getting restrictions on the work hours of the women and children whose work schedules interlocked with their own (Baer, 1978:25).

Thus, protective legislation had a dual advantage for men: it drove women out of certain occupations while it gained reduced hours for men in those occupations where women remained. Political factors facilitated these developments. Women had so little power in unions that legislation was viewed as the only remedy to their deplorable job conditions. But the fight became a vicious circle: because of male-dominated unions, working women had to turn to male legislators, who exploited the situation to their own advantage. Baer points out that discriminatory legislation was not necessarily the best remedy, because "if most of the workers subjected to bad conditions were women, legislation which applied to all workers, regardless of sex, would have achieved the desired results" (Baer, 1978:26).

For the most part, protective legislation began with maximum-hour laws and then branched out to other areas. The earliest maximum-hour laws provided for a ten-hour day, in the absence of a contract to the contrary. This provision often rendered the laws useless, because employees who would not agree to a contract providing for longer hours were often dismissed. By the late nineteenth century, such laws were passed for eight-hour days. Some of these laws were designed specifically for women, as were laws prohibiting them from working certain hours, usually at night. Although one can argue that these laws were progressive in that they improved the working conditions of some women, they were quite difficult to enforce. "Out of the twenty-six maximum-hour and night-work laws in twenty-five states, then, only four—the Massachusetts ten-hour and night-work laws, the Maine ten-hour law, and the New Jersey eleven-hour law—could be enforced with any regularity or predictability" (Baer, 1978:32).

Other types of protective legislation entirely barred women from entering certain occupations. Mining, smelting, working in taverns, cleaning, and moving machinery were occupations closed to women by laws in fourteen states. Unions also found ways to keep women out of the trades by enforcing apprenticeship rules and, ironically, by demanding equal pay for women—so that employers would not hire women just because they could be paid lower wages. Sachs and Wilson (1978) point out that in the fight for suffrage in the early twentieth century, even women's groups tended to ignore the other constraints of the law. Questions of personhood, divorce settlements, and child custody (Sachs and Wilson, 1978:111), which had far-reaching implications for working women, were virtually ignored, while protective legislation was viewed by many women's groups as a boon rather than a burden.

Court cases

Numerous court cases upheld these protective practices. Perhaps the most important of these was the *Muller* v. *Oregon* (208 U.S. 412, 1908) decision: "Prior to this decision a number of state supreme courts had issued decisions both validating and invalidating protective legislation for women" (Sachs and Wilson, 1978:113). This Court ruling upheld an Oregon statute that placed limits on the number of hours a woman could work, on the theory that the Court has a right to protect the "procreative functions" of all working women. The Court decided to grant special treatment to women because of their physical limitations and maternal functions. The *Muller* decision reasoned that women were at a disadvantage in the "struggle for subsistence" because of their "physical structure and the performance of maternal functions" and that this was "especially true when the burdens of motherhood are upon her." Furthermore, it argued that

> By abundant testimony of the medical fraternity continuance for a long time on her feet at work, repeating this from day to day, tends to injurious effects upon the body, and as healthy mothers are essential to vigorous offspring, the physical well-being of women becomes an object of public interest and care in order to preserve the strength and vigor of the race.
>
> Still again, history discloses the fact that woman has always been dependent upon man. He established his control at the outset by superior physical strength, and this control in various forms, with diminishing intensity, has con-

tinued to the present. As minors, though not to the same extent, she has been looked upon in the courts as needing especial care that her rights may be preserved . . . even with the consequent increase of capacity for business affairs it is still true that in the struggle for subsistence she is not an equal competitor with her brother. Though limitations upon personal and contractual rights may be removed by legislation, there is that in her disposition and habits of life which will operate against a full assertion of those rights. . . . Differentiated by these matters from the other sex, she is properly placed in a class by herself, and legislation designed for her protection may be sustained, even when like legislation is not necessary for men and could not be sustained. (*Muller* v. *Oregon*, 208 U.S. 412 [1908], quoted in Sachs and Wilson, 1978 : 113–114)

This decision had an important impact on the history of protective legislation. Some of the states that had previously taken a stand against protective legislation reversed their positions, and others instituted protective and restrictive laws covering women's work hours (Sachs and Wilson, 1978 : 114). Although the intention of these laws was originally to protect women's interests, they limited women's job opportunities (Lloyd and Niemi, 1979). Protective legislation after the Muller decision served less to protect women and more to protect men's jobs and to reinforce occupational sex segregation. It has served as an excuse for refusing to hire women. For example, the American Telephone and Telegraph Company (AT&T), which was investigated in 1970 for its almost total segregation of jobs, relied for its defense on state protective laws. The company asserted that this legislation prevented them from employing women in the craft jobs that led to managerial positions (Gates, 1976).

Protective legislation (especially those laws prohibiting women's employment in jobs requiring long hours, night work, weight lifting, and so on) not only contributed to sex segregation of occupations, but also served to reduce women's wages compared to men's. These laws reduce women's wages by reinforcing their concentration into a small number of sex-typed occupations (Lloyd and Niemi, 1979 : 301). The "crowding" of women into a limited number of occupations creates an oversupply of employees for a small number of opportunities, and this in turn reduces wages in these female-typed jobs.

Domestic-Relations Laws and Other Legislation

Beyond protective labor-legislation laws, domestic-relations laws also reinforce women's traditional role and perpetuate sex segregation in employment. Perhaps the most fundamental of these domestic-relations laws is the marriage contract, whose origins go back to common law.

In 1853, Elizabeth Cady Stanton wrote to Susan B. Anthony, "I feel, as never before, that this whole question of women's rights turns on the pivot of the marriage relation, and mark my word, sooner or later it will be the topic for discussion" (quoted by Sachs and Wilson, 1978:148). Stanton foresaw the subtle ways in which the marriage contract could undermine women's rights by perpetuating and reinforcing the existing inequalities between men and women. The marriage contract, as interpreted by the courts, clearly gives higher status to men. As late as 1970, an Ohio Supreme Court held that a wife was

> "at most a superior servant to her husband . . . only chattel with no personality, no property, and no legally recognized feelings or rights." As recently as 1974, the Georgia legislature approved a statute that defined the husband as "head of the family" with the wife . . . "subject to him; her legal existence . . . merged in the husband, except so far as the law recognizes her separately, either for her own protection, or for her benefit, or for the preservation of the public order." (*The Spokeswoman*, January 15, 1977, p. 11, quoted by Sachs and Wilson, 1978:149)

The marriage contract and other domestic-relations laws (for example, those concerning property and credit rights, Social Security and other pension benefits, pregnancy and other disability insurance, as well as maternity-leave policies and benefits) have also reinforced and perpetuated "women's place at home" and "men's place at work." This legislation also makes it more difficult to counteract employers' attitudes concerning the ability of women workers:

> Because a man is the legally appointed breadwinner, he is considered to be serious about his work, ambitious, and responsible. Jobs with a future must be reserved for him so that he can meet the financial needs of his growing family. . . . A woman, on the other hand, makes a poor foreman or sergeant if she is not even boss in her own home.
> If marriage were legally a partnership, a real contractual relationship, employers might be less inclined to channel young men and women into jobs believed to be appropriate for them as stereotypical husbands and wives. (Gates, 1976:68)

Still other legislation penalizes women more directly. Among these are laws that specifically pertain to working mothers, such as those regarding maternity leave. For example, in *General Electric Co.* v. *Gilbert* (1976) (321 U.S. 125), the court ruled that employers did not need to compensate women for maternity-related disabilities as they compensate employees for other disabilities (Sachs and Wilson, 1978:155). This type of legislation penalizes a woman directly by placing a financial penalty on her for being pregnant and reinforces society's message that a woman, especially a mother, belongs at home rather than at a paying job. Partly in response to this ruling, recent legislation has been passed that secures the rights of pregnant workers. This law (Public Law 95-555) was approved October 31, 1978, amending Title VII to ban discrimination based on pregnancy.

Recent Legislation: Sex Discrimination
and Equal Opportunity

It was not until the early 1960s that protective legislation was overridden by the Equal Pay Act (1963) and the equal employment-opportunity provisions of Title VII of the Civil Rights Act of 1964. These new laws and regulations nullified the protective labor laws of the states and provided a different legal environment, one that legally prohibited overt sex discrimination.

The Equal Pay Act (1963), the oldest federal legislation that deals with sex discrimination, stipulates that men and women must receive equal pay "on jobs the performance of which requires equal skill, effort and responsibility and which are performed under similar working conditions" (Task Force on Working Women, 1975:87). Differences in pay rates are only allowed in relation to a nondiscriminatory seniority system, a merit system, or one that measures earnings by quality or quantity of production as well as a differential based on any factor other than sex (Task Force on Working Women, 1975:57).

The Equal Pay Act does not address the more pervasive discrimination affecting women whose work, though different from work performed by men, is perceived to be of equal value (Deckard, 1979). Nor does the Equal Pay Act prohibit discrimination in hiring, promotions, or work assignments. The Act's major objective was to help women who were doing work substantially equal to that done by men but who were being paid less for it.

Perhaps the more important legislation dealing with discriminatory practices was enacted under Title VII of the Civil Rights Act of 1964, making it unlawful to

> discriminate because of race, color, religion, or national origin, in hiring or firing; wages; fringe benefits; classifying, referring, assigning, or promoting employees; extending or assigning facilities; training or retraining or apprenticeship; or any other terms, conditions, or privileges in employment. (U.S. Department of Labor, Women's Bureau, 1980:9)

Sex was added to this list in 1967 by Executive Order 11375.

Problems with enforcing
equal-opportunity laws

The Equal Employment Opportunity Commission (EEOC) was created specifically to enforce Title VII. However, the EEOC not only initially resisted enforcing the provisions concerning sexual discrimination, but even encouraged such discrimination by publishing guidelines that expressly allowed employers to publish employment ads in classified columns labeled by sex (Eastwood, 1978:114). The EEOC's limited budget and administrative problems further hampered Title VII's enforcement, and efforts to force compliance were "still left primarily to the private individuals who had been discriminated against, through private lawsuits in the courts" (Cahn, 1977:76).

How effective is Title VII? Cahn observes that the pattern of sex discrimination, unequal pay, and underutilization have continued. One indicator of the "inadequacy of legal remedy is that from 1965 to 1975, only 13 percent of all sex discrimination court cases were awarded 'class relief'" (Cahn, 1977:5). This was true despite the fact that, under Title VII, class relief is to be awarded "whenever a policy or practice has harmed a protected group by discrimination, necessitating relief to the class to make it whole" (Cahn, 1977:5).

Research about the effectiveness of the EEO laws is controversial. Beller (1977) has pointed out that the male/female earnings differential remained virtually unchanged between 1967 and 1974:

> One might be tempted to conclude . . . that the decade of enforcement of EEO laws has been a failure in reducing discrimination against women in the labor market. Yet there is an obvious explanation for the persistence in the earnings differential over this period. Because of the rising labor force participation rates of women, one would expect . . . an increase in the earnings differential. In general, new entrants into the labor market have less labor market experience than those already in and therefore command lower wages. That the earnings differential remained constant in the face of this significant trend in the labor force participation rate of women suggests that some underlying factors have been responsible. (Beller, 1977:1)

In contrast to Cahn's (1977) view, Beller claims that one such factor was the enforcement of Title VII. According to Beller, the male/female earnings differential would have widened approximately 7 percentage points between 1967 and 1974 had it not been for the enforcement of Title VII (Beller, 1977:2).

It was only when women's action groups such as the National Organization for Women (NOW) began to bring political and legal pressure at the local, state, and federal levels in the late 1960s and 1970s that the EEOC was compelled to enforce these laws (Eastwood, 1978; Sachs and Wilson, 1978). And, since 1972, the EEOC has been empowered to bring civil-action suits against private firms engaged in discriminatory practices (Barrett, 1979a:56).

Although the EEOC still lacks effective enforcement power and is overloaded with cases, its guidelines have clarified important issues. For example, the new guidelines make it illegal for firms to assign characteristics to individuals on the basis of the attributes of a group (Barrett, 1979a:56). Thus the guidelines address the "statistical discrimination" practices described earlier in this chapter.

Affirmative action

The 1970s witnessed a gradual shift in the legal context from prohibition of discrimination to affirmative-action laws. Employers were required to seek out and give preference to women and minorities for those occupations in which they were underrepresented, even if male candidates appeared to have better credentials (Barrett, 1979a:57). This practice, of course, invites charges of "reverse discrimination."[4]

> [Affirmative action] means more than passive nondiscrimination. It means that various [public and private] organizations must act positively, affirmatively, and aggressively to remove all barriers, however informal or subtle, that prevent access by minorities and women to their rightful places in employment and educational institutions of the United States. (Benokraitis and Feagin, 1978:1)

Many critics of affirmative action feel that women and minorities ought not to be hired under affirmative-action policies because they would thus end up in positions for which they are not qualified. These critics suggest, in accordance with their assumption that the causes lie within the individual, that women and minorities need to become better prepared for jobs. Benokraitis and Feagin (1978) note that what is "particularly strange" about this argument is that the evidence is to the contrary. They note that "when the population is canvassed, there is hardly a scarcity of qualified women and minorities for many, if not most, jobs" (pp. 205–206), and that many companies had reportedly found significant numbers of qualified women and minorities.

The impact of affirmative-action laws is difficult to assess directly, or to separate from other factors that have influenced the situation. For example, there is now a higher proportion of women in the labor market, their educational level is higher, and various civil-rights and women's groups have been active in pressuring for improvement (Benokraitis and Feagin, 1978). Improvement in many employment sectors has been negligible. The situation in some public-sector occupations has improved, but women and minority-group members still dominate the low-level, low-salary, and low-status jobs in government employment. In business and industry, the numbers of women and minority-group members have increased in white-collar jobs, but most are still concentrated at the lowest blue- and white-collar occupational categories. In the academic world, women and minorities are still holding lower positions in academic rank, are likely to be in the lower-paying areas of specialization, have lower salaries, and be at the smaller educational institutions that have less prestige (Benokraitis and Feagin, 1978).

In the opinion of some researchers, affirmative action is still insufficiently enforced, partly because the government's commitment to civil-rights implementation is generally low (Rodgers and Bullock, 1972:195; Benokraitis and Feagin, 1978:193). Perhaps affirmative action has worked best as a "protective shield" (Benokraitis and Feagin, 1978:194) against discrimination in employment, as witnessed by the increasing number of complaints filed at the EEOC. Many of the gains in equal employment opportunity reflect individual rather than institutional initiative. "Theoretically, affirmative action policies were designed to help the system help the victim. In practice, however, the victims still find that they have to fight a system that does not want to help" (Benokraitis and Feagin, 1978:194).

SUMMARY

This chapter has examined the economic and legal factors that help explain women's position in the labor force. Economic explanations may be categorized as individual or structural, in terms of their focus on the individual woman workers versus a focus on structural features of the economy.

The individual approach assumes that women themselves are responsible for the fact that they wind up in low-paying, dead-end jobs. Human-capital theory is an example of the individual approach. It argues that women are concentrated in such jobs because they do not have the qualifications for better-paying positions with higher responsibility, commitment, and prestige. Women are less well qualified than men, it is assumed, because women have invested less in their human-capital assets, such as education and on-the-job training—assets that lead to the better jobs. Women's prior socialization fosters their choice of jobs requiring little training or expertise; such jobs allow more flexibility, which permits women to spend more time with their families.

This approach in effect blames the victims for their own predicament and ignores the influence of the wider context—the structural features of the labor market and the economy.

A structural approach focuses on the structural aspects of the economy and labor market that constrain women's work situation. Even if women were better qualified for the higher-paying jobs typically held by men, they would meet with resistance related to their position within the structure of the labor force. A prime example of a structuralist approach is dual labor-market theory. According to this view, the labor market is stratified into a primary sector (jobs with high wages and status, good working conditions, and opportunity for advancement) and a secondary sector (low wages and status, poor working conditions, little chance for advancement). Women are concentrated in secondary-sector jobs by the discriminatory attitudes and policies (such as statistical discrimination) of both employers and employees.

Structural change is often effected through legal means. The law, however, has more often supported the status quo and has thus been an additional source of structural resistance. Throughout history, the law has initiated and sanctioned discriminatory practices that have perpetuated the occupational segregation and earnings differentials between men and women. Protective legislation is a case in point. With the coming of the industrial revolution and women's entrance into the work force, protective laws and regulations governed the hours women were permitted to work and the type of work they could perform. These laws originally arose out of the efforts of feminists, labor unions, and social reformers to protect women and children from sweatshop conditions. The legislation soon became an excuse that employers used to discriminate against women when they chose to do so. Domestic-relations laws also contributed to women's poorer labor-market standing.

Protective legislation was overridden by the Equal Pay Act in 1963 and by Title VII of the Civil Rights Act of 1964. These laws helped overcome some of the more blatant forms of discrimination, but their effectiveness has been limited. In the 1970s, the legal climate shifted from antidiscrimination legislation to affirmative-action laws that require employers to seek out and give preference to women and minorities in hiring for those occupations in which they have been underrepresented.

Although during the last two decades there has been some legal action promoting equality between the sexes, these changes have not evolved as one might have hoped. The legal structure does, after all, reflect and reinforce the prevailing social and economic structure, and changes have come not from within the legal system, but from outside—from, for example, pressure on the legal system from the women's movement. Members of the legal profession claim that the law supports equality and individual rights, but the law and the judges, who are primarily male, have acted more "as a barrier to, rather than a guarantee of, equality between men and women" (Sachs and Wilson, 1978:225).

The economic and legal context are but two of the important structural influences (see Chapter 3 concerning the family and education institutions) affecting women's inferior labor-market position. Although women need to gain the resources (education, on-the-job training, and so forth) to compete effectively on the job market, their qualifications are only a part of the problem. Society itself, and its economic and legal institutions, are also responsible for setting up and maintaining barriers to women's full economic participation. It is only by effecting change on both the individual and structural level that women can begin to enjoy equal employment and economic opportunity.

5 · The "Ordinary" Woman at Work: Clerical and Blue-Collar Occupations

Research on women workers has focused primarily on two groups: (1) professional and academic women (those in the top occupational classifications) and (2) poor and welfare-client women (those at the bottom of the occupational ladder). These groups comprise a small proportion of the female work force. The majority of working women are neither at the top nor at the bottom, but somewhere in the middle—in the ordinary white- and blue-collar jobs. These workers have only infrequently been the subject of extensive research efforts (for exceptions, see Roby, 1974, 1976; Seifer, 1973, 1976; Komarovsky, 1967; Rubin, 1976; Howe, 1977.)

WHO IS THE ORDINARY WOMAN WORKER?

The ordinary working woman is typically a working mother in her thirties; she attended and probably graduated from high school. She has little or no college experience, and therefore does not work in those higher-paying professional, technical, or managerial occupations that require college degrees and specialized training. She works, for example, in the typing pool of a large corporation, on the assembly line of a manufacturing firm, or she is a file clerk in an insurance company. She is the woman who waits on you when you shop for clothing—or she is the woman who stitched the clothing. She is also the woman who serves you at your favorite restaurant, cashes your check at the bank, answers your telephone call for information, or washes and cuts your hair at the beauty parlor.

Most likely, however, she holds a white-collar job (42 percent of employed women are in white-collar occupations), and most likely the job is clerical. The majority of women workers are typists, secretaries, bookkeepers, and clerks (the "pink-collar" occupations—white-collar occupations held predominantly by women). Thirty-five percent of employed women hold clerical positions, and women account for more than three-fourths of all clerical workers. The other major white-collar occupation for women is sales. Most women in sales work are in the retail trades, where they hold the lower-paying positions; for example, as clerks and department-store saleswomen (see Table 5.1).

The next largest occupational category for women is the services field (20 percent of employed women in 1979), where, again, women outnumber men. Within the services occupations, women work mostly in the food-services field as waitresses or in the health- and personal-services field as nurses' aides, orderlies, attendants, hairdressers, and cosmetologists. Cleaning and private-household service work is also common.

Blue-collar occupations, where male workers predominate, account for only about 15 percent of employed women. Most blue-collar women workers hold the lower-paying operative jobs; they are the assemblers, inspectors, wrappers and packers, or operators of machinery (such as sewing machines). Few women are employed in the more lucrative blue-collar craft jobs.

Although the occupations of "ordinary" women workers are quite diversified, they share some important characteristics. They are highly segregated by sex—most women are employed in occupations that are dominated by women. Furthermore, the skills or attributes required by their work are usually considered "female traits," and such beliefs guide the hiring practices of employers. For example, women in blue-collar occupations are hired as operatives because women are believed to have greater manual dexterity than men. Women are sewers and stitchers because they are believed to be better suited to do "fine detail" work. Similarly, most typists are women because it is said that their "superior" manual dexterity allows them to type faster than any man. (The belief that women have greater manual dexterity than men is supported by some research. However, manual dexterity is certainly as important for surgery, for example, as for sewing or typing, but we hear little argument that surgery is therefore "women's work.")

Another characteristic shared by these diverse occupations is that they

T a b l e 5 . 1 / *The "Ordinary" Woman Worker: A Profile, 1979*

	Percentage of Employed Women	Degree of Segregation: Women as a percentage of total employment in occupational groups
Typical white-collar occupations		
Sales	7	45.1
Clerical	35	80.3
Typical blue-collar occupations		
Craft and kindred workers	2	5.7
Operatives, except transport	11	39.9
Transport equipment operatives	0.5	8.1
Service workers	20	59.2

SOURCE: Adapted from U.S. Department of Labor, Women's Bureau, *Employment Goals of the World Plan of Action: Developments and Issues in the United States* (Washington, D.C.: U.S. Government Printing Office, July 1980), Table 11; U.S. Department of Labor, Bureau of Labor Statistics, *Perspectives on Working Women: A Databook*, Bulletin 2080 (Washington, D.C.: U.S. Government Printing Office, October 1980), Table 10, p. 9.

NOTE: These figures exclude women who work in professional, technical, and managerial and administrative jobs as well as those who work as farmers.

tend to be dead-end positions that are unstable and among the lowest paid. Within white-collar, blue-collar, and service categories, women earn about three-fifths the wages paid to men in the same occupational groups (see Figure 5.1), and women's unemployment rates are higher. Women's jobs also provide little opportunity for advancement in the organizational hierarchy. And it is rare that a woman's job requires that she supervise male workers.

Thus the ordinary woman worker performs support and service work. These are important tasks within the society, in that the "higher-level" occupations depend on the performance of such support and service tasks, but the work itself is not taken seriously. In this chapter, we focus on the working conditions and job prospects of two groups of ordinary women workers—those in clerical occupations, where the vast majority of women work, and those in blue-collar occupations, a category often overlooked by social-science research.

WOMEN IN CLERICAL OCCUPATIONS

The largest single occupational category for women today is clerical work: women are the stenographers, typists, secretaries, bookkeepers, and clerks. Clerical work has both changed in nature and grown enormously in

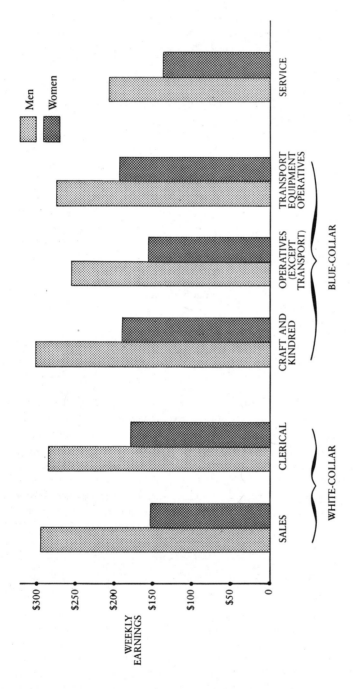

F i g u r e 5 . 1 / *Median Usual Weekly Earnings of Full-Time Wage and Salary Workers*

SOURCE: Prepared from data in U.S. Department of Labor, Bureau of Labor Statistics, *Perspectives on Working Women: A Databook*, Bulletin 2080 (Washington, D.C.: U.S. Government Printing Office, October 1980), Table 10, p. 9.

the last century. Since World War II, clerical work has tripled, reflecting a shift in the U.S. economic structure from manufacturing to the distributive, financial, and service organizations (Seidman, 1978).

Clerical Work at the Turn of the Century

Although the typical clerical worker is now female, this was not always the case. In the nineteenth century, clerks were almost exclusively male. The 1870 census reported that of 76,639 office workers in the United States, only 1,860 (3.5 percent) were women (Davies, 1975). Despite their numbers and the demand for their services, nineteenth-century clerks were not organized as an occupational group. They did not join unions as a way to improve their working conditions or increase their economic benefits. Trade unions were considered a working-class phenomenon, and many clerks wanted to distance themselves from the industrial proletariat (working class). The position of clerk had an aura of respectability, and it provided a means of obtaining the external trappings of the gentleman.

The typical male clerk had a highly personal relationship with his boss, a relationship developed over the forty or fifty years he spent working in the same small office. A clerkship also served as an apprenticeship for the young man who was to "learn the ropes" before moving up to a managerial position. Frequently the clerk was a son of the firm's owner, and the clerkship was considered training for the eventual takeover of the business. Those who were not so lucky as to be the boss's son nevertheless remained loyal to the company, hoping that their loyalty would be rewarded with promotions and raises in pay, if not a stake in the company (Davies, 1975; McNally, 1979).

How did this previously male-dominated occupation become so thoroughly feminized? The expansion of corporations at the end of the nineteenth century increased the demand for clerical workers, and technological innovations (the typewriter and the telephone) were important factors in the feminization of office work. Typing, as a new occupation, was originally considered "sex-neutral," but it quickly became a feminine specialty.

The Remington Company trained women to demonstrate their new machines. Therefore, from the beginning, typewriters were operated by women, facilitating their identification as a "feminine specialty" (Glenn and Feldberg, 1979:318). This was important, because women typists thus did not encounter the criticism that they were "taking over men's work." Typing and telephoning became women's work—after all, women were more dexterous and "chatty" than men. At that time also, the supply of eligible women had increased, because more women than men were graduating from high school. Women were typically excluded from the professions, while educated men had a wider range of job opportunities. Clerical work was attractive to the educated woman, who had relatively few options. Factory and sales work had lower social status and paid less well. Teaching was the only attractive alternative for educated women, and it was believed that clerical work paid better (Davies, 1975; Glenn and Feldberg, 1979; McNally, 1979; Tepperman, n.d.). At first, women's office work was confined to typing and telephoning, but women eventually invaded male domains. Shorthand, a skill previously associated with male office workers, was taken over by women who attended courses and learned the skill.

At the turn of the century, women's labor was in demand. Women constituted an educated pool of workers who could meet the needs of the expanding corporations. Women's reasons for seeking work were primarily economic. In the early twentieth century, most clerical workers were single women from middle-class backgrounds who needed jobs to support themselves, at least until they married. Working-class women soon joined the clerical ranks. Among the newer immigrants, working-class single and married women worked to help their families avoid poverty.

Office work in the large corporations was a far cry from the clerkship positions in the small intimate offices of the nineteenth-century firm. The responsibility and status of the clerk had diminished considerably, and the position was no longer that of an apprentice with the possibility of upward mobility. The large organizations created a more complex hierarchy, one in which the clerk's job became increasingly subdivided into a series of low-level, dead-end jobs. The remaining male clerical population was disadvantaged in terms of depressed status (a male clerk was now "one of the girls") and depressed pay (women were willing to work for lower pay, thus reducing the pay scale for all clerks). In the long run, however, male clerks benefited from the feminization of office work. Corresponding to the increase in dead-end, low-level office jobs was the development of low- and middle-management positions—a "managerial revolution" was taking place (Burnham, 1941). Because these managerial positions required lengthy training and broad qualifications, women were usually excluded from consideration and were concentrated instead in the lower levels of the office hierarchy. As the managers increasingly replaced the owner-manager, they came to be a level of workers between the top company officials and the clerks, often taking over the planning and decision making of the company (McNally, 1979).

The Clerical Worker Today

The contemporary nature of office work has dramatically changed, especially since World War II. Offices have grown in size and have become more impersonal and automated. Some regard the modern office as a "clerical factory," where tasks have been divided and subdivided, leaving the clerk with dull and repetitious work:

The modern office with its tens of thousands of square feet and its factory-like flow of work is not an informal, friendly place. The drag and beat of work, the "production unit" tempo, require that time consumed by anything but business at hand be explained and apologized for. (Mills, 1951:204)

The quality of work life is a problem, especially for women employed in the medium-level clerical jobs—which the vast majority are. Such problems are especially acute in big offices such as the large financial and insurance headquarters. In many such places, clerical activities are arranged as small, standardized tasks, usually with automated office machines to speed up the work process. Pools of workers (the secretarial office pool) or individual workers specialize in one set of small tasks, performing these limited activities over and over again (Glenn and Feldberg, 1977). Recent developments in the computer industry also promise to have a profound impact on the office worker. The invention of the silicon chip (a tiny wafer of silicon on which it is possible to store as much information as was once stored by a large computer) and of other computer innovations are now facilitating the production of small, very inexpensive data-processing systems, putting automation within the reach of even small firms (McNally, 1979:32). Although more and more companies, including the smaller ones, are installing highly automated equipment, the continued availability of a large pool of cheap female labor may slow down the extent of capital investment in office equipment (McNally, 1979:31).

Some observers believe that the growth of office mechanization, coupled with the division of office tasks into smaller and smaller routine operations, has blurred the distinction between manual and nonmanual work, making white- and blue-collar jobs more similar. In this view, the clerk can be considered a "helper's attendant" of a highly mechanized, high-speed process (Braverman, 1974). For example, it has been suggested that the introduction of new computer technology into the office—especially those microprocessor-based systems such as the word processor—eliminates some of the boring routine tasks of the office, but can also create a factorylike atmosphere in the office.[1]

Many claim that the word processor will free the secretary-clerk from dull and routine tasks, permit a shorter workweek, and allow time for more responsible and challenging administrative tasks. But it is more likely that the more responsible and challenging administrative tasks will be taken on by male employees. It is also feared that word processors and other automated office equipment will further widen the gap between men's and women's work by deskilling the female clerical employee (no longer requiring skills of her) and increasing managerial control of clerical workers (Morgall, 1981; West, 1982). "When a word processor enters the office, an automated time and motion man may come along with it. In order to capitalize on their investment, management may decide to increase shiftwork and speed up the work process. A piece rate system may be introduced" (Morgall, 1981: 94–95).

The new automated office equipment does reduce some of the old dull, routine tasks associated with many jobs, but operating the equipment can be just as dull and routine, and just as dehumanizing, although perhaps in a different way. The efficiency and the capacity of these machines to track errors make many operators uneasy. In the following quote, Nora, employed in what would be considered a medium- to low-level clerical position, describes her job operating a check-sorting machine in a large bank. The machine is programmed to "read" the magnetic-ink code numbers printed at the bottom of checks; it then sorts them into piles according to the bank branch:

> In our area we have about sixty or seventy people working. . . . A lot of checks are not supposed to go through—like certain checks that should go to another bank or forged ones or some that the number isn't quite clear on. Unfortunately, once in a while some of them slip through. Then you have to ring the buzzer and they have to come over and rebatch everything. And they know that sorter such-and-such let them go through. Now they have error sheets, so every time you make an error it gets marked down. People are making more errors now because they're so nervous about not making them. It's for performance reviews. They want statistics when it comes time for raises or promotions. They started marking down errors in January, but they didn't let us know until almost the end of the month. All of a sudden they hand you an error sheet. We didn't think it was fair not to let you know. It's almost like Big Brother. . . . These performance reviews . . . people are very upset about them. You're working faster because "times per hour" is going to be part of the statistics in your review. . . . Most of the people agree with me that they don't give you enough training on what happens to the check. They'll say, "You're running D.D.A. today." Fine, I know that D.D.A. means you're running the main type of work with the orange separator card, but I don't know what "D.D.A." means . . . or "D.V." or "S.D.A." or "G.G.E." . . . It would be nice if you knew what they were or where the checks come from or where they're going. It's just a feeling of not knowing. It's like the machine running you. You're like a computer. "We'll run D.D.A. today." (Tepperman, 1976:26–27)

Yet one should not conclude that clerical workers derive no satisfaction from their work. An in-depth study of women clerical workers (Glenn and Feldberg, 1979) reported that, in addition to the income, the "opportunities to form and maintain social connections" were important. Work was also reported to give "direction and purpose to their lives by structuring their time and getting them involved in 'useful' activity" (p. 33). For married women, the work also provided "an identity separate from their family roles" (p. 33). Thus, although it is hard to generalize about all clerical work, certain characteristics can be identified as important to the clerical worker's

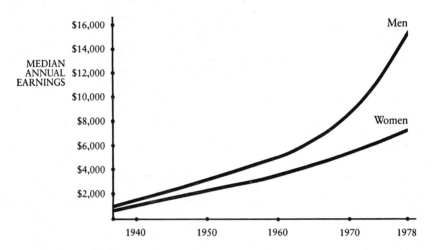

Note: Data for 1949 are for year-round workers; all other data are for full-time, year-round workers.

F i g u r e   5 . 2 / *Annual Earnings of Male and Female Clerical Workers, 1939–1978*

SOURCE: Prepared from data in Evelyn Glenn and Rosalyn Feldberg, "Clerical Work: The Female Occupation," in Jo Freeman, ed., *Women: A Feminist Perspective*, 2nd ed. (Palo Alto, Calif.: Mayfield, 1979), p. 322; and U.S. Department of Labor, Bureau of Labor Statistics, *Perspectives on Working Women: A Databook*, Bulletin 2080 (Washington, D.C.: U.S. Government Printing Office, October 1980), Table 62, p. 59.

job satisfaction. For example, the jobs that are most mechanized and routine are least likely to be satisfying, for several reasons:

> In the first place, this is because these jobs are associated with uncomfortable levels of noise and a variety of unpleasant stresses and strains on the human body. Secondly, the lack of variety entailed in such jobs is likely to induce a sense of boredom. . . . Thirdly, these are the jobs which are most likely to be physically segregated and thus diminish the opportunities for personal contacts. (McNally, 1979:83)

Financial rewards and job benefits

The wages of women clerical workers are low and have declined relative to those of other women in the paid labor force. From 1958 to 1970, the median wage of the women clerical workers declined from four-fifths to less than two-thirds the wages of women in the professional and technical occupations (Seidman, 1978:75). Clerical wages differ considerably, however, depending on whether the employee is male or female. Figure 5.2 shows that women's earnings are substantially lower than those of men. Even when fe-

Table 5.2 / *Education and Income of Clerical Workers, 1970*

Occupation	Education: Percentage by which median education is above or below median of all U.S. male workers		Income: Percentage by which median earnings are above or below median of all U.S. male workers	
	Men	Women	Men	Women
Bank teller	+4	+2	−25	−45
Bookkeeper	+4	+2	−3	−41
Cashier	0	−2	−59	−68
File clerk	+2	+1	−35	−55
Library attendant and assistant	+13	+7	−80	−73
Key-punch operator	+2	+2	−2	−40
Payroll and time-keeping clerk	+2	+2	+3	−32
Receptionist	+5	+2	−44	−56
Secretary	+5	+3	−1	−37
Telephone operator	+2	+1	−15	−44
Typist	+2	+2	−21	−47

SOURCE: Barbara Sinclair Deckard, *The Women's Movement: Political, Socioeconomic, and Psychological Issues* (New York: Harper & Row, 1979), p. 111.

NOTE: In all occupations listed, women are a majority of the total.

male clerical workers have education and job qualifications similar to their male counterparts, their wages are lower (see Table 5.2).

Part of the reason for these depressed wages is the tremendous over-crowding and continued segregation of women into the clerical field. Even *within* clerical work, the labor is segregated on the basis of sex. Male clerical workers are post-office mail carriers, shipping and receiving clerks, stock clerks, and storekeepers—all categories with a minority of women. Secretaries, typists, telephone operators, bank tellers, and bookkeepers, on the other hand, are almost exclusively women (U.S. Department of Labor, Women's Bureau, 1980a). As a result, even though the demand for clerical workers is high, the segregation and the influx of women into clerical work have lowered wages and made it difficult for such women to find jobs. The unemployment rate among clerical workers is high: in 1965, clerical workers represented 11 percent of all unemployed workers; in 1977, 15 percent (Barrett, 1979a:50).

Women clerical workers often lack the other compensations available to men and available within other occupations. Because most clerical work is nonunionized, such benefits as sick pay and pension plans, for example, are given at the discretion of the employer: "Some companies give supervisors the power to suspend a person's sick leave 'privileges.' Many places give clericals as few as five sick days a year or hassle people if they take sick leave to which they're supposedly entitled" (Tepperman, n.d.: 5).

Job advancement

Clerical jobs do not usually provide opportunities for advancement. The clerical work force is surrounded by "dead space," in that it "lacks links to other areas in most employing organizations" (Seidman, 1978: 77). Clerical workers rarely get the chance to move up in their organizations or receive on-the-job training. Positions that do open up are more likely to be filled by people from outside the company who have already been trained elsewhere.

There are several ways in which women miss out on job promotions. Seidman (1978) identified three different opportunity gaps in the clerical job market (see Figure 5.3). The first gap occurs at entry-level positions, when women lack the basic skills required to enter the clerical field as an alternative to blue-collar or service work. Those women who enter the clerical field at this level (as messengers or file clerks) then experience a second opportunity gap. The clerk finds she needs additional skills to move beyond her entry-level job, but she can rarely obtain these skills on her job—a Catch-22 situation. Clerical workers who have an upper-level clerical job (for example, executive secretary or clerk-supervisor) often discover a third opportunity gap. It is almost impossible for this group to move into the higher-paying, higher-prestige managerial or semiprofessional occupations (Seidman, 1978). This has been especially true in the American Telephone and Telegraph Company (AT&T, also affectionately known as Ma Bell), the single largest employer of women in the United States. AT&T has systematically excluded women from both higher-level management jobs and from the better-paying craft jobs, such as construction and repair jobs (see Wallace, 1976a). Statistics from AT&T in New York show that in 1970, only 1.1 percent of all craft jobs in the entire Bell System were held by women, while telephone operators were 99.9 percent female (Deckard, 1979: 92). Banks are also big offenders. A recent survey of twenty-four major banks revealed that women represented 63 percent of all workers, but only 13 percent of bank officers (Deckard, 1979: 93).

Barriers to promotions, while partly a result of job opportunity structure (see the opportunity gaps in Figure 5.3) and the disinclination of employers to promote from within, are also reinforced by a variety of stereotypes about women. Perhaps the most damaging is the belief that women workers are unstable and unreliable. Employers are often reluctant to promote or train their female employees because they fear the women will not remain very long—they will quit when they marry or when they have children. Yet, as Tepperman (1976) has pointed out, the notion of the female office worker as young and single, ready to get married and leave work, is false. The me-

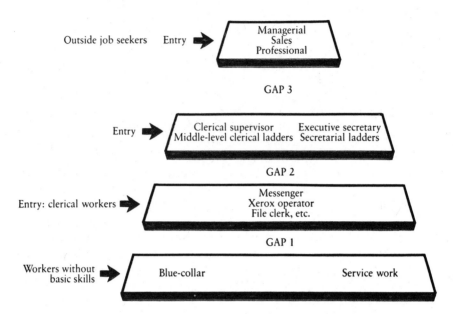

F i g u r e   5 . 3 / *Opportunity Gaps in Clerical Work: Employment Levels in Hiring of Clerical Workers*

SOURCE: Adapted from Ann Seidman, *Working Women: A Study of Women in Paid Jobs* (Boulder, Colo.: Westview Press, 1978), p. 78.

dian age of clerical workers is approximately thirty-five, and over half of all clerical workers are married. Today fewer women leave their jobs when they get married, and fewer quit to have children; those who do, return to work sooner (Tepperman, 1976). Available data also indicate that differences in turnover rates of men and women employees are small. As for absenteeism, one U.S. Public Health Service study showed an average of 5.6 days lost by women and 5.3 days by men (U.S. Department of Health, Education, and Welfare, Public Health Service, 1967). McNally has pointed out that the accuracy of the stereotypes held by employers concerning women workers may be less important than the fact that their beliefs operate as self-fulfilling prophecies:

> Since employers anticipate that women are likely to leave their jobs, they do not give them responsible positions, nor train them for more interesting and more skilled work. Many women become frustrated and bored in these undemanding occupations and eventually leave for what they hope will be greener pastures, and in the process confirm the views of the employers that women are unstable members of the labor force. (McNally, 1979:60–61)

Nonclerical tasks that "go with the job"

Issues other than mechanization, rationalization, and lack of pay and advancement also plague clerical workers. Clerical workers are often required to do work and perform tasks that are not reasonably included within the definition of clerical activities.

Clerical workers are often expected and sometimes required to make the morning coffee and run personal errands for the boss. One woman clerk was told by her boss to go and find and try on a nursing bra for his wife, who didn't have the time to purchase one. And many clerks resent the assumption that they should provide a "shoulder" for the boss to cry on.[2] These activities are experienced as demeaning, and clerks feel that they are patronized and not respected. Secretaries often end up in the role of "office wife," especially in the smaller, more traditional offices (Benet, 1972; Kanter, 1977a; Parsons and Bales, 1956; Rowe, 1958). In many ways, the clerical worker's job outside the home parallels her traditional homemaker role. The "perfect" secretary is expected to have certain basic secretarial skills, just as wives are expected to have certain basic cooking and housekeeping skills. She is expected to "understand" her boss and be alert to his moods, needs, whims, tastes, and personal quirks—paralleling the expectations of husbands concerning wives (McNally, 1979:56). Although it is often assumed that female office workers should provide a range of personal services for the boss, they themselves are treated as nonpersons: "Secretaries are viewed totally as machines. They are ignored. For instance, if an attorney brings a client into his office, he will introduce everybody but the secretary. Unless he wants coffee he won't speak to her" (Tepperman, n.d.:7).

Sexual harassment

Sexual harassment is a growing occupational hazard of clerical life. Although such harassment occurs in every occupation, from professional to blue-collar and service work, we discuss it here because the majority of women workers *are* clerical workers and thus it is most common in this setting. Sometimes, of course, flirtations and romantic involvements are welcome, and some people hope that their jobs will provide opportunities to meet potential partners (see, for example, Neugarten and Shafritz, 1980). But sexual harassment on the job is something else again:

> I was a typist, and one of the men I worked for is always caressing my hair, or rubbing my back or trying to hug me when he comes into the office. I pull away and tell him to stop, but he never seems to get the message. He acts hurt and says he's only being friendly. It's really upsetting and I can't work when he is around. Having to face him every day ties my stomach into knots. I need to work—I got two kids; but you can't work like that, you just can't. (Working Women United Institute, 1980:1)

Sexual harassment on the job is said to be so common that many consider it an inevitable condition of women's employment. It can take many forms, from verbal harassment and abuse to pressure to engage in sexual activity and even attempted rape (Lindsey, 1977). Sexual harassment has been defined as "any unwanted pressure for sexual activity" and includes "verbal innuendos and suggestive comments, luring gestures, unwanted physical contact (touching, pinching, and so on), rape, and attempted rape. It is a form of harassment mainly perpetrated by men against women" (Bularzik, 1978:25). Despite the sexual element, such harassment is best understood as an expression of power and domination of the more powerful (men) over the less powerful (women).

The pervasiveness of the problem is indicated by the pioneering survey of 155 women that was conducted by the Working Women's United Institute in 1975, in the Ithaca, New York, region. Seventy percent of the women surveyed reported that they had experienced sexual harassment at least once (Silverman, 1976–1977). Most frequently, harassment comes from superiors on the job, although co-workers and clients are also frequent offenders. Of the 155 women sampled in the Ithaca study, 40 percent reported having been harassed by a work superior, 22 percent by a co-worker, 29 percent by a client, customer, or person who had no direct working relationship with them; 1 percent reported being harassed by a subordinate. In addition, a recent survey by *Redbook* magazine (Safrain, 1976) reported that of the 9,000 readers responding to their questionnaire on sexual harassment in work settings, 88 percent reported having experienced such harassment.

The specific forms of sexual harassment vary according to occupation and social class. Bularzik (1978) notes that, historically, all women have been "subject to at least the subtler forms of sexual harassment (suggestive remarks, dress codes)" but that "physical violence was more common and expected by women in menial jobs" (Bularzik, 1978:38). Research on the contemporary situation reveals a similar pattern (see, for example, Silverman, 1976–1977, and Gruber and Björn, 1982). Women at the bottom of the occupational hierarchy are subjected to more blatant expressions of sexual harassment—crude suggestive remarks and physical assaults. For professional and managerial women, the treatment is more subtle: they receive offers for after-work drinks, expensive lunches, business trips—with the implicit message that sexual favors are expected (Backhouse and Cohen, 1981:33).

MacKinnon (1979) distinguishes two types of sexual harassment: (1) quid pro quo, a situation in which "sexual compliance is exchanged, or proposed to be exchanged, for an employment opportunity," and (2) "sexual harassment as a persistent condition of work" (p. 32). The first type, the quid pro quo, tends to arise in contexts in which men are supervisors and managers of female employees. The terms of such an exchange can be expressed ambiguously or explicitly, but the message usually gets through. Some examples quoted by MacKinnon: "[If] I wasn't going to sleep with him, I wasn't going to get my promotion"; "I think he meant that I had a job if I played along"; "You've got to make love to get a day off" (p. 32). The second type of harassment is more pervasive, in that it permeates the entire working environment, often making it unbearable:

> Unwanted sexual advances, made simply because she has a woman's body, can be a daily part of a woman's work life. She may be constantly felt or pinched, visually undressed or stared at, surreptitiously kissed, commented upon, manipulated into being found alone, and generally taken advantage of at work. (MacKinnon, 1979:40)

MacKinnon notes that this form of harassment is common with both "token women"—those in nontraditional jobs, such as a female truck driver or a female manager (where visibility often presents a challenge to the male co-workers)—as well as in the more typically traditional female jobs (p. 40).

To date, the information on the incidence of sexual harassment is uneven. Much of it consists of anecdotes from members of a wide range of working populations, making it difficult to generalize. The general picture, however, is that sexual harassment is widespread and that it occurs among all women workers, regardless of their age, marital status, occupation, or ethnic background (Neugarten and Shafritz, 1980:6).

Dealing with sexual harassment presents problems. In the Ithaca study, 75 percent of those who had been harassed did nothing about it (Silverman, 1976–1977). Many women are fearful and reluctant to confront the issues directly:

> Women are either embarrassed or humiliated that they are the targets of sexually coercive behavior. But more than that, they are intimidated as subordinates in the hierarchical structure, fearing that a direct confrontation would result in threats to their livelihood. Finally, women generally do not want their husbands, boyfriends, parents, and children to know of their predicament. They fear that they will be ridiculed or made to feel guilty that they in some way were responsible by encouraging the harasser. (Backhouse and Cohen, 1981:35)

These fears are not unfounded:

> Most male superiors treat it as a joke, at best it's not serious. . . . Even more frightening, the woman who speaks out against her tormenters runs the risk of suddenly being seen as crazy, a weirdo, or even worse, a loose woman! Company officials often laugh it off or consider the woman now available to themselves. (MacKinnon, 1979:49)

The occasional court case involving sexual harassment provides some illustration of the difficulties encountered in attempts to deal with the problem. Adrienne Tomkins (see Farley, 1978) took the Public Service Electric and Gas and Herbert D. Reppen to court, seeking compensatory and punitive damages and equitable relief:

Tomkins, a former office worker for the Newark, New Jersey, offices of PSE&G, alleges that after she became eligible for promotion to secretary her supervisor, Herbert Reppin, requested she lunch with him to discuss her prospects with the firm. At that time, she alleges, he made sexual advances and that she was detained by him against her will through economic threats and physical force. She also alleges her complaints to the company about the incident resulted in a transfer to a less desirable position in the company, and retaliation against her in the form of disciplinary layoffs, threats of demotion, salary cuts, and eventual termination. (Farley, 1978:185)

Sexual harassment clearly presents a major problem for women workers. It would seem appropriate that employers would assume responsibility for investigating and taking action when a worker reports sexual harassment. Yet many corporations are reluctant to let such incidents surface "for fear of maligning the reputation of the organization" (Neugarten and Shafritz, 1980:7). Organizations often lack adequate policies or guidelines for dealing with the problem and are likely to treat the few complaints that do surface as though they were complaints of sexual discrimination (Neugarten and Shafritz, 1980:7).

Some progress with this problem is reflected in the interim guidelines published by the Equal Employment Opportunity Commission in March 1980, reaffirming sexual harassment as an unlawful practice. These guidelines hold an "employer, employment agency, joint apprenticeship committee or labor organization, accountable for its acts and those of its agents and supervisory employees" (U.S. Department of Labor, Women's Bureau, 1980a:24). The guidelines further state that an employer should take the necessary steps to prevent sexual harassment from occurring, investigate all complaints alleging sexual harassment, inform employees that such harassment will not be tolerated, and initiate appropriate penalties (U.S. Department of Labor, Women's Bureau, 1980a:24).

The employee often endures sexual harassment because of the difficulties in dealing with it adequately and because she fears jeopardizing her job. Other problems in clerical occupations—such as being treated as a personal servant, being expected to run personal errands, the "office wife" role, and the dull, monotonous, and boring nature of most clerical tasks—are also endured because the employee needs the job. Workers rationalize dull and low-paying jobs because they meet new friends and acquaintances at work. These alternative satisfactions can function as reasons for not doing anything about the situation (McNally, 1979:85).

Alternatives and Prospects for Clerical Work

One of the obvious alternatives to a difficult job situation is finding a different job, in the same or a similar field. This option is in reality rather limited, given the rising levels of unemployment among clerical workers. In addition, job hopping can reinforce the stereotype of women as unstable and unreliable employees. Getting a totally different job is still another alternative, yet this option is also limited for clerical workers, given the dead-end nature of such occupations. A new job may require retraining, which makes it a costly option, especially if the family depends on the income, which is the case for the majority of working women. One may then ask, "What are the alternatives?" For the most part, other traditional female jobs are equally problematic in working conditions, remuneration, and status.

One kind of solution:
"Temporary" office work

An alternative that has become increasingly popular for many clerical workers is regular temporary office work. Placement in a series of different work settings through temporary agencies allows the worker to survey the range of options open to her. She can also leave a difficult job without fear of reprisals from the employer. Temporary office work can also be used as a "way station to another occupation or personal niche" (Olesen and Katsuranis, 1978:331). For others it is a way to overcome the boredom and lack of power and control over one's job. For still others the permanent life as a temporary provides them with a means of supporting other interests in their lives, such as another career or activity (Olesen and Katsuranis, 1978). For the working mother with small children, temporary employment offers the flexibility unavailable in full-time nine-to-five jobs. She is willing to trade the security of a full-time occupation for the ability to arrange workdays and hours to be free for other activities and responsibilities (McNally, 1979:97).

From every indication, the temporary-service industry will continue to grow (Olesen and Katsuranis, 1978:320), yet its growth has drawbacks:

> So long as agencies and temporary workers exist there is no pressure upon employers to adopt more flexible attitudes themselves. An employer who makes a concession to one permanent worker is obliged to extend this facility to all the others—let one married secretary come in at 9:30 and they will all want to. (McNally, 1979:98)

A temporary work force may also reduce the pressure on employers to accommodate particular needs of some women workers, such as child-care facilities within the firms, or maternity- and paternity-leave policies. A temporary workforce may also ensure that employers will not have to worry about working conditions, salary, upward mobility, or even training programs for their workers.

Unionization

The poor working conditions and lack of adequate pay and job-advancement opportunities have intensified the efforts of organizations such as Nine-to-Five (Local 925, Union of Clerical Workers) to push for the unionization of more clerical workers. Yet clerical workers are the largest category of workers who are *not* fully unionized (Glenn and Feldberg, 1979:331). A number of factors impede efforts to organize the clerical work force: "Unions, management, and others have assumed that this group is hard to organize because they are women, because they consider themselves semiprofessionals rather than workers and because they have close ties with their employers on the job" (Seidman, 1978:83).

The assumption that women's primary commitment is to their homes and family life has led organizers to believe that clerical workers' concerns about working conditions "are not of sufficient importance to motivate them to join unions" (Glenn and Feldberg, 1979:331). Women are socialized to be apolitical—to view their position (subordinate to men) as unchangeable by themselves. Therefore, it is assumed that their situation in the office will not strike them as unfair and that they are unlikely to organize in opposition to authority (Glenn and Feldberg, 1979:331). It is also assumed that many clerical workers are reluctant to take an oppositional stance toward their bosses, because they identify too much with management. The role of secretary, for example, is a supportive role; an oppositional stance toward the boss would effectively render their relationship unworkable (McNally, 1979:87).

Yet, as several observers have pointed out (Glenn and Feldberg, 1979; Howe, 1977), the conditions of clerical workers are changing:

> Things aren't the same anymore. Women's attitudes toward work are changing, and the office itself is changing. Becoming more mechanized. In addition, many of today's clerical workers are the daughters and sisters of blue-collar workers: they know first-hand the difference a union can make, particularly in terms of the paycheck. And for those still worried about the class stigma of a union, there are now the successes of teachers and nurses and other recently organized professions to point to. . . . Twenty years from now the majority of clerical workers will be in unions. (Howe, 1977:161)

The movement toward clerical unionization is growing (Tepperman, 1976), and statistics indicate an increase in the percentage of white-collar workers in unions. For example, in 1974 "white-collar workers voted for unions more than [in] any other year since records were kept. The fastest growing unions are those with a high percentage of office workers, especially unions of public employees" (Tepperman, 1976:95). Also emerging are grass-roots organizations, which are helping office workers overcome their fears of organizing.

The unionization of clerical workers promises to be an important strategy for ensuring the upgrading of the economic position of the clerical worker. Karen Nussbaum, an organizer of Nine-to-Five, typifies the promise of this tool for helping workers confront their employers and fight against inequities:

> The first thing people say to me is "Nothing ever happens here because *nobody* ever wants to do anything. I'm the only person who cares. How can I do anything? I'm all alone." Now, that's a defense. I mean, it's hard to think of what to do, for one thing. And it's also true that people are "apathetic," but that apathy comes from real sources. The sources are fear of losing your job and cynicism about change. People haven't seen people effectively work to change things. The steps for moving from a gripe to a solution aren't clear to them. You have to move from feeling that you are all alone to recognizing that your gripes are common ones and that you can also *act* on the gripe by building a group.
>
> What I do is try to help people go the first step and get an idea for the second step. To realize that if you come up against what seems to be a brick wall, there's a way to get around it. There aren't unsolvable problems. They don't exist! (Tepperman, 1976:150)

Training for women who are interested in organizing clerical workers is an important first step toward improving the quality of working life for the clerical worker. Researchers have suggested that training programs should focus on "skills in presenting information on legal rights, developing networks of interested employees within an organization, researching the position of clerical workers within an organization, and handling grievances" (Seidman, 1978:151; see also Union for Radical Political Economics, 1978).

BLUE-COLLAR WOMEN AT WORK

Blue-collar work covers the census category known as "craft and kindred workers, operatives, and nonfarm laborers." These categories emphasize manual skills—blue-collar workers are the stitchers, assembly-line workers, packers, and so on. About 15 percent of working women are employed in blue-collar occupations, mostly as operatives.

The employment of women in blue-collar work can be traced to the beginning of the industrial revolution, with the recruitment of young single women into the textile industries that were springing up in New England in the 1830s and 1840s (see Chapter 2). With the growth of new manufacturing industries, women began to be employed in the garment industry, shoe manufacturing, and food processing. By the beginning of the twentieth century, there were few industrial occupations in which women were not represented in at least some capacity (Baker, 1964). Yet most women were not allowed to enter the skilled trades; most were excluded from company trade-union apprenticeship programs, and most were ineligible for the vocational training programs present in some public schools (Abbott, 1910; Henry, 1915).

Working Conditions

Factory working conditions at the turn of the century were pretty grim. Sweatshops were real, as we can see in the following description by an employee of the Triangle Shirtwaist Company, Pauline Newmann, who became an ILGWU organizer (International Ladies Garment Workers Union):

> I went to work for the Triangle Shirtwaist Company in 1901. The corner of a shop would resemble a kindergarten because we were young, eight, nine, ten years old. It was a world of greed; the human being didn't mean anything. The hours were from 7:30 in the morning to 6:30 at night when it wasn't busy. When the season was on we worked until 9 o'clock. No overtime pay, not even supper money. . . . My wages as a youngster were $1.50 for a seven-day week . . . by the time I left the Triangle Waist Company in 1909, my wages went up to $5.50. . . . The early sweatshops were usually so dark that gas jets (for light) burned day and night. There was no insulation in the winter, only a pot-bellied stove in the middle of the factory. . . . Of course in the summer you suffocated with practically no ventilation. (Wertheimer, 1977: 294–295)

Perhaps the grimmest reminder of the poor working conditions is the fire that broke out in this same factory in 1911. The building had no sprinkler system, and the factory's doors were locked each working day to "keep the women in and the union organizers out" (Wertheimer, 1977:310). When the fire broke out, the workers, mostly women and girls, jumped to their deaths, were burned, or suffocated in the fire; 146 people were killed.

Although conditions have improved dramatically since the turn of this century, factory working conditions are still poor. For the most part the work remains underpaid and dull, routine and repetitive, usually leading nowhere (Seifer, 1973). The alienation experienced by the contemporary factory woman is vividly described by Tepperman (1970), who worked in a Chicago factory:

> The woman who worked next to me on the line at Nadir was named Pat. She had two children and two grandchildren, and she would talk to me about them, about getting her hair done, and about cooking. Every morning, just before the bell rang to start work, she would give me a little "Well, here we go" look. One morning she said, "Every day you think you can't possibly hate it any more, and then the next day you hate it more." Then the bell rang and it was like going underwater and holding your breath for two hours (until the break). I worked on an assembly line of about forty women. I put little things on wires into something else, with wirecutters. After a while, I found out what the little things were, but I never found out what they were used for. . . . Most of the jobs in the plant were like mine, a series of the same ten or so motions all day.

All the men who were factory workers admitted that the women had the worst jobs, and that they (the men) would go crazy if they had to do that stuff. (Tepperman, 1970:116–117)

Reasons for Working; Job Satisfaction

Paid employment for blue-collar women is typically represented as a difficult choice weighed against the primary role of wife and mother. The blue-collar woman's decision to go out to work is said to be dictated by economic need and is really an extension of her primary family role (Walshok, 1978:14). But, contrary to this image, paid employment is simply a fact of life for many women. There is no conflict with marriage and family roles; having a job is taken for granted. The income is essential, but beyond economic motives, paid employment is as important to the personal satisfaction of blue-collar women as it is for men or for professional women (Baker, 1978; Komarovsky, 1967; O'Farrell and Harlan, 1980; Walshok, 1978, 1981). Komarovsky's (1967) case study of fifty-eight blue-collar families in the late 1950s reveals the importance of the "sheer pride of earning." As one blue-collar woman noted, "I like to think I am bringing in some money too" (Komarovsky, 1967:68). Apart from money, working wives enjoyed the social life, the satisfaction of completing tasks, and relief from constant association with home and children (Komarovsky, 1967).

An in-depth three-year longitudinal study of blue-collar women (see Walshok, 1978) in both traditional and nontraditional work confirms the range of these satisfactions. Walshok's study revealed a cluster of motives for working: the most frequently mentioned reason was "money" (over 90 percent), but "getting out of the house and doing something," the "desire for outside communication and friendship," the "desire for challenge and personal satisfaction," and the "need for achievement" also figured as important motivations. For women entering nontraditional fields of work, the challenges and rewards are even more significant (Walshok, 1978:17). Many of the women in Walshok's study indicated that they would continue working even if they did not need the money.

Other research indicates that the woman with a full-time job is happier and feels herself to be better off than the full-time housewife, even though carrying a double role is difficult. Part-time workers were found to be most satisfied with their job situations and most interested in nonmonetary aspects of their work (Ferree, 1976:430). Research on this issue, however, does not produce consistent findings. For instance, evidence from six national surveys between 1971 and 1976 indicates that many working women see advantages to the housewife role, such as more free time, while they also enjoy the benefits of outside income and the increased independence (Wright, 1978:312).

These positive views of worker satisfaction among blue-collar women are contrary to the social scientist's view that, beyond the economic benefits, blue-collar work is not highly appealing. Yet we have shown that employment that is not particularly appealing from a social scientist's point of view may be highly appealing from a blue-collar woman's perspective. It appears that blue-collar women, as Walshok (1981) notes, "judge their present opportunities differently than do men or well-educated women. It is not only because of better money that they are satisfied. It is also the challenging qualities the nontraditional work experience offers, in contrast to traditional women's work" (Walshok, 1981:153).

While we have revealed a positive picture of worker satisfaction among blue-collar women, there are some indications that an important distinction needs to be made between skilled blue-collar work (typically women who enter nontraditional blue-collar work, such as craft jobs) and those women who enter less-skilled work (such as packers or assembly-line workers). Recent research has shown that job satisfaction among blue-collar women appears to be related to skill level. Women who are in skilled craft jobs report high levels of work satisfaction (O'Farrell and Harlan, 1980; Walshok, 1978), especially in comparison to those women in unskilled jobs. Rosen's (1981) study of unskilled blue-collar women workers in old manufacturing industries in eastern New England, for example, found extremely low levels of work satisfaction. Most of the women in this study indicated that they would rather not be working and that they would prefer to stay home and take care of the family (Rosen, 1982:23–24).

Sex Segregation, Income, and Job Security

Blue-collar women have been largely excluded from the skilled craft occupations and have been concentrated in the low-paying unskilled jobs (except during World Wars I and II). Most are employed as operatives— 48.7 percent of all assemblers are women, 94.8 percent of dressmakers are women, and 93.8 percent of sewers and stitchers are women (U.S. Department of Labor, Women's Bureau, 1980a). Even within craft occupations, women have the lower-paid, low-prestige jobs. For example, 72.9 percent of window dressers are women, but only 1.3 percent of carpenters are women. Men are generally concentrated in the higher-paying crafts; they are the electricians, carpenters, machinists, and tailors.

Women have made some inroads into the male-dominated skilled job categories. In 1960, only 2.9 percent of all craft workers were women; by 1979, they were 5.7 percent of these workers (see U.S. Department of Labor, Bureau of Labor Statistics, 1980:10). Affirmative-action laws enacted in the 1970s helped to eliminate some blatant discriminatory practices such as discrimination in hiring and recruitment of women workers. Entry-level positions are now opening up to women. However, there is also evidence that organizational practices within companies may be circumventing these laws by segregating women within organizations. For example, women are assigned to jobs with low mobility potential and to jobs that prevent women from obtaining the training and experience necessary to move up. Harlan and O'Farrell's (1982) study of women in nontraditional blue-collar work has revealed that while equal-employment policies increased the number of women who were hired, new patterns of segregation by sex (as well as race) emerged.

The range of industries employing blue-collar women is also more limited. Blue-collar men generally work in manufacturing, mining and construction, retail, transportation, and public utilities. Blue-collar women, on the other hand, work primarily in manufacturing. Within the manufacturing industry, women are concentrated in clothes-manufacturing firms, which are often marginal. These firms are small, and their capital investment is little more than sewing machines, cutting equipment, and material. Profits in this industry are minimal and uncertain because of the intense competition and changing tastes in fashion. The majority of jobs in these firms are semiskilled operative occupations, characterized by low pay, seasonal work, and little opportunity for advancement (Baker, 1978:349–350).

In all categories of blue-collar work, women earn less than men. Sex segregation within occupational categories is an important factor in limiting women's incomes. Operative jobs, for example, are "male" or "female" operative jobs; those held predominantly by women pay 61 percent of what those held predominantly by men pay (refer to Figure 5.1). Roby (1974) describes some examples:

> In the sewing divisions of auto industries, for example, women and black men have the hard, heavy, lower-paid jobs involved in sewing and lifting upholstery. White men have the lighter, high-paid jobs: guiding automated cutting machines, changing sewing machine parts and driving tractors onto which women and black men have loaded upholstery. Similarly, in textile mills, all loom fixers are men and loom tenders are women, and their pay difference is considerable. In the garment industry, women sew and men cut. Cutters and sewers within the same plant even belong to separate union locals. (Roby, 1974:25)

Since the enactment by Congress of the Equal Pay Act and other employment-rights legislation, the names of many job categories have simply been changed from "male" and "female" to "heavy" and "light." "Heavy" jobs are, of course, the same jobs formerly identified as "male"; they are the jobs that pay more. Other changes in job titles work the same way: women are "electronic assemblers," and men are "electronic technicians." The jobs entail identical work but "assemblers" are paid less (Roby, 1974:27). These tactics undermine the intent of the law—equality in wages —and perpetuate the wage inequalities between men and women. Such practices are illegal, yet they often go undetected unless a complaint is filed (Roby, 1974:27). According to Roby, only a "small fraction of the existing wage inequalities come to the attention of the Wage and Hour Division of the U.S. Department of Labor" (Roby, 1974:28). Few women realize that enforcement of the equal-rights laws depends on their making complaints.

The rating of expertise required by specific jobs is yet another source of wage inequality. The Dictionary of Occupational Titles (DOT) describes and rates the complexity level of the tasks involved in approximately 30,000 different job titles. The accuracy of these ratings is crucial, because the DOT is used by a variety of agencies (public and private employment agencies) to set wages and determine career-ladder criteria (Howe, 1977:236; Roby, 1974:29). Yet the DOT consistently underrates the complexity level of those jobs held primarily by women (Howe, 1977; Whitt and Naherny, 1975). For example, the job of child-care attendant has the same rated level of complexity as that of parking-lot attendant. A nursery-school teacher's job is rated as much less complex than that of a marine-mammal handler (Howe, 1977:238). Nurses, kindergarten teachers, and foster mothers are classified at the same level as restroom attendants; all are classified below pet-shop attendants.

An added economic issue for blue-collar women is the high rate of unemployment compared to that of blue-collar men. In 1979, the unemployment rate for blue-collar men was approximately 6 percent, while for women the rate was nearly 10 percent (Leon and Rones, 1980). Rosen (1982) has pointed out that the job security of blue-collar women is even more threatened because many of the industries in which they are employed tend to relocate their production sites. Many manufacturers have moved their plants from the north and east to the Sun Belt (especially Texas, California, and Florida); others have relocated outside U.S. borders (Rosen, 1982:30).

Alternatives and Prospects for Blue-Collar Women

A big part of the overall economic problem for blue-collar women is their limited access to the higher-paid skilled-craft occupations. Access to these occupations is typically gained through apprenticeship programs and vocational education or training. In construction and other trades, apprenticeship programs are usually conducted by employers and unions through joint apprenticeship committees. Traditionally, women have been excluded from apprenticeship programs because of the attitude that the journeyman status is a "male only" preserve (Briggs, 1977:226; Seidman, 1978). In 1976, women comprised slightly over 1 percent of all registered apprentices (Briggs, 1977:225), but the apprenticed fields were predominantly the female-dominated ones such as hairdressing and cosmetology.

As with the white-collar work world, some of the most difficult barriers to overcome are the stereotyped perceptions of women as blue-collar workers. A 1974 survey of apprenticeship programs that sampled seventy-eight organizations training Wisconsin state-registered apprentices showed that almost half the respondents in all-male establishments felt women did not perform as satisfactorily in production work as men, and over one-fourth of the respondents indicated that there were some jobs in a plant that women wouldn't be able to do (Briggs, 1977:227). Over three-fourths believed women were suited only for certain skilled trades (most frequently mentioned were sewing, upholstery, interior decorating, and drafting), while two-thirds stated that they would hesitate to consider a woman for certain other apprenticeable trades. Over half stated that their reluctance was based on the "unsuitability" of the work, in that it involved long hours and was "dirty" or "heavy" (U.S. Department of Labor, 1974; Briggs, 1977:227).

Research on women in blue-collar jobs is scarce. O'Farrell (1978:8) notes,

> Most of the work done in this area was done between 1900 and 1925. From then until 1974, researchers had not devoted a single book to women in blue-collar jobs. . . . Research indicates no significant sex differences in aptitude and knowledge areas studied. Where differences existed, men excelled in two (structural visualization and grip) and women excelled in six, e.g., abstract visualization and accounting aptitude. No significant sex differences appeared for analytic reasoning. (O'Farrell, 1978)

The few recent studies done on blue-collar women in nontraditional jobs reveals "that women are interested in nontraditional blue-collar jobs and are performing them adequately" (O'Farrell, 1978:12).

Other barriers hinder the woman blue-collar worker's efforts to enter nontraditional apprenticeship programs. Women often lack the information they need to enter such programs, and many women who want to enter at a later point in their life cycle (after marriage and children are raised) find they are past the apprenticeable age limit, which is twenty-six to twenty-seven (Briggs, 1977; Seidman, 1978).

Vocational education has been an important avenue to improved job opportunities for working-class men. As we noted in Chapter 3, women are concentrated in the homemaking, retailing, and clerical programs in vocational education. Very few women are being trained for the better-paying trades and for industrial or technical jobs (Roby, 1977:205). The same stereotypes that limit women's access to many blue-collar jobs and apprenticeship programs limit their full participation in vocational education programs. These stereotypes are reflected in institutional barriers such as the policies of educational systems that used to routinely exclude high-school females from carpentry and shop courses.

Career guidance, reflecting these same stereotypes about appropriate "masculine" and "feminine" work, has also limited women's access to non-traditional blue-collar work (Roby, 1977).

Unionization

Another way to improve working-class women's situation is through unionization. Although more women are now joining unions, their numbers have not kept pace with the increasing number of women entering the work force. It has been estimated that only one of seven working women is a union member, and, conversely, approximately one out of five union members is female (Seifer, 1973:33).

One of the reasons for the lag in women's unionization is fear of reprisals: "Women are still sometimes fired, or threatened with firing for attempting to get organized. In 1972 . . . a manufacturer of men's slacks in El Paso, Texas, discharged seventy-five women for trying to set up a union in the factory" (Seifer, 1973:33).

Other reasons include attitudes held by the women themselves or their husbands. Many women are reluctant to join a union because it is "unladylike" or because their husbands object to their "entering what remains largely a male domain." Other women assume that the union is not relevant because they perceive their employment as temporary (Seifer, 1973:33).

Wertheimer and Nelson (1975), in their study of women's participation and leadership in thirteen New York union locals, found that many women had inadequate information about unions and that men's prejudice (in both the leadership and rank-and-file) concerning women's roles hinders unionization of women blue-collar workers. The union hierarchy itself is male dominated—few high-level union positions are held by women. This creates a sense of powerlessness that can further discourage women from full union participation.

However, women blue-collar workers are making some progress in making unions more responsive to the needs of female workers. Seifer (1973) notes that a number of women's caucuses and departments that emerged in the 1960s have as their main goals the promotion of the special interests of women workers, such as equal pay, day care, training and opportunities, and maternity leave. Many of these caucuses have linked up with one another to form local federations.

Another landmark development has been the formation of the first nationwide organization of women unionists—the Coalition of Labor Union Women (CLUW, established in 1974). The CLUW could become an important force in improving working conditions for women. At present, approximately forty chapters have been chartered in the United States and are served by a national coordinator. CLUW is currently engaged in a foundation-funded project, "The Empowerment of Union Women," addressing the limited leadership roles of women in American labor unions (U.S. Department of Labor, Women's Bureau, 1980a:51).

Hopeful signs and recommendations for change

Although current research has documented that women who hold nontraditional jobs face resentment from both co-workers and management—with hostility ranging from practical joking to the threat or use of violence—research reveals a decrease over time in such harassment and shows that the harassment involves only a small number of men. Some women report that men are helpful to them in learning and carrying out their work (O'Farrell, 1982:152–153).

Some research suggests that concerns about challenging and succeeding in a nontraditional setting, including concerns about getting along with male co-workers, may diminish over time. A study of a sample of women in nontraditional skilled and semiskilled occupations revealed that "Those women who remained in a non-traditional job one year later had become less concerned with these aspects of the job, and more concerned with the traditional sources of satisfaction and dissatisfaction common to blue-collar workers" (McIlwee, 1982:299).

Sophenia Maxwell, who was taken on as an apprentice electrical mechanic for the Southern Pacific Railroad in November 1974, typifies the promise of the future: Maxwell is the only black female electrician apprentice employed by Southern Pacific. In an interview with Terry Wetherby (1977:163–164), she describes her work situation:

[Wetherby:] Have you had any psychological problems with your work?
[Maxwell:] When I started, . . . I felt a racial thing, certainly. My fears were about being black and working with the kind of men I was going to be working with. They haven't always been earning a decent salary, and those are the ones that feel the greatest threat. Being black and being a woman, I thought I would feel that. But they did a very good job of covering it up, because I didn't experience any of that. See, we have been taught . . . we've been put against each other. And then when we see each other and I talk to them, and they talk to me, we find out, "Hey! You're not so bad! You're not lazy! And you don't do this and do that." And it was okay. It was all right . . .
[Wetherby:] Do the men at work accept you?
[Maxwell:] I've had a fantastic reception! Beautiful! I always work with men. Sometimes I work with three or four, if there's trouble. If they've finished their work and they see you still working on something, they'll come and help you. Really beautiful! Really fine! . . .
[Wetherby:] You are totally accepted?
[Maxwell:] You can't change a person altogether, and they've grown up with

certain outlooks and things that are ingrained in them about women. I am a woman, so they still open doors for me and I definitely let them. If they see me carrying something heavy, they'll take it. If I see them carrying something heavy, I'll come and help them with it. They have little names that they call me, like "Little one." . . . As big as I am. I feel embarrassed. I think you run into those types—one who says, "Well, if you're a women's libber, you do it!" So they'll give you everything to do. There's the one that won't let you do anything. And then the one will understand and help you if you need it. I think the men really want me to be a good mechanic. They give me little tips and hints about doing things. Right now I'm working with a fellow on an outside job wiring someone's house. That's really been a change! I'm learning how to bend conduit and things like that.

Maxwell's experience indicates that there are grounds for hope. She has managed to break through the barriers to women in apprenticeship programs and is finding a relatively high degree of acceptance from the men with whom she works.

Training policies and programs (apprenticeship and vocational) to accommodate the needs of the working mother would be a helpful step. For example, apprenticeship age limits should be revised to accommodate women who wish to enter training programs after their children are raised.

It is also vital to encourage the growth of grass-roots organizations, which already show promise of playing an important role in training and hiring women. For example, organizations such as Better Jobs for Women (BJW, founded in 1971 by the Denver, Colorado, YWCA) have already helped to recruit, tutor, counsel, and place women in skilled trade apprenticeships. Another organization, CATALYST (founded in 1962 in New York, with a career-resource network comprising over 150 local resource centers), has provided job referrals and placement services for women. This organization is especially concerned with promoting upward mobility and flexibility in women's work schedules.

The proliferation of such nongovernmental grass-roots organizations has already been a positive force for social change:

> Several nongovernmental organizations have as their principal focus widening the job options and promotional opportunities of women. Such organizations have provided much of the impetus for establishing goals and timetables for women in federally financed construction and in apprenticeships in the skilled trades. They have also actively participated in experimental or ongoing projects—usually requiring some degree of governmental support to move women into better-paying nontraditional jobs. (U.S. Department of Labor, Women's Bureau, 1980a:40)

Increasing women's membership and promoting women as leaders within unions is yet another vital step in upgrading the situation. Research shows that, in all industries, earnings of organized women are higher than those of unorganized women by nearly 30 percent (even though union women still earn less than union men).

It is also important to reach out to young women in the school system through improved career counseling so that women will have the necessary information on nontraditional work opportunities (including vocational and apprenticeship opportunities) as well as a better understanding of their own abilities. Women need to have the option of freely choosing from a full range of lifestyles and employment options. We need to ensure that women will enter their work with full knowledge of the alternatives and consequences of their decisions.

SUMMARY

The literature on working women typically focuses on women at the extremes: those at the top (corporation executives, lawyers) and those at the bottom (welfare recipients). The vast majority of women, however, are somewhere in between, employed in routine, ordinary jobs. These women and their occupations have received relatively little attention from researchers.

Most of the jobs held by women have become identified *as* "women's" jobs; that is, relatively few men hold these jobs. The sex segregation of these occupations has important ramifications: women's jobs are the low-level, low-prestige, low-paying, low-benefit, dead-end jobs. Even when women and men do hold the same or similar occupations, women receive less pay than men.

Clerical work is the largest single occupational category in which women are employed (35 percent). The field is so dominated by women that we tend to associate clerical work exclusively with women. However, during the nineteenth century, clerical work was a male-dominated occupation. The position was highly respected; clerks performed functions typical of a present-day office manager. With the introduction of new technologies (the telephone, the typewriter), a widespread demand for clerical workers, and a shortage of men at the time, women entered the clerical field in such numbers that by the early twentieth century clerical work had become a thoroughly feminized occupation. The nature of the position changed considerably. Clerical activities increasingly became subdivided into smaller and smaller routine tasks. Clerical work became a low-status, low-paying, dead-end position, identified as typically "women's work." Few women moved into the newly emerging managerial-level positions.

Clerical workers face a number of problems in addition to those that affect all working women, among which are the expectations that a secretary should run personal errands for the boss, make coffee, and provide a shoulder to cry on, while being treated as a nonperson in most other respects.

Some women have found that working through a temporary-office-help agency is preferable to holding a regular full-time job in that it allows them to survey other job possibilities, it provides a flexible schedule, and it permits relatively easy exit from unsatisfactory work settings. Unionization is another channel that offers hope of improving conditions for clerical workers.

Sexual harassment is a growing occupational hazard that affects women in every occupational category. Efforts to cope with sexual harassment on the job are fraught with a variety of special problems—occupational, social, and legal.

Blue-collar women workers comprise 15 percent of all women who work. These women are concentrated primarily in the unskilled job categories; they have little access to the higher-paid skilled craft positions. Increased access to such positions could be gained through acceptance in apprenticeship and vocational education and/or training programs, but access to these programs has also been limited. Unionization offers hope here too, but unions have traditionally been male preserves, which has slowed their responsiveness to the needs of working-class women.

Equal-employment laws and equal-wage legislation offer hope of correcting some of the inequities, but enforcement of these laws is problematic. One of the difficulties is that enforcement depends ultimately on individuals filing complaints. Grass-roots organizations have helped bring the range of inequities to public consciousness and have tried to modify the basic attitudes and stereotypes regarding women's employment. Stereotypes concerning appropriate work and sex roles are a fundamental part of the problem.

Although conditions have improved in some respects for women in clerical and blue-collar jobs, their status in salary, benefits, and opportunity for advancement remains depressed and far from equitable. These women are concentrated in sex-typed jobs and have limited access to the male-dominated jobs with higher status, better pay, and broader opportunity.

6 • Women in Professional and Managerial Occupations

Professional and managerial occupations attract a lot of attention. They are visible; they have relatively high status and salaries; and their images are reinforced by media and literature (see Hall, 1975). Understandably, then, women's participation in these occupations arouses publicity and popular commentary.[1] However, in pointing to a few notable cases of female success in management and professions, the media has overlooked the status of the vast majority of the women in management and professions. In these occupations, as elsewhere, women occupy the low-ranking and low-paying positions and are concentrated in areas, fields, and locations with limited power and influence.

The professional and managerial occupations share certain characteristics. Both occupations have relatively high status and educational requirements. Their job functions emphasize problem solving, planning, and decision making. And they are both "male-dominated" occupations. Yet particular features of the professions set them apart from managerial, as well as other, occupations. Because of these particularities we separate, in the first part of the chapter, our discussions of the professional and managerial occupations and women's position within them. However, in accounting for the status of women in these two occupational categories, we shall see in the second half of the chapter that common explanatory factors and arguments—cultural attitudes, occupational demands, and the male culture of organizations—apply to both groups.

Moreover, we shall see that individual-level characteristics—such as women's motivation, beliefs, and occupational orientations—can only go part of the way in explaining the depressed status of women in professions and management. To fully understand women's position in these occupations, and to redress their disadvantage, we must look to structural and organizational factors. Compared to men, women have restricted opportunities in management and professions. They work in different settings, hold different kinds of jobs, and are assigned different types of tasks from those of men (Kanter, 1977a). These organizational and structural factors provide a key to analysis and understanding of women's depressed status in these occupations.

PROFESSIONAL OCCUPATIONS

Most people are readily able to identify certain occupations—medicine, law, or the ministry—as professions. But from the social scientist's perspective, the public also misidentifies as professional some groups such as "professional" athletes, artists, or performers (Hall, 1975). The term *professional* is not to be applied loosely to occupations with large fees or high status. Rather, the term refers to occupations with particular attributes or characteristics. These attributes were first systematically identified and analyzed in the early part of this century by A. M. Carr-Saunders and P. A. Wilson of Oxford University. Although that early model has been expanded and elaborated, social scientists have continued to focus on certain core characteristics of the profession.

To begin with, the major criterion distinguishing an occupation as professional is its *systematic theory* or base of knowledge, which is acquired during long and intensive training. It is important to distinguish here between skills and theoretical knowledge as they relate to professions versus other occupations. To illustrate: although both botany and gardening may be occupations, the first is often a profession and the second is not. At the basis of botany is a systematic theory involving, among other things, a detailed classification of plants and soils. And although gardening may involve intricate skills of planting, pruning, and fertilizing, those particular skills are not necessarily founded on the abstract and interrelated propositions that provide the theoretical basis for a profession.

Another attribute of the profession is its *authority*. This means that the occupational group, itself, has a mandate to prescribe a particular course of action and decide what is, or is not, in the interests of its clients. Related to the authority is professional *autonomy*. This component refers to the capacity to make decisions and exercise judgment without interference from clients and from others who are not members of the profession. Autonomy is reflected in the profession's control of its training programs, licensing, and accreditation, as well as in peer evaluation of its members. Thus, the profession governs the length and content of its education, the requirements for graduation, and the certification necessary for practice.

For autonomy, the profession's authority must be guaranteed by *community sanction*—another important attribute. The community must give approval to the profession's right to govern itself and set its own standards. That sanction is manifested in the profession's exclusive right to title; one cannot use the title "physician" or "attorney" without being granted right to that title by the profession, itself. The community enforces, or sanctions, that right by bringing its police power to bear on those who might try to practice law or medicine without the credentials bestowed by the respective profession. However, the professions themselves also protect the public with *codes of ethics* and censure their members for violations of standards. This self-policing protects not only the client but also the profession, because gross infractions would result in the withdrawal of community support and sanction. Furthermore, the community's regulatory agencies are composed largely of the members of the profession, and hence public approval is controlled in part by the profession itself.

Finally, the profession is an *occupational subculture* and colleagueship, with its own language and symbols and with a network of formal and informal relationships. The greater the development of this subculture, the stronger will be its members' involvement with, and commitment to, the group, and the greater social distance there will be between the profession and public.

Thus the profession represents an "ideal type," a baseline for comparison and evaluation. Comparing a given occupation with this baseline allows us to determine how well the occupation approximates the model, and "how professional" it may be considered to be. Occupations that come closest to the ideal type include medicine, law, and academia, as well as ministry, dentistry, and architecture. We shall see that the very characteristics (such as complex training, authority, and subculture) which, according to the ideal type, make an occupation a profession, are also factors that inhibit women's participation within them.

Women in the Professions

In this country, 10 percent of the physicians are women, as are 12 percent of the attorneys and 17 percent of the university academics. Although these proportions show the relatively small numbers of women, the position of professional women becomes more vivid when we begin to examine their particular location and specializations *within* the professions. In medicine, for example, women are concentrated in pediatrics, psychiatry, public health, and other relatively low-status specialties, such as anesthesiology and pathology (see Table 6.1). Women are absent from the most prestigious and remunerative subfields—cardiovascular medicine, gastroenterology,

T a b l e 6 . 1 / *Percentage Distribution of Women Physicians, by Specialty*

| Specialty | Percentage | |
	Actual (N = 20,304)	Expected[a]
General practice	12.1	19.4
Medical specialties (subtotal)	31.9	23.7
Allergy	0.6	0.6
Cardiovascular	0.8	2.0
Dermatology	1.3	1.3
Gastroenterology	0.2	0.6
Internal medicine	10.2	12.6
Pediatrics	17.9	5.9
Pulmonary	0.9	0.7
Surgical specialties (subtotal)	9.9[b]	27.4[b]
General surgery	1.4	9.4
Obstetrics, gynecology	6.2	6.0
Ophthalmology	1.5	3.2
Orthopedic surgery	0.2	3.0
Otolaryngology	0.3	1.7
Plastic surgery	0.2	0.5
Other surgery	0.2	3.5
Other specialties (subtotal)	39.0	25.1
Anesthesiology	7.2	3.4
Neurology	1.0	0.9
Occupational medicine	0.4	0.9
Pathology	5.7	3.3
Psychiatry	13.7	7.3
Physical medicine	1.1	0.5
Preventive medicine	0.5	0.3
Public health	2.8	1.0
Radiology	2.9	4.1
Other specialty	3.7	3.3
Unspecified	7.1	4.4

SOURCE: Adapted from Michelle Patterson and Laurie Engleberg, "Women in Male-Dominated Professions," in Ann H. Stromberg and Shirley Harkess, eds., *Women Working: Theories and Facts in Perspective* (Palo Alto, Calif.: Mayfield, 1978), Table 1, p. 273.

[a]This is the percentage of women that would practice the specialty if the sex composition of each specialty reflected the sex composition of the profession as a whole.

[b]The sum of component specialties does not equal the subtotal, because of rounding.

and especially surgery (Epstein, 1970; Kutner and Brogan, 1979; Patterson and Engleberg, 1978). In medicine, as elsewhere, we find a negative relationship between female composition and occupational-prestige levels: Fields with higher female proportions are lower-status areas. The causal mechanism, however, is uncertain. As discussed in Chapter 4, it isn't clear whether women enter low-prestige fields or whether the fields have low prestige because women are located within them.

Women's position in law resembles their status within medicine. Female attorneys are concentrated in the low-status and less lucrative and powerful fields—trust, estates, and domestic relations. These are the more invisible specialties, which are practiced in the background and in the back rooms, away from contact with powerful clients and institutions. Furthermore, because these specialties are less profitable and are considered less important, it is difficult for the women within them to gain distinction or to advance by contributing substantially to the firm's profits and prestige (Epstein, 1970).

Likewise in academia, the status of women is much below men's. Academic women are located disproportionately in four-year colleges and state universities with heavy teaching loads and undergraduate enrollments unconducive to the research and publication that lead to professional eminence and recognition (Astin, 1969, 1978; Hornig, 1979; Tsuchigane and Dodge, 1974). Academic women also hold lower-ranking positions than do men. Across all colleges and universities, as the rank decreases, the proportion of women increases: Women represent only about 10 percent of the full professors, but nearly 30 percent of the assistant professors, and in the lowest ranks—instructor and lecturer positions—women represent almost 50 percent of the faculty (Patterson and Engleberg, 1978). Furthermore, we find critical sex differences in academic fields. Men are concentrated in the sciences and social sciences, and in professional schools aligned with powerful institutions such as business, technology, and medicine; while women are in the arts, humanities, and fields associated with the more marginal areas of education, health, and welfare (Fox, 1981a). Finally, academic women are greatly disadvantaged in their salaries. Even after taking into account their credentials and qualifications, and their rank, field, and institutional locations, women in academia are paid significantly less than men (Astin and Bayer, 1979; Bayer and Astin, 1975; Fox, 1981a; Gordon, Morton, and Braden, 1974).

Women in the Semiprofessions

Thus, across the various professions, women tend to share a common plight of low-status specializations, low-ranking positions, and location in places where they have little visibility and slight chances for recognition. Yet even more fundamental is the very small group of women who are employed at all in the full professions. The vast proportion of women classified as pro-

T a b l e 6.2 / *Women as Percent of Total*
Employment in Selected Professional and Technical
Occupations, 1979

Occupation	Women as a Percentage of Total
Registered nurses	97.0%
Elementary teachers	84.3
Librarians	81.0
Social workers	63.0
Secondary teachers	50.7
Life and physical scientists	18.9
University teachers (academics)	17.0
Lawyers and judges	12.4
Physicians	10.7
Industrial engineers	7.3
Surveyors	3.5
Total professional and technical	43.0

SOURCE: U.S. Department of Labor, Bureau of Labor Statistics, "Employment and Earnings" (Washington, D.C.: U.S. Department of Labor, Bureau of Labor Statistics, June 1979).

fessional workers are not in the full professions, but rather in the semi-professions—nursing, social work, teaching, and librarianship. In fact, these semiprofessional fields are dominated numerically by women, who in this country, constitute 97 percent of the nurses, 84 percent of the elementary-school teachers, 81 percent of the librarians, and 63 percent of the social workers (Table 6.2).

These fields are called *semiprofessions* because they are much further from the professional model than are occupations such as law or medicine. First, the female-dominated semiprofessions, such as social work, have weakly developed theoretical bases of knowledge, and lack a monopoly over the knowledge of the occupation. Rather, the public itself claims knowledge about such areas as social welfare, service, and benefits, and does not grant a mandate on these matters to a specialized occupational group.

The semiprofessions also lack authority and autonomy. Semiprofessionals, alone, are not authorized to decide what is, or is not, in the interest of their clients. Instead, their decisions are held accountable to superiors, and their superiors are accountable, in turn, to an outside authority. Likewise, occupational entry and evaluation are subject to outside forces, such as the community board of education for teachers or hospital administrators for nurses:

> Nursing is called a "profession," but in fact nurses are employees of hospitals. Physicians [on the other hand] are in partnership with hospitals. Physicians are accorded admissions privileges; they admit "their" patients to hospitals for service according to physician's orders. The physician is also a boss. The physician writes the "orders" and expects them to be implemented. (Stevenson, 1981:9)

In addition, the training in the semiprofessions is much shorter and less intensive than in the full professions, and educational credentials are not a firm prerequisite for employment. Accordingly, although one must have a medical or law degree in order to practice these professions, only a minority of those doing social work have M.S.W. degrees, and only 15 percent of school librarians have graduate degrees in librarianship (Grimm, 1978).

As a consequence of their weaker knowledge and training and their lower authority and autonomy, the semiprofessions tend to emphasize hierarchical ranks and differentiated duties. Among these ranks, the higher the semiprofessional position, the greater the involvement with supervisory and administrative, rather than primary, tasks (Simpson and Simpson, 1969). Thus, in marked contrast to the established professions, success in the semiprofessions implies administrative, rather than practicing, roles. This high regard and esteem for administration reflects the semiprofessions' absence of distinctive primary skills, and the reaction among clients and the public that administrative skills deserve more rewards than the groups' specifically professional skills (Simpson and Simpson, 1969).

Although the semiprofessions are dominated numerically by women, these higher-ranking administrative positions are held disproportionately by men. So, even in the "female fields" of nursing, teaching, social work, and librarianship, we find that women have the lower-level, and men the higher-level, positions (see Table 6.3).

For example, in its sex composition nursing is almost entirely a "female field": 97 percent of the nurses are women. Yet, of the small numbers of men in nursing, nearly 50 percent have administrative positions, while only 29 percent of the women hold these positions (Grimm and Stern, 1974). This doesn't mean that nursing is controlled by men, but rather that a disproportionate number of males are the administrators, supervisors, and head nurses. Furthermore, the male proportion in nursing has been increasing over the past twenty years (Grimm and Stern, 1974).

In teaching, too, the percentage of males has been increasing steadily. But even more indicative of the growing power of men and declining control by women are the sex proportions among the educational administrators. More specifically, the proportion of females in school administration has been decreasing since 1930; and currently, although women are over 80

T a b l e 6.3 / *Intraoccupational Stratification by Sex, for Selected Semi-Professions*

	Occupation				
	Nursing[a]	Elementary Teaching[b]	Secondary Teaching[b]	Academic Librarian-ship[a]	Social Work[c]
Percentage of men within occupation	1.1	16	50	37	37
Percentage of men in administration within occupation	45.7	80	94	70	66

[a] Data from James W. Grimm and Robert Stern, "Sex Roles and the Internal Labor Market Structures: The 'Female' Semi-Professions," *Social Problems* 21(June 1974):690–705.

[b] Data from Ann Parker Parelius and Robert Parelius, *The Sociology of Education* (Englewood Cliffs, N.J.: Prentice-Hall, 1978).

[c] Data from Diane Kravetz, "Sexism in a Woman's Profession," *Social Work* 21(November 1976):421–426.

percent of the elementary-school teachers, they are only 20 percent of the principals. In secondary schools, the sex disparities are even more marked: women are half of the teachers, but a mere 6 percent of the principals (Parelius and Parelius, 1978).

Similarly, in the female occupations of librarianship and social work the tasks are carried out predominately by women but are planned, supervised, and directed by men. In a study of college and university librarians in the United States, males represented only 37 percent of the sample, but 70 percent of these men held administrative positions (Schiller, 1969). Men were more likely than women to be assistant and associate directors and were twice as apt to be chief librarians.

Likewise in social work, a much higher proportion of women than men are in the lower-status direct services, such as casework and group work, while a higher proportion of men are in some form of administration or community organization (Grimm and Stern, 1974). In fact, although almost two-thirds of the members of the National Association of Social Workers are women, two-thirds of the administrative positions are held by men (Kravetz, 1976). Correspondingly, male social workers obtain higher salaries than women, and this salary gap is not accounted for by differences in men's and women's education and seniority (Grimm, 1978; Kravetz, 1976). In one discussion of the distributions of men and women in social work, we can see the assumptions that underlie the link between male sex, high rank, and advantageous salary in the profession:

Salaries of community organizers are undoubtedly higher because men are preferred for organizing positions, for reasons stemming from the requirements of community organization practice. Organizers are more likely than practitioners in other methods to interact with executives, businessmen, professionals, public officials, and others influential in community affairs. Men fill these roles in American society, and men are usually believed to be more effective in working with other men. (Brager and Michael, 1969:596)

MANAGERIAL OCCUPATIONS

People employed in management positions are usually enumerated in the U.S. Census Bureau's category as "managers and administrators." The managerial classification encompasses occupations requiring personnel who set broad policies, execute policies, and direct the departments and the phases of an organization's operations (U.S. Department of Labor, Women's Bureau, 1980b). But not all people who perform management functions—planning, directing, and deciding—are subsumed under this category. Some may be listed as professional and technical workers, if, for example, they administer a scientific laboratory, and classify themselves as scientists rather than administrators (U.S. Department of Labor, 1977). Nonetheless, the census categories allow us to make comparisons of the female and male participation.

In management, as in the professions, we find that women are conspicuous by their absence. Although women are 42 percent of all workers, they are only 25 percent of the country's managers and adminstrators. And among all employed women, only 6 percent work in managerial positions (Table 6.4). The small proportion of employed women holding managerial jobs has remained at a nearly constant level since 1947, when 5 percent of all employed women had managerial or administrative positions. Thus, while female labor-force participation has increased greatly in the postwar decades, "the growth in the number of female managers has not been proportional to the overall influx of women in the work force" (Brown, 1981: 14). Beyond their small proportions, however, women's status in management becomes clearer when we look at their particular rank and status.

As in the professions, the women are concentrated in the low-ranking, low-paying, and less powerful positions within management. Only 1 percent of the positions as high as vice president, and just 6 percent of the nation's middle-management positions are held by women. Rather, women are concentrated in the first-level and supervisory ranks in low-level positions, such as buyer, restaurant manager, general office manager, or department head in retail trade. This concentration of women at the low ranks reflects, in part, their recent entry into business and industry after years of being excluded

Table 6.4 / *Women Nonfarm Managers and Officials, 1979 Annual Averages*

| Number (in thousands) | Women as Percent of | | |
	Total Managers and Officials	Total Labor Force	Total Employed Women
2,586	24.6%	42.2%	6.4%

SOURCE: U.S. Department of Labor, Women's Bureau, *Women in Management* (Washington, D.C.: U.S. Government Printing Office, 1980), p. 2.

NOTE: Figures are for women aged 16 and over.

altogether. Yet even when women do have high-ranking titles, their positions seldom lead to top management, but rather are on ancillary, dead-end routes (Epstein, 1975). For example, a woman may be called vice president but be assigned only to limited functions such as administration of affirmative action or recruitment of female personnel. Or women may be placed in positions without the backup needed to effect consequences or change in the organization. In his book *Male Chauvinism and How it Works*, Korda describes one way this process operates: "When a woman deserves to be head of a department, and there is no alternative to promoting her, men tend to create a committee or alter an existing one, without making her a member of it, to control whatever it is she does" (Korda, 1972:31).

The salary levels of male and female managers also show the disparity in their statuses. In 1975, 80 percent of the male, but only 40 percent of the female, salaried managers earned at least $10,000 a year. In the highest-salary groups, the gap between the sexes is even greater, with 20 percent of the managerial men but a mere 2 percent of the women earning $25,000 or more (U.S. Department of Labor, 1977). Even those women who graduate from a top business school are subject to salary disparity. Among graduates of Harvard and Dartmouth M.B.A. programs, for example, women had lower salaries than men, and the salary gap between the sexes increased with time (Brown, 1981).

EXPLAINING WOMEN'S POSITION IN PROFESSIONS AND MANAGEMENT

Women's depressed status in the professions and management may be explained by at least three common factors—cultural attitudes and ensuing sex-role conflicts, occupational demands for career continuity and commitment, and the male culture of organizations. Beyond these factors, explanations diverge by a perspective that emphasizes individual factors such as women's attitudes and orientations and a perspective that emphasizes structural factors such as the characteristics of women's work groups, tasks, and settings.

Cultural Attitudes: Occupational and Sex-Role Links and Conflicts

The concentration of professional women in the semiprofessions and within certain specialties of the full professions represents, in part, a linking of the occupational and sex roles. Occupations are regarded as extensions of the sex and family roles, so that teaching, nursing, and social work serve as continuations of the nurturing, helping, and support expected of females. Similarly, pediatric medicine and psychiatry are patient-intensive fields, with the relatively strong social and emotional functions ascribed to the female role. In like manner, specialization in trust, estate, and domestic law links women with family-related areas, which are regarded as culturally appropriate female concerns. Thus, "as a focus for female aspirations, the three 'ks' of an earlier generation—kinder, kuche, kirche [children, kitchen, church]—have been replaced by the three 'hs'—healing, helping, and home management. The professions now open to women are in the main in the service sector" (Schork, 1978, quoted in Bernard, 1981:215).

The tendency toward this "linking" suggests potential sex-role and occupational conflicts for women (see Chapter 3). These conflicts stem from a clash between (1) a sex role demanding nurturance, empathy, and support, and (2) occupational roles demanding aggressiveness, competitiveness, and opportunism. The conflicts also stem from the heavy domestic responsibilities that create dual (home and market) work for employed women.

Accordingly, certain classic studies of professional women maintain that sex-typed specializations represent realistic adjustments to potential conflicts and that fields such as public health offer female physicians the advantage of stable working hours and possibilities for part-time employment (Kosa and Coker, 1965). Yet when we examine the working conditions of specializations held by women, we find *contradictions* in the pattern of sex and occupational typing. For example, fields such as obstetrics and gynecology, which would be "natural" for women, have few female practitioners. And medical fields such as ophthalmology, plastic surgery, and dermatology, which have regular work hours and few emergency calls, also have few female practitioners, while pediatrics, with its unscheduled demands and emergency cases, has the largest proportions of female physicians (Epstein, 1970; Kutner and Brogan, 1979). Thus, it seems more likely that it is the relatively low prestige of pediatrics, psychiatry, and public health that accounts for women's concentration in these, as opposed to other, medical areas (Kutner and Brogan, 1979).

Similarly, in management there are cultural conflicts between (1) expectations held for the female and (2) occupational work roles. More specifically, attitudes reflect perceived disparities between the characteristics and temperaments thought appropriate for women and those thought appropriate for managers. The ideal manager is perceived to be competitive, aggressive, and firm; women are characterized, however, as intuitive, emotional, personable, and dependable.

Thus, when male middle managers of insurance companies throughout the nation were asked to rate (1) women in general, (2) men in general, and (3) successful managers on ninety-two descriptive terms, their responses showed a significant resemblance between ratings of men and managers and no resemblance between ratings of women and managers (Schein, 1973). A replication of this study among *female* managers showed that they, too, perceived successful managers as possessing characteristics ascribed to men rather than women (Schein, 1975). Both male and female administrators have perceived "feminine" and "manager" as mutually exclusive terms, and this perception may influence management's selection, promotion, and placement of men versus women. In a work on *The Professional Manager*, Douglas McGregor's perception illustrates the assumed overlap between the male and the managerial roles:

> The model of the successful manager in our culture is a masculine one. The good manager is aggressive, competitive, firm, just. He is not feminine; he is not soft or yielding or dependent or intuitive in the womanly sense. The very expression of emotion is widely viewed as a feminine weakness that would interfere with effective business processes. (McGregor, 1967:23)

But the problem is not a simple matter of women in management lacking the attributes—such as assertiveness, practicality, and competitiveness—that are believed to be associated with managerial success. In fact, business managers—both male and female—exhibit these traits (Brief and Oliver, 1976; Harlan and Weiss, 1980; Lyle and Ross, 1973). And while the popular image of the manager is masculine, the *actual tasks* required of managers are not necessarily those identified with one sex or the other (Brown, 1981:31). Thus, along with certain "masculine traits," successful managers need female-typed skills, such as interpersonal warmth and understanding. Yet when assertiveness or competitiveness is displayed by women, the behavior may be perceived as inappropriate and outside the female role. Certain research indicates, for example, that employees are more satisfied with supervisors' aggressiveness when they are working for males than when they are working for females (Roussell, 1974). And in like manner, other studies reveal that employees are more satisfied with their manager's "considerate behavior" when their manager is female rather than male (Petty and Lee,

1975; Petty and Miles, 1976). In other words, employees may be more satisfied with supervisors' behavioral style when it conforms with the consistent, traditional sex role, male or female.

However, because a number of these studies on satisfaction fail to control for type, structure, and environment of the employees' work unit, it may not be supervisors' sex, as such, which is the sole cause of the response. Indeed, recent research suggests that employees' attitudes may be a reaction also to features of the work unit, and the relative power and status of the supervisor, rather than a response to supervisors' sex per se (Cashman, Dansereau, Green, and Haga, 1976; Kanter, 1977a; Osburn and Vicars, 1976). In other words, the situational context of the female versus male supervisor is an important factor governing employees' response.

Contradictory findings about the effect of supervisors' sex may also be, in part, an artifact of different methodological techniques employed. The studies conducted in the laboratory, compared to field studies, are more likely to report the significant effect of supervisors' sex upon employee satisfaction. The effect may be stronger in the laboratory because these experiments are conducted with subjects who are strangers, interacting for only a brief time. Under these conditions, the manipulated sex variable may be one of the few available items for discrimination and response (Terborg, 1977).

Work Structures in Professions and Management

Beyond these cultural and organizational attitudes, females are also absent and less successful in the professions and management because of the set pressures operating on all women at work: family and educational constraints that restrict their possibilities, and an economic and political structure that limits their access and opportunities (see Chapters 3 and 4). But in addition, in professions and management, the very structure of the work disadvantages women.

Demands of time, continuity, and commitment

Professional and managerial work run at a rapid and relentless pace—and performance is measured against time. In these fields, one is expected to make big strides in one's late twenties, to take leaps in one's early thirties, and be fully advanced by age forty. Performing on this schedule requires single-minded pursuit and continuous participation. Furthermore, the work load is so large and the time demands so voracious that they leave little room for life outside of work.

The work pace and commitment of the professional and executive run beyond the nine-to-five weekday, and beyond weekdays into the weekends as well. Myra Strober, a professor of business administration at Stanford University, describes the consequences of this pace for women:

> Professional and managerial women with young children have little difficulty in working forty hours per week. In fact, increasingly, women with young children work full time. . . . But, it is well known that professionals and managers, especially those interested in promotion, work more than sixty hours per week on a full-time job. And a sixty-hour work week, of course, leaves little time for one's family. Many professional women with children have said wryly, "I'd like a part-time job. I'd like to work about forty hours a week." (Strober, 1975:87)

This relentless pace is possible because men, who constitute the vast majority of these workers, face little institutional interference with their work. Being husbands and fathers rarely hinders men's occupational involvement and commitment. In fact, the duties that a man does have to home and family fall primarily in the occupational sphere (Epstein, 1970), and a man who spends too much time with wife and children is thought a "slacker" who could better serve his family by advancing his career. Furthermore, many of these men have supporting partners (wives) to manage and maintain the life of the professional, who—though totally devoted to work and career—still requires cleaning, feeding, and refueling.

But for the professional and managerial woman, the domestic role competes with, rather than complements, her occupational role. Wifehood and motherhood vie for resources, which must be allocated among both the occupational and domestic roles. And these multiple demands inhibit the single-mindedness, continuous participation, and commitment required for success.

First of all, allocation of time to both family and work can create discontinuity in women's careers, especially if it results in withdrawal from employment for childbearing and child care. Compared with the occupational discontinuity of other female workers, the careers of professional women are remarkably stable (Astin, 1969; Zuckerman, 1971). But they are somewhat more discontinuous than men's (Ferber and Kordick, 1978). And discontinuity can create obsolescence of skills, as well as the loss of competitive position, participation, and personnel contacts.

In addition, because women's marriages are hypergamous (upwardly mobile or stable, in socioeconomic terms), married professional and managerial women invariably have husbands who, themselves, have high-level professional, administrative, or executive careers that may require transfers and relocations. And because family structure is virilocal (residence determined by males), there is greater pressure on wife to follow husband rather than vice versa (Theodore, 1971). These patterns, too, may impede a woman's career development.

With demands from all sides of life, professional and managerial women face choices rarely encountered by men. In order to manage work and life, women may have to dispense with the more optional occupational activities, such as meetings, conferences, and extraneous collegial relations. Hence, women are excluded indirectly from certain work activities by their multiple role demands. However, they are also excluded more directly by the "male subculture" that prevails in these occupations.

"Male culture" in management and the professions

As a consequence of men's numbers and dominance, the professional and managerial world is a male culture. The male members have grown up together, played, learned, and worked together. They share common "understandings" about rules and styles of competing, bartering, and succeeding. These understandings ease their communication and assure support and acceptance among them. But women are outsiders to this male milieu. They do not share men's settings and traditions—in locker room, bar, and playing field. As a result, it's difficult for women to partake of this male world, and as outsiders to the club it is thought they might weaken its intimacy and solidarity (Epstein, 1970). As one female professional puts it:

> No matter how skewed a man's individual upbringing might have been, to the extent that he has learned the male role imperatives, he will "fit" the organizational requirements. This is so because organizational life as we know it has been created by men: the economic structure of the country, its institutions, its processes, and its growth have all been developed by men. Consequently, *organizations are male culture-bound*, having been built by men, they expect what men bring to them. Any man who fulfills the basic male role can expect to find a place in organizational life. (Kosinar, 1981 : 35; italics added)

Women's exclusion from men's informal circles of communication and interaction has critical consequences for occupational success in the professions. First, it has consequences for women's professional socialization, because professional education and training is largely an informal process that occurs not in the classroom, but rather in the process of informal interaction between a faculty sponsor and student protégé, or a mentor and apprentice. From relationships with a senior person, a fledgling learns how to pose important questions, solve problems, and set goals. As Epstein (1974a) points out, a degree from a good school does not, in itself, guarantee a brilliant medical diagnostician, persuasive courtroom advocate, or insightful scientific investigator. Rather, in medicine, law, and science, such competence is created *selectively* by providing certain young members the opportunity to learn critical techniques and avoid costly pitfalls. Young men are much more apt than women to be chosen for these opportunities. The men are favored because professional education operates not simply to train personnel but also to assure continuity of its leadership. And the senior professional, nearly invariably a male himself, cannot identify a young woman as his eventual successor. Furthermore, ties between male sponsors and female protégés may prompt sexual suspicions that the professional wishes to avoid.

Women's exclusion from the informal circles of communication and interaction also cuts them off from the significant professional information that flows through these networks. In men's daily rounds through the office corridors, lunch room, and cocktail lounge, they exchange information about data and services, job prospects and possibilities, and research notes and news. Furthermore, they trade gossip about which of their colleagues and superiors are, and are not, helpful and trustworthy (Reskin, 1978). Women's limited access to these networks means that, for information, they must rely on the formal communication in publications, announcements, and official memos. But the informal gossip may never appear in these printed sources, or if it does, it may come too late to matter. Professional information is most valuable early on, when it gives an edge on a research finding, job prospect, or potential client.

As outsiders, women themselves feel awkward and self-conscious in the informal male milieu. This may make them hesitant to make contact, communicate, and interact. And, in turn, this hesitation may further their exclusion and heighten their marginality (Epstein, 1970; Reskin, 1978).

Moreover, the formal organization of the profession is, like its informal structure, a male universe. The programs, boards, publications, and advisory councils of the profession are controlled overwhelmingly by men, and women have limited access to the central resources and opportunities of the organizational structure.

By virtue of men's large numbers and superordinate position, a "male culture" also dominates corporate management. As in the professions, this culture arises out of men's common experiences and engenders among them a common language and understanding, which particularly manifest themselves in the organizations' informal social relations. However, the development of exclusive male business circles also stems from the uncertainty in managerial work and from the members' efforts to reduce that uncertainty (Kanter, 1977a:48–49). Bureaucracies are supposed to increase predictability and routine, but organizations are subject, nonetheless, to variable contingencies within both the organization and its environment. Under these conditions, members must depend frequently on individuals, rather than on impersonal procedures. Hence, management develops tight inner circles and prefers "ease of communication and . . . social certainty over the strains of dealing with people who are 'different'" (Kanter, 1977a:49). Women are among the "different" and do not share the common, male language, experience and behavioral styles that make for easy interaction and communication. So, even women who do hold managerial positions may be excluded from the informal settings where so much business actually is conducted.

There is some consensus about professional and managerial women's disadvantage from the three factors just discussed—cultural attitudes and ensuing sex-role conflicts, occupational demands for career continuity and commitment, and the male culture of organizations. But beyond these factors, the explanation of women's position splits into divergent perspectives emphasizing (1) individual variables and (2) structural variables. In the social-science literature, these perspectives have focused on managerial, rather than professional, women, but the arguments apply to women in both occupational categories.

The "Individual" Perspective

In accounting for social inequalities, the American tendency is to look for explanation within individuals (see Chapter 4). People's success is attributed to hard work, ability, and determination, and failure is attributed to indolence and incompetence. Likewise, the disparity in men's and women's status and position is attributed to differences in their character, attitudes, and orientations, which result from their biological nature, social experience, or both (Kanter, 1976).

Hence, in seeking an explanation for women's limited success in management, investigators have searched for answers in men's and women's individual attributes and characteristics. In one notable survey of corporate men and women, Hennig and Jardim (1976) conclude that the sexes do have different beliefs, attitudes, and assumptions about themselves and each other, and about organizations and managerial careers. These differences, they say, result in female styles, emphases, and responses that are dysfunctional for success in management. More specifically, Hennig and Jardim review certain sex differences in concepts of career, personal strategy, and subordinate role, which together reflect the "separate worlds of men and women in management."

Hennig and Jardim report that women see career development in terms of self-improvement and fulfillment, while men visualize a career, not as personal growth, but as a series of jobs or organizational promotions and advancements. The female emphasis on personal growth is related to a sense of career passivity, or "waiting to be chosen." The passivity, in turn, depends for its rationale on women's belief in the formal, organizational roles and policies—the ways things "should be done." At the same time, women overlook the informal system of relationships and exchanges—ties of loyalty, dependence, favors given and taken. Thus, in answering questions and surveys about their careers, women emphasize the importance of hard work, performance, and progressive achievement. But they fail to talk about the organizational environment, and the need to gain visibility and exposure and to build connections with bosses, peers, and subordinates.

Because women do depend on the formal structure, they are often disappointed and immobilized when it fails them, and they are unable to accept the informal system as a continuing element, rather than an aberration, in the organization. Men, on the other hand, recognize this organizational environment and build it into their careers: They act so that people will see them as having ability to move on; they attempt to influence those who can help them advance; they try to be needed by important people, and become necessary to them. And this behavior helps men advance.

A related sex difference centers around men's and women's concepts of personal strategy. Hennig and Jardim report that the men focus on achieving a goal, or reaching an objective, with the critical issue being "What's in it for me?" Women's definitions of strategy concentrate not on the goal but on the process of planning and finding the best methods of attainment. Hennig and Jardim suggest, then, that men are emphasizing objectives and cooperating to win in the world as it is, while women struggle in an ineffable quest of the best possible method and the best possible world.

They report a third central sex difference in the way males and females fill the subordinate role. Men concentrate on "their bosses' expectations of them" and women on "their own concept of themselves."[2] Men are alert to cues and signals from their superordinates as to what might be expected and hence to what might be in the interest of reward and advancement. However, because women's responses center on who they are, they are much less flexible in assuming a style or adopting behavior for a given situation. This inflexibility makes them less able to deal with their bosses and serve their self-interest.

Hennig and Jardim claim that these sex differences—in concepts of career, strategy, and subordinate role—are at the heart of women's difficulties advancing within management. The normal, managerial career path moves from a technical or specialist role, to the more general role of middle management, and from there upward toward a higher-level position requiring both specialization and broad decision making and problem solving. A first-level supervisor applies technical knowledge to routine problems, and meets specific goals set by superiors; in contrast, the middle manager must coordinate with counterparts in other departments in order to carry out broader organizational objectives. Movement into senior management depends on this pivotal transition from technical manager to middle manager. And Hennig and Jardim maintain that this transition is "extraordinarily painful" for women. Women may function as outstanding supervisors, but they lack flexibility and the capacity to focus on long-term objectives. Rather, women "concentrate upon task, skill, and job performance, and ignore the critically important behavioral variables." Especially missing from women's behavior is the development of alliances within the informal network of relationships. And this becomes a real hindrance because the activities of middle management are embedded in this informal network.

Shortcomings of the "individual" perspective

The message of the individual perspective is that women's own work behavior is holding them back and that, in order to advance, women must change (Kanter, 1977a). The perspective translates into policies and programs aimed to correct women's deficiencies and develop needed competencies. These programs range from self-help literature on decision making or communication, to assertiveness-training workshops, and seminars on career planning and improvement. However, although these programs may help develop personal esteem, job skills, and social support systems, it is not clear that they have any impact on the organization of industry or the work world. Furthermore, such programs may give an appearance of progress without really changing an organization's structure of hiring and promotion (Kanter, 1976, 1977a).

In addition, the individual perspective builds stereotypes and reinforces traditional beliefs about the sexes. Labeling certain organizational behavior as "male" and "female" tends to polarize the sexes and to exaggerate their differences (Kanter, 1976). Men's particular patterns are then regarded as the "standard" or "norm," and women's as "deviant" and "deficient." By implication, women's depressed position and status are attributed to sex— as both a biological and social category. Consequently, the individual perspective leads us to disregard the ways in which work behavior is a response, not to gender, but to organizational structure—the characteristics of the work unit, the task performed, position held, and the group doing the work. Yet it is the structural perspective that provides a key to analysis and understanding of women's depressed status in management and professions.

The Structural Perspective

In explaining organizational behavior, the structural perspective focuses on the very factors that the individual perspective overlooks: the characteristics of the work groups, their tasks, and interactions and relationships as they determine behavior. In an important case study, Rosabeth Kanter (1977a) applies this perspective to a study of men and women in the corporation. Kanter focuses on three particular variables in the organization: its structure of opportunity, structure of power, and proportional distributions of different kinds of people. Kanter maintains that these factors—opportunity, power, and numbers—explain the position of corporate women, men, or for that matter, any other group of workers.

From the structural perspective, the achievements of corporate men and women are not a simple function of their motivation or ability levels. Rather, they are a function also of men's and women's *opportunities* for mobility and growth. The extent or span of one's opportunity is determined by such factors as the promotion rates from particular jobs, the career paths from positions, and the access to challenge, skills, and rewards. Kanter reports that women are much more likely than men to be located in jobs with "short" chains of opportunity. This makes it difficult for women to "break into" management and to be promoted within the organization. And the limited opportunity, in turn, affects work attitudes and behaviors—including aspirations, commitment, and involvement. Thus, if women are less ambitious, task oriented, and work involved, it may be because of the characteristics of their jobs rather than because of their own shortcomings. Women are concentrated at the low end of the corporate ladder, in positions with less authority, control, and discretion, and their lower aspirations are, in part, a response to these restricted locations and to depressed chances for mobility.

Organizations are structures not only of opportunity but also of power. Although *power* has a number of connotations and meanings, Kanter uses the term to refer to the ability to get things done, mobilize resources, and get whatever one needs in order to accomplish goals. In order to manage effectively, one must have power; as a leader, one must be able to obtain a favorable share of resources, opportunities, and rewards for one's group.

Kanter maintains that, in a number of ways, bases of power are organizational, rather than personal. Power is determined by the characteristics of the job—the visibility of the position to superordinates, the relevance of the job function for current organizational problems, and the opportunity the job provides for demonstration of extraordinary activities. Power is accumulated, also, through informal alliances—with sponsors, peers, and subordinates. In like manner, power*lessness* results when the formal position provides few opportunities for visibility, extraordinary or relevant activities, and little access to sponsorship and influence.

Women tend to be located in these positions of powerlessness. The first-line supervisory positions, in which they are concentrated, offer women little chance to gain power through activities, because their job-functions do not lend themselves to visibility or the demonstration of extraordinary solutions to organizational problems. Furthermore, because they have few rewards to distribute, they cannot gain power through alliances with their peers and subordinates. And women have trouble gaining power through the sponsorship of superordinates, because male superiors cannot identify with a female protégé.

When people feel anxious, helpless, or insignificant—that is, when they are in positions of powerlessness—they tend to respond by becoming critical, controlling and coercive; by being rules-minded; or by jealously guarding their territory or domains of function and expertise. These responses to powerlessness—controlling, rules-minded, jealous behavior—are the stereotype of the female boss or leader. Kanter suggests that these stereotyped behaviors are a consequence not of a particular group's sex but rather of their level of power. The traits attributed to female bosses are actually characteristics of their relative powerlessness. Similarly, Kanter maintains that the reported preference for male, rather than female, bosses is actually a preference for powerful leaders—who are able to influence superiors, protect subordinates, get inside information, and ensure rewards. Restating the old cliché, Kanter says that "everyone loves a winner" and that "in large organizations, at least, people would rather work for winners than losers" (Kanter, 1977a:200). Women's restricted opportunity and power limits their chances as "winners."

In Kanter's scheme, the third structural factor determining organizational behavior is the proportion and distribution of groups of certain types—in this case, men and women. One of the most apparent conditions of the female managers is that there are so few of them; especially within the upper ranks, women are vastly outnumbered. Thus, while men continually find themselves in the comfortable company of their own kind, women find themselves alone among male peers at formal conferences and meetings, and at informal lunches and gatherings. As a consequence of their scarcity, women are visible, noticeable, and scrutinized.

Under these conditions, women have limited behavioral options: They may choose to overachieve and minimize peer concern, or to accept visibility and turn it to the advantage of publicity, or to find ways to limit visibility, minimize their social differences, and develop a low profile. However, each of these alternatives is costly. The first course requires not only unusual ability but also the outstanding demonstration of ability; the second runs against the peer acceptance that is so essential for effectiveness in management; and the third involves avoidance of conflict, controversy, and risk and ultimately results in social invisibility and limited recognition. In this way, the popular observations that, in group performance, women are emotional and reactive, and inflexible about error and mistake (both in others and in themselves), may be a function of their "outnumbered" circumstance rather than of their gender category.

STRATEGIES FOR IMPROVING
WOMEN'S POSITION IN PROFESSIONS
AND MANAGEMENT

By focusing on the characteristics of work groups, tasks, and interactions, the structural perspective helps us to see women's depressed position as an organizational, rather than simply an individual, problem. By implication, we see that solutions lie not so much in changing women's attitudes, beliefs, and assumptions as in changing the settings, structure, and composition of the jobs and the institutions in which they work.

It is through such reorganization of work, itself, that we begin to deal with the roots, not simply the surface, of the disparity in men's and women's statuses. Our strategies for improvement in women's status in professions and management focus on particular reorganizations of professional and managerial occupations and organizations, including (1) alteration of these careers, (2) modification of search and hiring procedures, (3) development of training programs, and (4) construction of support and communication systems for women.

The structure of professional and managerial work currently calls for single-minded and continuous participation and commitment. As previously discussed, this career design disadvantages women, who are often faced with domestic, as well as occupational, demands. To reduce this disadvantage, certain modifications must be made in the very structure of the professional and managerial work demands. First, organizations need to determine which jobs are amenable to less than the involvement of sixty hours per week now expected of professional and managerial employees. In fact, a study of professionals and executives by the Department of Health, Education, and Welfare (HEW) reveals the strong feasibility of part-time work in these occupations. In this study, HEW identified sixty target positions, examined several hundred job applicants, and from these applicants selected twenty-two employees on a part-time basis. The department found that these part-timers were highly productive workers who had few difficulties with their jobs and their supervisors (U.S. Department of Labor, Employment and Training Administration, 1977). The feasibility of this part-time management becomes apparent when we consider that although managers may be full-time employees, in actuality they are frequently traveling or attending meetings and hence are absent from their offices and those whom they manage.

As part of the restructuring of careers, organizations must also examine transfer policies to determine if current practices are, indeed, necessary for job performance. Such scrutiny is important, because transfers are especially disadvantageous to professional and managerial women. If married, these women almost always have husbands who are themselves high-level executives, administrators, or professionals with careers not amenable to sporadic relocation.

In addition, organizations need to examine the arrangement of hours worked during the day. The rearrangement of working times has been called "flex-time," because while the design does require employees to be at work during a particular core time (such as 9:30 A.M. to 3 P.M.), it allows for flexibility in starting and finishing times at the beginning and end of the workday. This flexibility can be especially useful to women and men with family responsibilities. Flex-time has been implemented only on a limited basis in this country. But in Europe, where it is far more common, researchers have found that flex-time has improved workers' satisfaction, motivation, and productivity, and has proved useful to the organization as well as to its employees (Kanter, 1976).

The second strategy for organizational change centers on modification of recruitment and hiring practices. Traditionally, the hiring of executives and professionals has been an informal process in which search and selection has been made through the "old-boy" network, on the basis of loosely specified, unwritten, and subjective criteria. Because women and other minorities are outsiders to these networks, they have lacked the chance to even compete for choice positions. For this reason, the posting and circulation of job openings is an extremely important factor in the movement toward occupational equity.

In order to provide a basis for these job postings and descriptions, it is further necessary to assess and specify the particular qualifications and characteristics required for the successful performance of a given job. This specification is critical, because when standards of performance are more clearly defined the effects of sex and other ascriptive[3] characteristics are minimized in organizational evaluation and reward (Epstein, 1970).

A third strategy for improvement of women's professional and managerial status focuses on programs to help train employees, plan their careers, and sharpen their skills. These programs are particularly important for women and minorities because these groups have been shut out of the informal sponsorship and mentoring in which professional and managerial skills have been customarily nurtured and developed. In order to facilitate organizational training programs, supervisors should be held as accountable for the instruction of their trainees as they are for their other job objectives, and those supervisors who provide good training should be rewarded accordingly (Harlan and Weiss, 1980). Moreover, in order to prevent the perception that women are "deficient employees" who require "favored treatment," training programs should be open to both men and women with similar needs (Harlan and Weiss, 1980).

A fourth strategy involves the development of support and communication systems for women in the organization. Because organizations have been created, maintained, and dominated by men, males entering the organization find a support system already intact and waiting for them (Forisha and Goldman, 1981). This gives men access to people and resources who can help them do their job and accomplish their goals. But because women have been excluded from the male business and professional world, and its social networks, they need their own parallel support groups. These groups provide the opportunity for women to break down their isolation, share common experiences, and solve problems.[4] A particularly important aspect of these support groups lies in the example that can be offered by older women, who serve as role models.

Beyond alterations in the structure of work, a fifth strategy would center on organizations' recognition of the importance of androgynous (both male and female) attributes in the performance of professional and managerial tasks. Emphasis on the importance of nurturant and expressive as well as analytical and competitive attributes would help link the managerial and professional roles to the cultural expectations for both sexes. Moreover, a mixture of traditionally female as well as male traits could greatly enhance the delivery of professional services. As one woman in medicine has put it, "Up to now it has been very difficult for women to rehabilitate [change] what would be our more affective nature. Medical school works against those feminine cultural traits that medicine really does not" (Dr. Elizabeth Sparks, quoted in Zeno, 1982:23). Accordingly, studies of personal attributes associated with effective and humane health care indicate that those qualities traditionally associated with the "feminine spirit"—such as understanding, compassion, and nurturance—do, in fact, notably improve patient care (Zeno, 1982:24).

CONCLUSION

The male-biased structures and processes within professions and management, and the marginal female position in these occupations, are linked partly to women's small numbers and proportions. As the levels of female participation increase, so, too, may their pay, power, and prestige. Recent educational trends offer encouraging prospects: in the decade between 1968 and 1978, the number of first professional degrees granted to women increased tenfold, and the number of doctorates earned by women nearly tripled (U.S. Department of Education, National Center for Education Statistics, 1980). To the extent that these degrees act as educational credentials for managerial and professional employment, we may expect to find increasing participation of women within these occupations. However, numbers alone do not ensure equity; we have observed, for example, that the semi-professions, such as those of social work and librarianship, are dominated numerically by women, while higher-ranking positions are controlled increasingly by men. Thus, improvement in women's status within professions and management will require, along with their increasing numbers, certain changes in the organization of their work—namely, (1) greater flexibility in the structure and design of work and careers, and (2) greater access to the key positions, critical functions, and supportive alliances that enable advancement.

SUMMARY

Women's status in the professions and management reflects their standing in the labor force at large. Within these occupations, as elsewhere, women are concentrated in the lower-ranking and lower-paying positions, and in the less powerful and prestigious places and locations. But beyond the general constraints and restrictions operating on all women at work, in the professions and management, women are disadvantaged by certain other problems.

First, women's participation and advancement in professions and management is hindered by cultural conflicts between a sex role requiring nurturance, empathy, and support and an occupational role demanding aggressiveness, competitiveness, and risk. Correspondingly, organizational attitudes reflect perceived disparities between (1) the characteristics and temperaments thought appropriate for women and (2) those thought appropriate for managers and professionals. As a result, women are constrained by perceptions and stereotypes about their abilities and capabilities and by attitudes about the appropriateness of their occupational participation.

Furthermore, these occupations make unusual demands on time and energy, which, when combined with family demands on women, create two imposing, and sometimes competitive, roles. The professions, especially, expect a single-minded pursuit and continuous participation suited to men's rather than women's needs. Thus, within academia, for example, leaves of absence for research and sabbatical "rest and refreshment" are normative, while leaves for childbearing and child care are unusual and regarded more skeptically.

Finally, as a consequence of men's numbers and dominance, the professional and managerial occupations are male cultures in more general, but equally critical, ways. In these occupations, the male members share common "understandings" about rules and styles of competing, bartering, and succeeding. These understandings ease men's communication and assure their support and acceptance. But they exclude women as outsiders to the club. This has consequences for women's socialization into the professions and for their communication and interaction within them. Similarly, in management the dominant (male) culture governs the informal social networks, where a great deal of business is conducted.

Moreover, from a structural perspective, women are constrained by their location in jobs with "short" chains of opportunity. They are concentrated at the low end of the corporate ladder, in peripheral positions in law firms, and in marginal ranks within academia and other professions. In these locations, women have restricted opportunities for mobility, limited access to organizational resources and alliances, and very few chances to demonstrate talent or ability. Under these conditions, women's aspirations may sink to their level of opportunity and hence may reflect the characteristics of their jobs rather than of their sex.

To improve women's status in professions and management, we must alter the organizational and occupational stuctures that currently depress women's opportunities. These reorganizations include the (1) alteration of careers, (2) modification of search and hiring procedures, (3) development of training programs, and (4) construction of support and communication systems for women. In addition, organizations and occupations need to recognize the importance of androgynous (both male and female) traits in the successful performance of professional and managerial tasks and goals.

7 ◆ The Minority Woman at Work

The minority woman worker has much in common with other working women. The most obvious bond is, of course, the problem of sexism. As we have seen throughout previous chapters, all women are disadvantaged compared with men in terms of earnings, occupational status, and job mobility. However, minority women face additional problems—problems related to race and national origin.

A minority woman is, in the widest terms for our society, practically any woman who is not white. Significant minority populations in the United States include blacks, Hispanics,[1] Asian-Americans, and Native Americans. Minority women account for approximately 18 percent of the female U.S. population, and for about 16 percent of all women who work. There are more than 5 million minority women in the labor force (Almquist, 1979). The largest proportion of minority women workers are blacks, followed by women of Spanish origin and then women of Asian origin (see Figure 7.1). From Table 7.1 we can see that the overall labor-force participation rate of minority women is greater than that of white women, and varies among the different minority groups. Filipino women have the highest labor-force participation rates, followed (in order) by Cubans, Japanese, Chinese, blacks, whites, Mexican-Americans, Native Americans, and Puerto Ricans. Participation rates also vary by marital status. Among married women, Japanese women have the highest labor-force participation rate, followed by Cubans, then blacks and Chinese. Overall, it appears that Asian, Cuban, and black women have consistently high labor-force participation rates; Native American, Mexican-American, and Puerto Rican women have consistently lower rates (Almquist, 1979).

In general, minority women hold the same kinds of jobs that all women hold—that is, they are employed predominantly in clerical, operative, and service occupations (see Table 7.1). There are, however, some important differences. Women of Asian origin, for example, are heavily concentrated in

153

Figure 7 . 1 / Minority and White Women's Labor-Force Participation Rates, 1970

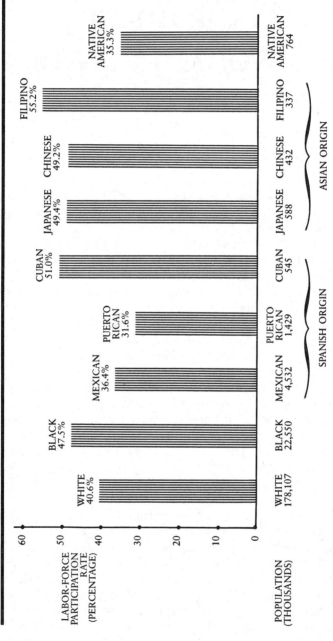

Note: Data include women 16 years of age and over.

SOURCE: Prepared from data in Elizabeth M. Almquist and Juanita L. Wehrle-Einhorn, "The Double Disadvantaged: Minority Women in the Labor Force," in Ann H. Stromberg and Shirley Harkess, eds., *Women Working: Theories and Facts in Perspective* (Palo Alto, Calif.: Mayfield, 1978), pp. 66–67.

T a b l e 7.1 / Comparison of Occupational Distribution and Income of White and Minority Men and Women (1970)

| | Median Income | | | White | | Black | | Spanish Origin | | | | | | Asian Origin | | | | | | American Indian | |
| | | | | | | | | Mexican | | Puerto Rican | | Cuban | | Japanese | | Chinese | | Filipino | | | |
	Men	Women	%[a]	M	W	M	W	M	W	M	W	M	W	M	W	M	W	M	W	M	W
Professionals, technical workers	$11,577	$6,675	58	15	16	6	11	5	6	5	7	13	9	21	16	29	19	18	32	9	11
Managers, administrators (except farm)	11,292	5,523	49	12	4	3	1	4	2	4	2	7	1	12	4	11	4	3	2	5	2
Sales workers	8,321	2,279	27	7	6	2	3	3	6	4	4	6	5	6	7	4	5	2	4	2	4
Clerical workers	7,965	4,646	58	8	37	8	21	6	26	11	30	25	26	9	34	9	32	9	29	6	25
Craftworkers, foremen	8,833	4,276	48	22	2	15	1	21	2	16	2	18	3	20	2	7	1	13	1	22	2
Operatives	7,017	3,885	55	19	14	30	17	27	26	34	40	24	43	10	13	10	23	14	11	24	19
Nonfarm laborers	4,839	3,151	65	6	1	16	1	13	2	8	1	6	1	10	1	3	1	8	1	13	1
Farmers, farm managers	3,859	—	—	3	0	1	—	1	0	0	0	0	0	3	1	4	0	1	0	2	1
Farm laborers, foremen	2,238	1,166	52	1	0	3	1	9	4	1	0	0	0	2	1	0	0	11	2	6	2
Nonhousehold service workers	5,568	2,541	46	7	14	16	25	10	21	17	12	14	11	6	17	24	13	20	17	10	26
Private service workers	—	825	—	0	2	0	18	0	5	0	1	0	1	0	4	0	2	0	2	0	7

Percentage of Labor Force

SOURCE: Adapted from Elizabeth M. Almquist and Juanita L. Wehrle-Einhorn, "The Doubly Disadvantaged: Minority Women in the Labor Force," in Ann H. Stromberg and Shirley Harkess, eds., *Women Working: Theories and Facts in Perspective* (Palo Alto, Calif.: Mayfield, 1978), pp. 68–69. Data are from U.S. Department of Commerce, Bureau of the Census, *Subject Reports of the 1970 Census* (Washington, D.C.: U.S. Government Printing Office, 1973).

[a]Women's median income as a percentage of men's.

the lower-level professional and technical jobs. Other minority women are most heavily concentrated in the operative and service categories. Within the service category, black women are more likely to be private household workers.

The dual oppression of racism and sexism is of major importance to minority women's status in the labor market. Which is the greater problem, racism or sexism? How are they related? Is there any basis for the increasingly popular notion that for certain minority women—blacks, for example—the dual oppressed status has become an advantage in the labor market? This chapter examines these issues, focusing primarily on black women workers because they represent the majority of all minority women and because black women's history of slavery is especially relevant to the double oppression of racism and sexism. We then look at the labor-force experience of other minority women, and compare their experience with that of black and white women to shed some light on these important questions.

THE BLACK WOMAN WORKER

Black women in the labor market suffer a double burden—that of being female and being black (Beale, 1970). They are subject to racial as well as sexual discrimination. If we include discrimination based on social-class membership, black women may be said to suffer from "triple jeopardy" (Ladner, 1977:32). This is characteristic of other minority women as well.

The problem of sexism and racism (and social class) confronting minority women is, to a large extent, rooted in established social attitudes and practices. The plight of black women in our society, however, has a special history. As we all know, blacks did not immigrate to this country voluntarily; they did not flee oppression in their home country to seek freedom in the "land of opportunity." They were imported as slaves. The employment status of blacks is distinctive in that this slave heritage has shaped their position in the labor market.

The Legacy of Slavery

Nowhere is the double oppression of racism and sexism more clearly demonstrated than within the institution of slavery. Slave women were exploited not only as workers but as breeders of slaves and as sex objects for white men (Lerner, 1979:70). Like male slaves, they were considered intrinsically inferior. Slaves were property, not people. They faced severe cultural and legal restrictions: their family lives were controlled by their owners, their children were not their own, and their educational opportunities were almost nonexistent (Almquist, 1979:46). After emancipation, their employment and economic opportunities were limited, because the skills they had learned on the plantation transferred to relatively few jobs, and only to jobs of low pay and status.

The legacy of slavery may partly account for the relatively high labor-force participation rate of black women. Although in general, women's labor-force participation rate is lower than men's, black women's participation rate is higher than that of white women. However, this gap has been narrowing in recent years: white women's labor-force participation between 1890 and 1976 rose from 16.3 to 46.3 percent, while black women's rate has been high (increasing from 39.7 percent in 1890 to 50.3 percent by 1976) throughout this period. (In absolute terms, however, the major labor-market gains for women in recent years were achieved by married white women—see Goldin, 1977:87). Black women have always been represented in the labor market—first as slaves and subsequently as freed people (Goldin, 1977:87).

The traditional stereotypes concerning femininity did not apply in the case of black women slaves. Black women were not considered "weak" females, but were treated more like beasts of burden (King, 1975:121). They were not included in the image of the "delicate female" or the "American housewife." Black women were not part of the "cult of true womanhood" we discussed in Chapter 2. While middle and upper class women had entered into this lifestyle by the late nineteenth and early twentieth centuries, the black woman was "not sheltered or protected; she would not remain oblivious to the desperate struggle for existence unfolding outside the 'home'" (Davis, 1981:7). Chafe (1977) further noted, "While many white daughters were raised in genteel refined circumstances, most black daughters were forced to deal with poverty, violence and a hostile outside world from childhood on" (Chafe, 1977:53). Sojourner Truth, formerly a slave and an activist in the abolitionist and women's rights movements, eloquently expressed the differences in treatment, under slavery, of black and white women: "That man over there says that women need to be helped into carriages and lifted over ditches, and to have the best place everywhere. Nobody ever helped me into carriages, or over mud puddles, or gives me any best place . . . and ain't I a woman?" (Truth, 1851, quoted in Almquist, 1979:61).

If we consider only the present time period, it may appear that black and white women have certain experiences in common—low economic position, being the target of discriminatory practices in education and in work, and overall marginality in the power structure. But black and white women have reached their present circumstances through very different histories. Although feminists have urged black and white women to unite in the fight against sexism, black women felt little in common with the movement (especially in its early days) and were put off by its racial and class composition. Women in the movement "looked too much like 'Miss Ann,' the employer and oppressor of the black woman domestic" (Deckard, 1979:378). Black women are less likely to forget that white women benefited from black women's slave labor and shared with their husbands the role of oppressor. Black women rarely had the option of choosing between work and leisure, as did white women. Although white women's status was clearly inferior to that of white men, they were treated with deference and they shared in the status privileges of their husbands. The status and power hierarchy certainly separated (as it still does) men and women, but the status of blacks was that of property, and the relationships between black and white women were always ambiguous (see Lerner, 1979; Jones, 1980). Nevertheless, Chafe (1977:125) notes, "Despite major differences in priority and perspective between black and white women, a National Black Feminist Organization formed in 1973 both to assert the distinctive interests of black women in the struggle for women's rights and to provide a base for cooperative action on those issues which affected women across racial lines."

Reasons for Working

Black women's reasons for working are basically those reasons cited historically. Since the days of slavery, black women have worked to support themselves and their families (Lerner, 1979:74). Most women work because of economic necessity, but a much higher proportion of black women than white have been, throughout our history, under pressure to earn a living (Bell, 1974).

This high participation rate has been true for married women as well as single women. The labor-force participation rate for black wives with husband present was 70 percent in 1970, compared with 49 percent for white wives (U.S. Department of Labor, Bureau of Labor Statistics, 1980). Minority male heads of households earn less than white male heads of households. The median income of black male heads of families in 1975 was $11,380—approximately 25 percent lower than the $14,094 median income for white male heads of families (Cahn, 1977:33). In addition, since World War II the unemployment rate for minority heads of families has been about double that for white heads of families (Cahn, 1977).

Because of the husband's poor economic position in the labor force, the black family is more dependent on the black woman's wages. In 1978, black wives' earnings (those who worked full time, year round) contributed 41 percent of their family's income, compared with 37 percent for white wives (U.S. Department of Labor, Bureau of Labor Statistics, 1980:76).

Added to these economic pressures is the fact that black female-headed households are more numerous than white, which puts black women in the role of primary wage earner much more often than white women. (One should not conclude, however, that the typical black family is matriarchal— see Staples, 1970. The majority of black families fit the husband/wife nuclear family model—see Lerner, 1979:74.) In March 1979, 40.5 percent of all black families were maintained by women, compared with 11.6 percent of white families (U.S. Department of Labor, Bureau of Labor Statistics, 1980:78). Among families maintained by women in 1977, 51 percent of those headed by black women were below the poverty level, compared with 24 percent of white-female-headed households (U.S. Department of Commerce, Bureau of the Census, 1980:95). Furthermore, the vulnerable economic position of black males—their low wages and uncertain employment—continues to push black married women, even those with small children, into the work force. Overall, the black woman's labor-force pattern is similar to men's, in that black women are likely to work more continuously and for more years than are white women (Wallace, 1980:4).

The "Superhuman" Black Woman and Her "Favored" Status

In contrast to the idea of double (or triple) jeopardy, there is also the increasingly popular image of the black woman as possessing nearly superhuman qualities. She is the economic mainstay of her family as well as its matriarch, she assumes all major responsibilities, she holds the family together through all kinds of economic and social hardship. She is "stronger than other women and certainly stronger than black men" (Ladner, 1971:30).

Factual information on these matters tends to be skimpy, partly because information on blacks in the labor force applies primarily to black men (Almquist, 1979:53). Most of the social-science sources that do treat black women either concentrate on those outside the labor market—women on welfare, for example (Wallace, 1980:2)—or treat them in terms of the myths and stereotypes just mentioned. It is often said that the black woman has a favored economic position in that she can almost always get a job, even if only at the most menial occupations. She is said to have all the advantages in terms of securing employment with significant status and in terms of the ease with which she climbs the occupational ladder (Aldridge, 1975:49). Thus she is believed to have an economic advantage over black men, and some social scientists consider black women to be among the most economically successful groups (along with white men) in our society (Aldridge, 1975; Jackson, 1975; Nelson, 1975). Nelson (1975) attributes these myths to the economic role black women have played within the black family, summed up thus by Joyce Ladner:

> The highly functional role that the black female has historically played has caused her to be erroneously stereotyped as a matriarchate, and this label has been injurious to black women and men. It has caused a considerable amount of frustration and emasculation within black men because it implies that they are incapable of fulfilling the responsibilities for the care and protection of their families. (Ladner, 1971:29)

Part of the reason for these myths, then, stems from the myth of the black matriarchy—the idea that the black woman is put in a superordinate position in the family by the "historical vicissitudes of slavery" (Staples, 1970:8).

Unfortunately, many people accept these impressions without regard to their basis in fact. What do we know about black women's employment status? Does the double (or triple) burden somehow result in a favored workforce situation, and if so, how?

Occupational distribution

The relevant statistics do not support the popular notion of the black woman's favored status. According to U.S. Department of Labor figures, black women have more unemployment than any other group—white men, white women, or black men. In 1970, for example, the unemployment rate for black women was 12.3 percent, compared with 10.3 percent for black men, 5.9 percent for white women, and 4.4 percent for white men (U.S. Department of Labor, Bureau of Labor Statistics, 1980:62–63). Unemployment statistics, however, are only one measure of the employment problems black women face. Underemployment is also an issue. Classified by Bureau of Labor Statistics as "involuntary part-time workers," the underemployed are those who have some kind of work but who cannot find full-time jobs because of structural labor-market factors such as slack work, material shortages, and the like (U.S. Department of Labor, Employment Standards Administration, Women's Bureau, 1977:3). Such factors affect everyone, of course, not only blacks and other minority-group members, but they affect minority workers disproportionately. In 1976, one-fifth of white women and one-third of black and other minority women working part-time did so involuntarily. The "discouraged worker" is another category in which we find a disproportionate number of black and other minority women. These workers either do not enter the labor force or, having entered, withdraw from it because they are discouraged by dismal job prospects (U.S. Department of Labor, Employment Standards Administration, Women's Bureau, 1977).

Looking at black women's occupational distribution over time (Table 7.2), it is clear that until recently black women have been concentrated in unskilled or semiskilled work. In 1910, 90.5 percent of black women worked as agricultural laborers or domestics, compared with 29.3 percent of white women.

Black women's concentration in service work—especially domestic work—was largely a result of limited opportunities available to them following the Civil War. The only factory employment open to them was in the Southern tobacco and textile industries, and until World War I most black

T a b l e   7 . 2 / Occupational Status of Women 14 Years of Age and Over, by Race, 1910, 1940, 1950, 1960, 1970, and 1979 (Percentages)

Occupational Category	1910		1940		1950		1960		1970		1979[a]	
	White	Black	White	Black	White	Black	White	Black	White	Black	White	Black
Professional	11.6	1.5	14.7	4.3	13.3	5.3	14.1	7.7	15.5	10.0	16.9	12.7
Managerial and administrative	1.5	0.2	4.3	0.7	4.7	1.3	4.2	1.1	4.7	1.4	6.7	3.0
Clerical and sales	17.5	0.3	32.8	1.3	39.3	5.4	43.2	9.8	43.4	21.4	43.5	31.7
Craft	8.2	2.0	1.1	0.2	1.7	0.7	1.4	0.7	1.1	0.8	1.8	1.3
Operatives (including transport)	21.2	1.4	20.3	6.2	21.5	15.2	17.6	14.3	14.5	16.8	10.7	14.4
Nonfarm laborers	1.5	0.9	0.9	0.8	0.7	1.6	0.5	1.2	0.4	0.9	1.1	1.7
Private household workers	17.2	38.5	10.9	59.9	4.3	42.0	4.4	38.1	3.7	19.5	2.1	8.0
Other service workers	9.2	3.2	12.7	11.1	11.6	19.1	13.1	23.0	15.1	28.5	34.5	61.6
Farm laborers	12.1	52.0	2.3	15.9	2.9	9.4	1.5	4.1	1.6	0.5	1.0	0.5

SOURCE: Adapted from Delores Aldridge, "Black Women in the Economic Marketplace: A Battle Unfinished," *Journal of Social and Behavioral Sciences* 21 (Winter 1975): 53; and from U.S. Department of Labor, Bureau of Labor Statistics, *Perspective on Working Women: A Databook*, Bulletin 2080 (Washington, D.C.: U.S. Government Printing Office, October 1980).

[a] Data for 1979 applies only to women 16 years of age and over.

women were farm laborers, domestics, or laundresses. Life as a domestic worker in 1912 sounds remarkably like life as a slave:

> I am a negro woman, and I was born and reared in the South. I am now past forty years of age and am the mother of three children. My husband died nearly fifteen years ago. . . . For more than thirty years—or since I was ten years old—I have been a servant . . . in white families. . . . During the last ten years I have been a nurse . . . . I frequently work from fourteen to sixteen hours a day. . . . I am allowed to go home to my children, the oldest of whom is a girl of 18 years, only once in two weeks, every other Sunday afternoon—even then I'm not permitted to stay all night. I not only have to nurse a little white child, now eleven months old, but I have to act as playmate . . . to three other children in the home, the oldest of whom is only nine years of age. . . . I see my own children only when they happen to see me on the streets when I am out with the children, or when my children come to the "yard" to see me, which isn't often. . . . You might as well say that I'm on duty all the time—from sunrise to sunrise, every day of the week. I am the slave, body and soul, of this family, and what do I get for this work? . . . ten dollars a month. (Anonymous, 1912, quoted in Lerner, 1972:227–228)

Although World War I opened up some factory jobs, these were typically limited to the most menial, least desirable, and often the most dangerous jobs—jobs already rejected by white women. These jobs included some of the most dangerous tasks in industry, such as carrying glass to hot ovens in glass factories and dyeing furs in the furrier industry (see Greenwald, 1980:26). During the period from 1910 to 1940, white women's occupational status began to improve; the proportion of white women employed in clerical and sales positions almost doubled, and there was a decline in the numbers of white women in domestic work (see Chapter 2). Private household work then became the province of black women: the percentage of black household workers increased from 38.5 percent in 1910 to 59.9 percent in 1940, as shown in Table 7.2 (Aldridge, 1975:52). Black women remained for many decades the single largest group in domestic service (see Katzman, 1978).

During World War II, racial restrictions in hiring were relaxed because of severe labor shortages, and black women began to find blue-collar positions in the war industries (Aldridge, 1975:54). From the 1950s to the present, black women have made significant gains in occupational status. There has been a steady decrease since 1940 in the number of black domestic workers and an increase in clerical positions as many younger, better-educated black women found employment in these clerical occupations, as shown in Table 7.2 (Aldridge, 1975:54).

Although there are similarities in the occupational structure and distribution of black and white women—especially over the last decades, as more and more black women have moved into white-collar positions—these similarities are limited. By 1979, black women were still more likely than white women to be employed in service and blue-collar positions, as shown in Table 7.2 (Wallace, 1980:23). In the blue-collar sector, black women are still primarily operatives, while the higher-paying, higher-status craft jobs are held by white men. Similarly in the white-collar sector, black women have made headway in clerical and professional positions (mostly nursing and teaching), while the lucrative managerial, administrative, and sales jobs are held by white men. When black women's occupational status is compared with that of black men, a similar pattern emerges: black men enjoy a markedly greater diversification of jobs with higher prestige and status. Although a higher percentage of black women are professionals than black men, they are concentrated in the "female professions." Black men participate in a wider variety of professions. (See Figure 7.2.)

Douglas (1980) also points out that even *within* the same occupations, or within the same "women's work," the positions held by black women are likely to be inferior to those held by white women (see also Stevenson, 1975c). In domestic work, for example, black women are likely to have the more menial tasks—scrubbing and laundry—while the white domestic worker is more likely to be the chambermaid. In clerical work too, white women are more likely to be employed as receptionists or executive secretaries; black women are more likely to work in the secretarial pool, supervised by a white woman (Douglas, 1980:37).

The gains made by black women may appear impressive in some respects, but we should bear in mind that the data indicating these trends comes from cross-sectional studies. Often such trends are not exemplified in any individual employment experience. For example, a national longitudinal survey observed a group of mature women (thirty to forty-four years of age) at three different points in their employment history: first job after leaving school, once again in 1967, and again in 1972. The survey sought information concerning the determinants of these women's occupational position at these three different times in their work lives. Results indicated that the status of a woman's first job was associated with race even after other important explanatory factors (such as level of education, age, marital status, family status) were considered. The results also indicated that the occupational status of black women workers relative to white women deteriorated substantially over the period between their first job and the 1967 follow-up. The racial differences continued over time, so that when these women were reinterviewed in 1972, their occupational status had declined even further (Parnes and Nestel, 1975:85).

F i g u r e 7 . 2 / *Occupational Distribution of Employed Black Men and Women, March 1979*

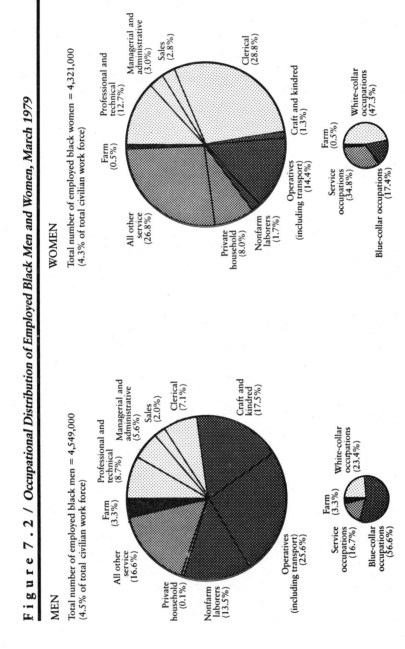

MEN

Total number of employed black men = 4,549,000
(4.5% of total civilian work force)

WOMEN

Total number of employed black women = 4,321,000
(4.3% of total civilian work force)

SOURCE: Prepared from data in U.S. Department of Labor, Bureau of Labor Statistics, *Perspectives on Working Women: A Databook*, Bulletin 2080 (Wasington, D.C.: U.S. Government Printing Office, 1980), p. 74; and U.S. Department of Labor, Bureau of Labor Statistics, *Marital and Family Characteristics of the Labor Force, March 1979* (Washington, D.C.: U.S. Government Printing Office, 1981), p. A-9.

Earnings

A popular image of the black woman worker is that she and white men "have it made" economically (Nelson, 1975:13). An important indicator of "having it made" is income. During the last decade, black women have made greater gains than have white women, but, having started from further back, their earnings have merely begun to approach the level of white women's earnings (Smith, 1979).

Smith points out some reasons for the rise in black women's economic status: the increased similarity in the educational distributions between races, the rapid rise in black wages in the South, and the concentration of black women in public-sector jobs. Smith also suggests that the elimination of domestic service as black women's primary occupation was an important factor, but he does not fully explore this variable. We should note that Smith's analysis deals only with married women living with their husbands (see Smith, 1979:201–202).

Over a nearly forty-year span of time, the median wage or salary income of black women who worked full time, year round, increased from 38 percent of white women workers' incomes in 1939 to nearly 94 percent in 1978. The earnings of black men during this same time period (1939–1978) did not come so close: they increased from 45 to 74 percent of white males' incomes (Wallace, 1980:59). Data such as these are sometimes interpreted (see, for example, Levitan, Johnson, and Taggart, 1975:55) as evidence that black women have an income advantage over black men because they have closed the gap on white women's earnings at a more rapid pace than black males have closed the gap on white males' earnings (Wallace, 1980:58). (But meanwhile, the earnings gap between white men and women has increased—see Chapters 2 and 4.)

Such statistics give a distorted impression of black women's economic situation, but it is the type of comparison that social scientists often make. By comparing white women with black women and black men with white men, the double oppression of black women is hidden. The overall lower economic status of blacks compared with whites obscures the fact that black women suffer racial discrimination in addition to sexual discrimination (Gurin and Gaylord, 1976:190). As Figure 7.3 illustrates, black women are *not* doing well in any absolute sense—they earn less than white men, black men, or white women.

In every occupational category, black women earn less than either white or black men (see Table 7.3). The earnings of black and white *women*, however, are the same in clerical, service, and in elementary and secondary education jobs. The largest gap in earnings between black and white women is in the operative category. Of special interest is that among professional and technical workers and managers, black women had somewhat higher earnings, on the average, than white women (Young, 1979:37–38). Some re-

F i g u r e 7 . 3 / *Median Earnings of Year-Round, Full-Time Workers with Income, by Race and Sex, 1970–1977*

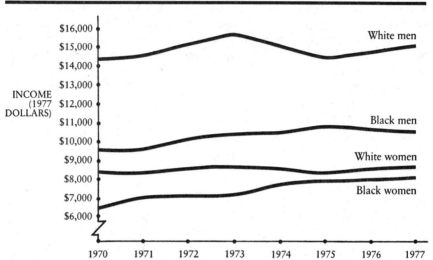

Note: Data include workers 14 years of age and over.

SOURCE: Adapted from U.S. Department of Commerce, Bureau of the Census, *Current Population Reports*, Series P-60, Nos. 118 and 80 (Washington, D.C.: U.S. Government Printing Office, 1977).

searchers have attributed this anomaly to the more interrupted work histories of white professional women. Wallace, for example, points out that older black women professionals have a longer and more consistent work history, which would account for their higher hourly pay rates (Wallace, 1980:61).

Our analysis of the labor-force status of black women reveals little that supports the popular myth that black women have somehow benefited from their double oppression: they rank lowest on measures of economic status (occupational rank, earnings, and unemployment rates) compared with black men and white men and women. Some researchers have pointed to the greater concentration of black women in the professions as evidence of their "unnatural superiority," and, indeed, if there were any supporting data, one should expect to find it in studies of black professional women.

Black Women in the Professions:
Their "Unnatural Superiority"

Black women have constituted more than half of all black professionals since 1940, while women in general have comprised only 38 to 41 percent of all professionals during this same time period (Kilson, 1977). Furthermore,

T a b l e 7.3 / *Median Earnings of Wage and Salary Workers Who Worked All of 1977 at Full-Time Jobs, by Sex and Race*

Occupational Category	White		Black	
	Men	Women	Men	Women
Professional and technical	$17,745	$11,947	$14,861	$12,212
Managers and administrators, except farm	19,138	10,150	15,024	12,225
Sales workers	16,049	6,814	a	a
Clerical workers	14,436	8,410	11,208	8,474
Craft and kindred workers	15,031	8,903	11,252	b
Operatives, except transport	12,704	7,358	11,038	6,507
Transport equipment operatives	13,689	b	10,154	b
Laborers, except farm	11,663	7,428	7,987	b
Private household workers	b	c	b	3,354
Service workers, except private household	10,965	6,248	8,072	6,095

SOURCE: Adapted from Anne McDougall Young, "Median Earnings in 1977 Reported for Year-Round, Full-Time Workers," *Monthly Labor Review* 102 (June 1977): 38.
NOTE: Figures are for workers aged 16 and over.
a Data unavailable.
b Data not shown for occupations with fewer than 75,000 people employed.
c Median less than $3,000.

black women's superiority is said to have "devastating" consequences for the psychological well-being and occupational attainment of black men (Hare and Hare, 1970:66).

One researcher concluded that the black woman was so threatening to black men that the training programs for black women should be slowed down while those for black men should be intensified, because of the possibility that black women "would increase their disproportional contributions to the professions and possibly magnify 'their unnatural superiority' over black males" (Bock, 1971:128; see also Bernard, 1966:69).

Social scientists have differed in their explanations for black women's superiority in the professions. Bock (1971) has attributed their higher concentration in the professions to advantaged educational opportunities. He noted that black women took advantage of a "farmer's daughter" effect. Like the nineteenth-century white farmers who allowed their daughters rather than their sons to stay in school, black parents educated their daughters at the expense of their sons. Racial discrimination in education and employment has operated less severely against black women than men. A college education for black women was considered a better investment. Lerner

(1972, 1979) describes this as a "sex loophole" in racial discrimination: when opportunities in education and employment become available to blacks, they are more likely to be awarded to black women than to black men.

Perhaps the most extensive explanation for the success of black professional women comes from Epstein's (1973) study of thirty-one professional women and black college senior women. Epstein does not state that black women are "dominant" or have fared well in the labor market, but she does view the black professional woman as having achieved unusual success, especially in high-prestige occupations such as law and medicine. She attributes their success to the "positive effects" of the "double negative"— being black and female. These effects are said to operate as follows:

1. Focusing on one of the negatively valued statuses may cancel the negative effect of the other—that is, raise its "worth." For instance, in a white professional milieu, a black woman is viewed as lacking the "womanly" occupational deficiencies of white women (seeking a husband, for example), and the black woman's sex status is given a higher evaluation.
2. Two statuses in combination create a new status (for example, the hyphenated status of black-woman-lawyer), which may have no established "price" because it is unique. In this situation, the person has a better bargaining position in setting his or her own worth. This pattern may also place the person in the role of a "stranger," outside the normal exchange system and able to exact a higher than usual price.
3. Because the "stranger" is outside the normal opportunity structure, he or she can choose (or may be forced to choose) an alternate life-style. This choice was made by many black women forced to enter the occupational world because of economic need, and, in turn, it created selective barriers, which insulated the women from diversions from occupational success and from ghetto culture, thus strengthening ambition and motivation. (Epstein, 1973:152)

Embedded in these explanations are some questionable assertions: (1) that black women have benefited professionally because they have an educational advantage over black men, (2) that black women are better prepared to deal with white society—especially white employers—because they may be in a better bargaining position, and (3) that black women derive unusual motivational strength and ambition from their dual status. These assertions are examined in the following subsections.

Black women's educational "advantage"
Beginning with elementary school, inadequate public education (particularly in ghetto areas) severely limits career choices, as black girls have only

T a b l e 7 . 4 / *Median Number of Years of School Completed, by Race and Sex, 1940–1979*

	White		Black	
Year	Men	Women	Men	Women
1940	8.7	8.8	5.4	6.1
1950	9.3	10.0	6.4	7.2
1960	10.6	11.0	7.9	8.5
1970	12.2	12.2	9.6	10.2
1979	12.5	12.4	11.7	12.0

SOURCE: Adapted from La Frances Rodgers-Rose, "Some Demographic Characteristics of the Black Woman: 1940–1975," in La Frances Rodgers-Rose, ed., *The Black Woman* (Beverly Hills, Calif.: Sage Publications, 1980), p. 33. Data for 1979 from U.S. Department of Labor, Bureau of Labor Statistics, *Perspectives on Working Women: A Databook*, Bulletin 2080 (Washington, D.C.: U.S. Government Printing Office, October 1980).

limited access to training in the skills necessary to compete effectively in the job market. Large classes and teachers whose attitudes often reflect the racism and sexism of our culture narrow rather than broaden the job horizons for young black girls. At the high-school level, the problems continue. Baker and Levenson's study of the placement practices of a vocational working-class high school in New York City revealed that the school's referral and placement procedures restricted the job opportunities of minorities, despite their qualifications. Placement counselors were unduly influenced by the racial stereotypes of employers, and black women were generally tracked into lower-level blue-collar jobs, in contrast to their white female counterparts, who were more likely to be placed in white-collar occupations (Baker and Levenson, 1975).

At the college level, conditions are not much better. Biased counseling and other factors influence the choice of courses and channel minority women into nonscientific academic majors or keep them out of college altogether (Alexander, 1979:29). Little or no encouragement and information about graduate education and fellowships, exclusion from the network of scientists and professional organizations, and lack of funding for research projects are also factors that contribute to minority women's limited access to the professions. Anxiety about being "special admits"—a derogatory way of saying they fulfill affirmative-action quotas—also plagues many black women (Gibbs, 1979).

According to Rodgers-Rose's (1980) figures, the educational attainments of black women and men are similar. Table 7.4 shows that the average number of years of school completed are a little higher for black women than

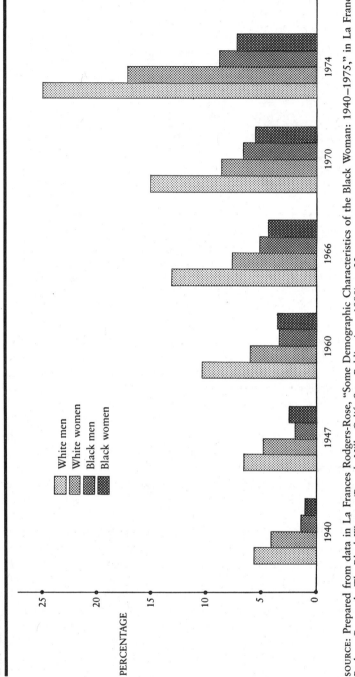

F i g u r e   7 . 4 / *Percentage of the Population over Age 25 That Completed Four or More Years of College, by Race and Sex, 1945–1974*

SOURCE: Prepared from data in La Frances Rodgers-Rose, "Some Demographic Characteristics of the Black Woman: 1940–1975," in La Frances Rodgers-Rose, ed., *The Black Woman* (Beverly Hills, Calif.: Sage Publications, 1980), p. 33.

men, but these differences are not statistically significant. The percentages of black men and women finishing four or more years of college are also similar: in 1974, 8.8 percent of black men completed college, compared to 7.6 percent of black women (see Figure 7.4).

These data do not support the assertion that black daughters have been preferred over black sons in terms of education. What *is* clear is that differences by race are much greater than differences by sex. In 1974, 24.9 percent of white males finished college, compared with 8.8 percent of black males; 17.2 percent of white females finished college, compared with 7.6 percent of black females (see Rodgers-Rose, 1980:32–33).

Black women's "better" bargaining position

Epstein (1973) argues that the combination of two negative statuses create a new, positive status. The black woman is said to be in a better bargaining position because she is not perceived by white employers as having the same occupational deficiencies as white women, who, for example, are said to be out to "get a husband." Black women are thus less likely to be perceived in terms of these sex-role stereotypes.

Epstein cites the black woman lawyer as an example of the black woman professional who, because of her unique status, has no established price. But, as the following account illustrates, this unique status does not necessarily lead to a favored status:

> A woman obtained my name from the American Bar Association and sent her husband to me. He knew that I was a woman, but when he arrived and I introduced myself and he saw that I am Black, he said, "I knew you were a woman, but this is too much," and he turned and left. (from interview cited in Leggon, 1980:195)

Although it is true that more than half of all black professionals since 1940 have been women, the dominant professions have been the low-paying, low-status ones. The major profession for black women between 1890 and 1970 was teaching; social work and nursing were far behind as second and third (Kilson, 1977:38).

This distribution within the professions is similar to the distribution of white women in the professions, as described in the previous chapter. For the most part, black women, like all women, are concentrated in a few traditionally "female" professions (Kilson, 1977). But professional opportunities for black men have become much greater than for black women, especially since World War II (Kilson, 1977:40). Whereas the most popular profession for black males used to be the clergy, black males are now represented in a variety of professional occupations, including school and college teaching, engineering, accounting, and medicine.

Black women's "unusual" motivational strength

Epstein (1973) argued that black women possess unusual motivational strength, which better prepares them for obtaining professional employment. Evidence from other research, however, does not support Epstein's argument. Studies by Gurin and Epps (1975) and by Gurin and Gaylord (1976) found that black college men had higher levels of aspiration, both educationally and occupationally, than did black college women. Black women's goals reflected lower levels of aspiration on almost every measure (Gurin and Epps, 1975 : 395). Although black college men and women were similar in more general motivation (such as need for achievement, desire for security, and need for recognition), women channeled these general motives into sex-stereotyped goals (Gurin and Gaylord, 1976 : 14). Although the number of black women expecting to attend graduate school in 1964 and 1970 was almost the same as that of black men, fewer women intended to pursue professional degrees. Also, more women expected to finish graduate school at the master's-degree level (Gurin and Gaylord, 1976).

The occupational aspirations reveal a similar picture. Black women aspired to the lower-level occupations—those requiring less ability, those with lower status and prestige, and those less subject to racial discrimination. Black women also aspired to a narrower range of occupations, and their choices of occupation closely resembled traditional female fields. In fact, sex-role influences were found to influence the career and educational aspirations of black women in the same ways as for white women. The differences between black men and women in these areas closely parallel the differences between white men and women (Gurin and Gaylord, 1976 : 15).

As we can see, Epstein's assertions concerning black professional women are not supported by other researchers' findings. And, as Almquist has pointed out, there are other limitations to Epstein's study: the size of Epstein's sample was small, and the study was "admittedly distorted by including numerous career-oriented immigrants from the West Indies" (Almquist, 1979 : 70). While Epstein's conclusions may apply to this special group, generalizations to the general U.S. population of black women seem inappropriate (see also Myers, 1980; Kemp, 1981).

For those black women who do make it through the many obstacles and gain entry into the professions, other difficulties remain, including unique psychological problems. The black professional woman is isolated—she may feel she belongs neither in the professional world nor in her minority community:

> As she gains in professional status, the ethnic minority woman cannot help but be aware that there are few like her. As she moves up the ladder, she simultaneously and experientially moves away from her community of origin. This results in . . . being perceived as an outsider by her community. (Collins, 1979 : 6)

The sense of isolation and discrimination experienced by a black woman economist is revealed in the following personal account:

> Another trap is the illusion of belonging. Although apprehensive at first, one often lets the guard down with time and becomes, at least superficially, "one of the crowd." That's until there is a need to remind you that you are, indeed, Black, female, and last. In one job situation, I felt especially close to others after a demanding report was produced on time, and then we had a cocktail party to celebrate. But the warmth and closeness were shattered when I overheard a "nigger" joke. . . . When my effort was needed, I was one of the crowd, but when the crunch was off, I was, again, just a Black woman. (Malveaux, 1979:53–54).

In some cases, the black professional woman must choose between her community and her career. At a 1979 Conference on Minority Women Lawyers (Minority Women Lawyers Regional Seminar, 1979), black women expressed concern that their very identities were threatened by becoming professional because the model for success was "to dress, think, talk and act as close to masculine and white as possible" (Collins, 1979:11). Fears of losing their ethnic identity or their femininity plague minority women, and to compensate, some try to live the "superwoman" myth—handling everything, in all spheres of their lives—in order to prove their link with their families and reaffirm their racial identities. In the minority community, there is often the sentiment that if a woman succeeds, she has somehow sold out (Flowers, 1979:48; see also Benjamin, 1982).

Thus the situation for black women, including black professional women, appears to be more complex and more negative than the image provided by the popular myths and stereotypes.

OTHER MINORITY WOMEN AT WORK

How does the dual oppression of sexism and racism affect other minority women? Native American, Hispanic, Asian, and other nonwhite women, while similar to black women in many ways, face circumstances unique to their ethnic groups. They share with black women the concerns of all women; they share with the men of their ethnic groups the problems of discrimination against ethnic minorities. Each minority group has had a different experience in American society and has faced different opportunities and obstacles.

Native American Women

Native American women, like blacks, have a history of oppression that shapes their present-day situation. European settlers pushed Native American tribes off their land and deprived them of food and livelihood, culture and traditions. For example, Navajo society was matrilineal, with extended families the norm; Navajo women owned property and played an important role in family decisions. But, beginning in the 1930s, government policy disrupted this system, giving land only to males. As more and more Navajo men had to seek employment off the reservations, nuclear families became the norm. As a result, Navajo women are often isolated and powerless. They have become dependent on male providers, but they often face divorce or desertion and thus economic difficulties, because the community frowns on women seeking work off the reservation.

The disruption of the traditional Native American society has left Native American women in very grim economic circumstances. Native American women's labor-force status participation rate is low; in 1970, it was only 35 percent (see Figure 7.1); their unemployment rate was double that for all women; and 80 percent of Indian women earned less than $4,000 per year, with a median income of $1,697. One-third of all Indian women are employed in the low-paying service occupations—1.7 times the national average (Urban Associates, 1974). The blatant discrimination in hiring practices is evident in the following report by a Native American woman describing her job search: "I was applying for a job as a waitress and they said they wanted all whites . . . they said they had a lot of office workers coming in and they preferred white girls" (Bahr, Chadwick, and Strauss, 1972).

To some extent, these conditions are the result of lack of opportunity for formal education. The Bureau of Indian Affairs (BIA) has a major role in any decisions concerning education for Indians and has stressed training in secretarial skills for women, and training in woodcutting, car repair, and farming for men (Metoyer, 1979:333). According to Metoyer (1979), education of the majority culture and of the Indian community would be one means of alleviating the prejudice and discrimination, but the prospects for this appear limited. The American Indian Movement has made some gains in increasing Native Americans' control over their environment and tribal affairs through lawsuits designed to regain acres of land to ensure water and mineral rights for the lands they already possess. However, these changes will not affect Native Americans' occupational and economic status (Almquist, 1979:44). It is doubtful that such efforts will even begin to conquer the overwhelming racism that all Native Americans experience or the combination of racism and sexism faced by Native American women.

Hispanic Women

Spanish-heritage groups are the "middle minorities" (Almquist, 1979), ranking higher in economic status than Native Americans and blacks but lower than Asian minorities. In 1970 the median family income for the major Hispanic groups was $6,962 for Mexican Americans, $6,165 for Puerto Ricans, and $8,529 for Cuban Americans (Almquist, 1979:36). Women's economic role in the support of the family differs from group to group. Mexican-American women have very low labor-force participation rates; they have few marketable skills and little education. The Catholic Church, with its emphasis on traditional family values, has also contributed to the subordination of these women. The Mexican-American woman's major role is keeping her family together (Lorenzana, 1979:337).

The labor-force participation of Puerto Rican women is even lower (32 percent, see Figure 7.1). Their employment is complicated by frequent migration between the island and the mainland, which often leads to instability both in work and in family life:

> It is not unusual to find women working in the U.S. whose children are cared for by grandmothers or other relatives in Puerto Rico or to find wives and children living in Puerto Rico while their husbands find work on the mainland, or to find working wives in Puerto Rico pioneering the resettlement of husband and children. (King, 1974)

Of all Hispanic groups, Cuban women have the highest labor-force participation rate: 51 percent (see Figure 7.1). Many Cuban women who had been housewives in Cuba sought work outside the home when they entered the United States. Their employment is primarily in blue-collar occupations, and many work as factory operatives. Like other Hispanic women, Cuban women are underrepresented in white-collar and clerical positions. The general economic status of Cuban families is somewhat better than that of other Hispanic families; their higher median family income is often attributed to the higher proportion of Cuban women working.

Hispanic women may, like black women, find that their social, cultural, and historic bonds with white women are somewhat tenuous (Nieto, 1974). Hispanic cultures tend to be even more male dominated than is U.S. culture, with women assigned an almost exclusively familial role. In addition, the discrimination that both Hispanic men and women have faced tends to draw them together in the struggle against racism, making sexism almost a peripheral issue for many of these women. Lorenzana (1979) describes this situation for Mexican-American women: "When a people are undernourished, ill, socially alienated, and powerless members of a society, male chauvinism is of trivial concern" (Lorenzana, 1979:336). Thus, affirmative-action programs are looked on skeptically because they are perceived as pitting Hispanic women against Hispanic men in the search for jobs. In Puerto Rican culture, as in black culture, there is the myth that the women are more successful, although the statistics show the opposite to be the case. Nevertheless, even women who are working to gain better treatment for Puerto Ricans assume that men should hold the positions of leadership (King, 1974). Almquist (1979) suggests that as Hispanic women's labor-force position becomes more like that of white women, they will become more involved in the feminist movement, but racism must be overcome first.

Asian-American Women

The employment situation for Asian-American women—those of Chinese, Japanese, and Filipino origin—is very different than it is for other minority women. They have high labor-force participation rates and relatively high economic status (compared to women of other minority groups). Both the men and women of these groups tend to hold jobs in the white-collar occupations.

The three highest occupational concentrations of Chinese and Japanese women are as clericals (highest), factory operatives, and professionals (lowest). Their labor-force position closely resembles that of white women. In general, Filipino women are similar to white women in occupational distribution—in fact, more similar than Filipino men are to white men; the only major difference is that 30 percent of Filipino women are professionals, while only 16 percent of white women are.

Almquist (1979) offers several reasons for Asian-American women's success. First, they are relatively few in number and more easily absorbed into the mainstream than the large population of blacks. Second, they do not have the black's history of slavery in this country. Third, they have been able to build strong, viable ethnic communities in the United States. Fourth, many reside in Hawaii, where discrimination against Asians is less relevant. And fifth, the level of education, especially of the most recent immigrants, has been quite high.

Acculturation has also helped: the longer the Asian-American woman has been in the United States, the more she accepts American sex-role standards and rejects the rigid patriarchial structure that characterizes traditional Asian societies.

PROSPECTS FOR CHANGE

Social scientists speculate that as the labor-market position of minority women becomes more like that of white women, their lot will improve. The assumption underlying this speculation is that racial discrimination is the major problem, and that to the extent that racist attitudes and practices diminish, minority women will be treated like white women and can expect to enjoy the same labor-market opportunities, occupational distribution, and earnings that white women now have. Asian-American women and some black women now experience such "success." And that certainly is an improvement, especially when we compare the present situation of white women with that of, for example, the Native American women. But minority women will find, if and when racial discrimination vanishes, that they face sexist discrimination as well. And, as one black woman has observed, it isn't always easy to tell what one is fighting: "Although it's difficult to distinguish between the two, most days I think it's sexual because I see white women experiencing the same things I am. . . . In the matter of salaries, you can't tell whether it is racist or sexist" (Leggon, 1980: 195).

Certainly it is necessary for minority women to have the necessary education and training, but, as many well-qualified minority women can attest, credentials are not necessarily enough. And certainly there has been progress, but real progress will come only when sexism and racism are confronted simultaneously and when educational and employment opportunities now available to white men become equally available to everyone.

SUMMARY

This chapter has examined the problems of the minority woman worker. Like all women, minority women are subject to sexist discrimination, but minority women face the additional problem of discrimination based on race and national origin. Like women in general, minority women tend to be employed in the low-level, low-status, and low-paying occupations, but minority women are (with a few notable exceptions) generally concentrated in the most menial jobs within these low-level occupational categories.

We have focused on the black woman worker because she represents the majority of all minority women workers in our culture and because black women's history of slavery is especially relevant to the double oppression of racism and sexism. Participation in the labor force was never a matter of choice for slaves, and black women's labor-force participation rates have always been high, first as slaves and later as paid employees. Another important factor is the vulnerable economic situation of black men: black women have been under more pressure than have white women to earn a living to support themselves and their families.

We have also examined research relevant to the increasingly popular notions that being both black and female produces a unique status that has special advantages in the labor market, that black women are particularly successful in economic terms, and that black women have advantages over black men in the labor market. Our examination reveals little to support such notions. In all respects, black women face double oppression. Although their dual negative status may create a unique third status, this unique status is equally negative. The interaction of sex and race, influenced by the heritage of slavery, places black women at a distinctly *disadvantaged* position in the labor force. Black women work more, and always have; their compensation is, and always has been, less. Black women have higher unemployment rates, and more black families headed by women are below the poverty line (U.S. Department of Labor, Bureau of Labor Statistics, 1980). Black women do not have more favored jobs than black men, but are employed in the least desirable traditional female occupations—the service jobs and lower-level clerical and operative jobs. Black women earn less than white women, who in turn earn less than men—white or black. There is little to support the myth about the special advantages of being both black and female.

The situation for other minority women is, in broadest terms, similar, in that they suffer discrimination on two counts. In addition, occupational opportunities may be limited because of inadequate training and education as well as cultural attitudes and restrictions, as among, for example, Native American women and women of Hispanic origin. These factors combine to produce their worst effects in the case of Native American women. Asian-American women represent an exception to the general picture of minority women, in that a relatively high proportion is employed in professional and technical occupations, albeit in low-level positions.

In general, the problems of occupational restrictions and discrimination are more severe for minority women than for white women. It is typically assumed that racial discrimination is the greater problem, and that once racism can be overcome, minority women will have the same economic and occupational advantages that white women now have. We have pointed out that although this will be a considerable improvement for many minority women, the problems of sexism remain: even with appropriate education, training, and credentials, women face restrictions and discriminatory practices in the labor market.

8 ◆ Problems and Strategies for Dual-Worker Families

Currently, only 6 percent of American families correspond to the traditional model of two parents, with husband as full-time employee in the labor force and wife as full-time homemaker in the home (Moroney, 1978; Pifer, 1978). The decline in the incidence of the traditional family is due in large part to the increasing participation of women in the labor force.[1] As discussed earlier, between 1890 and 1980 women's rate of participation in the labor force grew from 18 to 50 percent, and presently half of the mothers with children under age six are working outside of the home. In addition, the incidence of dual-career[2] (as well as two-job) families has also increased, particularly in the last decade (Rice, 1979:6–7).

But despite these changes in labor-force patterns, social institutions continue to be geared toward the traditional family model. As we shall see, employment institutions continue to operate as though households had just one full-time worker and the supportive services of a full-time homemaker. Sex-role values continue to emphasize the dominance of husband's employment needs and opportunities. And housework and child care are still allocated disproportionately to women, whether they are employed or not. In this way, we have lags in values and social institutions, which have not kept pace with changes in labor-force behavior.

For example, in many occupations the work demands are so high as to virtually assume the presence of a full-time partner at home to provide the support that makes the employee's work involvement possible. In other cases, inflexible work schedules that require that employees start work at a fixed time operate as though another partner were available to manage the often competing schedule of children and household. These lags in out-moded values and institutions result in stresses and problems—and, more specifically, conflicts and overloads—for men and women in their work and family roles, and in their relationship with each other.

Although we discuss certain aspects of these conflicts among family, work, and relationship in other chapters, this chapter focuses explicitly on the stresses and problems. The first part of the chapter analyzes the prob-lems, and the second part proposes resolutions. In both parts, we are guided by our perspective that work, family, and other institutions connect with and reflect each other, and that only by changing current institutional ar-rangements can we reduce the strain between work and family and substan-tially improve the labor-force position of women.

This chapter focuses on problems and resolutions for *husband/wife fami-lies*. The focus is on husband/wife families because while only a minority of American families have a full-time homemaking mother and a full-time em-ployed father, a majority (87 percent in 1977) do have a husband and wife present (Kamerman, 1981:12). Furthermore, most children (80 percent in 1976) live with two parents, although the proportion living with both of their *natural* parents is only 67 percent (Kamerman, 1981:12). This per-centage points to the high rate of both divorce and remarriage in American society.

ROLE CONFLICT AND OVERLOAD: FAMILY, WORK, AND RELATIONSHIP

In their dual roles[3] in work and family, men and women are confronted with demands from both of these spheres. As a result, they are often faced with conflicts and overloads (Rapoport and Rapoport, 1971). For example, demands to meet a business appointment can compete with a child's school performance or open house. Or a spouse's birthday may coincide with a professional conference or meeting. One can't be in two places at once, yet to meet both demands would require just that.

Furthermore, the conflicts are not just restricted to certain time points, but rather may be an ongoing occurrence. Work and employment may re-quire continuously high investments of time and energy, which are at odds with other investments, including those in personal and home life. Thus, a person trying to operate a business, build a professional practice, or manage an artistic career is subject to continuous and relentless demands on his or her resources. At the same time, one's family is also a "greedy institution" (Coser, 1974)—an institution that makes persistent demands on energy and resources. In describing these family demands, a harried mother says,

"When the kids go back to school, it's sheer hell. Everyone needs to buy clothes. There are fees to submit, forms to fill out, sports start, music lessons start, dancing lessons start, Scouts start, and I go crazy" (Hall and Hall, 1979:98). By themselves, such family demands are high, and when they combine with work claims the overload can be excessive.

As a result of accumulating, and sometimes unmet, demands and expectations, people may feel guilt and a sense of failure in living up to standards. And these reactions are especially marked for women compared to men. This is because women are not so free to compartmentalize their roles—leaving the demands of work at the doorstep when they come home, and conversely, putting the family on the back burner when work demands are high (Johnson and Johnson, 1980). Current research indicates that employed women continue to bear primary responsibility for home and family (Hofferth and Moore, 1979; Meissner, Humphreys, Meis, and Scheu, 1975; Pleck, 1981) and that they experience anxiety about failure in these roles (Johnson and Johnson, 1977). Men, on the other hand, spend relatively small amounts of time in housework—whether their wives are employed or not (Moore and Hofferth, 1979; Pleck, 1981). Moreover, women's household labor represents a great demand not just in the time required, but also in the pacing of those demands (Glazier-Malbin, 1975). Tasks such as food preparation that are performed by women represent constant and recurrent demands. In contrast, the chores likely to be handled by males, such as house painting and repairs, are not only less frequently performed, but are also more flexibly scheduled.

In addition, as a group, men tend to approach children and family in a more detached and nonemotional manner (see Johnson and Johnson, 1977). Hence, while we later discuss the problems of overburdened roles for both the men and women in dual-job families, it is important to remember that for women these burdens and conflicts are much greater both at home and at work.

Problems at Home

The strain and overload of the roles do vary, and depend on a number of domestic factors, such as personal housekeeping standards and style, the presence or absence of children, and the particular allocation of household tasks.

Housekeeping standards

In housekeeping standards, we find that married couples often try at first to give to cooking, entertaining, cleaning, decorating, and correspondence the same attention given to these tasks in a traditional home with a full-time housewife (Hall and Hall, 1979:120). But over time most lower their standards, and both men and women agree that some readjustment of domestic lifestyle is necessary for working couples. One way to deal with the problem is to determine exactly what is currently being done and then what can slip, what can be allocated to outside help, and what can be eliminated altogether (Hall and Hall, 1979). Particular strategies of household management and decisions about what to stress and what to eliminate depend, however, on individual values about matters of relative importance or nonimportance (as we discuss further in the second half of the chapter).

Children

Many employed people are able to manage the house, but feel less certain about the children. And surely children do add considerably to already over-loaded roles. To begin with, parenthood increases the number of tasks and chores to be performed, and involves certain responsibilities and commitments to children that can't really be counted or so assessed. Moreover, while housekeeping standards can be lowered, the notion of a lower parental, and especially maternal, standard is almost a contradiction of terms (Fogarty, Rapoport, and Rapoport, 1971:344).

Yet research indicates that children do not necessarily suffer from the mother's employment (Moore and Hofferth, 1979; Silverstein, 1981).[4] While employed compared to nonemployed mothers do spend less time with their children, it is not at all clear that sheer quantity of time is a critical determinant in child development (see Hoffman, 1974). Rather, other factors, such as stimulation, affectionate play, and responsiveness, constitute "quality" of parenting—and these factors do not appear to vary significantly with mother's employment status (Moore and Hofferth, 1979). Thus, parents have found that the demands of parenthood can be managed not only through supportive child care but also by reevaluation of time spent chauffeuring the kids, volunteering for school activities, and so forth.

Allocation of tasks

The extent of overload from house and family demands also depends on other factors such as the particular allocation of tasks between partners. The negotiation of household tasks between the sexes is not a straightforward matter, and studies in Scandinavia and Eastern Europe, as well as Britain and America, indicate that the allocation of housework is a very "touchy area" for working couples (Rapoport and Rapoport, 1976:306).

Under the traditional division of domestic labor, men work outside, and women inside, the home; and hence cleaning, cooking, and the like have been designated as "women's work." Yet when women become employed they do not relinquish housework for market work; rather, they add one role to the other. And in this way, a lag in the norms about division of domestic labor helps account for the inequitable burden on employed women.

Beyond these traditional role expectations, another factor explaining the unequal household labor of the sexes is the higher salary potential, and hence greater contribution to household income, of men compared to women. On the average, wives earn 60 percent of the amount earned by their husbands, and, importantly, that female proportion *decreases* with husband's socioeconomic status; so that among husbands with salaries between $12,000 and 15,000, wives' earnings represent 70 percent of the husbands', and among husbands with salaries between $15,000 and 20,000 and $20,000 and 25,000, the wives' proportionate earnings decrease to 60 and 50 percent, respectively (Benenson, 1981). In this way, the earning potential and economic contribution of husbands results in men being excused from housekeeping and in women being allocated these tasks.

Attempts to change the traditional division of labor at home are often highly motivated but still subject to difficulty (Hall and Hall, 1979:117; Nadelson and Nadelson, 1980). This is because intellectual commitment to equality between the sexes is one thing, while emotional and behavioral adjustment is another, and men and women tend to experience resistance and anxiety when stepping out of accustomed roles. Furthermore, couples who make these changes generally get little social support, and frequently get a good deal of social opposition. Carol and Theodore Nadelson (1980), who are themselves a dual-worker couple, describe this resistance of community and tradition to redefinitions of husband's and wife's roles:

> The husband who was brought up to believe that housework is women's work may be resentful of the demands on his time, or he may experience anxiety because of his perceived failure to live up to what he unconsciously believes to be a masculine role. Furthermore, he may find that colleagues at work are unsympathetic or even frankly hostile when he takes time off to take a child to the dentist or a parent's meeting. . . . The wife in this situation often experiences even greater conflict and anxiety, despite her commitment to an egalitarian model. (Nadelson and Nadelson, 1980:93)

Problems with Work

Working couples face problems not only in managing their home, but also in managing their work and their relationship with each other. For many of these couples, the fundamental work problem is simply finding two jobs that will provide satisfactory employment and still allow them to live in the same area and coordinate work and nonwork schedules. The traditional solution was to regard the husband's job as primary and the wife's secondary, so that even if both partners worked, the demands of the husband's employment determined locale and the wife just followed. And, in fact, this is still the dominant pattern among working couples (Berger, Foster, and Wall-ston, 1978). But it is becoming less common, and other factors, beyond simple sex-role directives, determine variation in the job-seeking problems of dual-worker couples.

In explaining variation in job-seeking problems, the first factor to consider is the couple's degree of occupational specialization. Locating two jobs in one locale is particularly difficult in specialized fields that may be practiced in only a limited number of settings or organizations. Location of jobs is less difficult in more general, and in certain free-lance, occupations. Thus, the husband and wife specializing, respectively, in restoration of classical antiquities and in microscopic biology are likely to encounter more difficulties locating employment in one locale than is the couple interested in more general areas within art or biology. Flexibility is afforded, particularly, to those couples among whom one or the other partner is a free-lance or autonomous worker—such as a writer, photographer, or artist—who is free to settle in any number of locales. However, the relative market demand for the occupational skills is also a factor, and while location flexibility may be afforded by certain general or free-lance fields such as elementary-school teaching or journalism, there must also be sufficient demand for the skills in order to make the relocation possible.

The relative difficulty encountered in coordination of partners' jobs is determined secondly by the centrality of work in their lives (Berger et al., 1978; Hall and Hall, 1979). Among partners for whom work is a mutually central and primary life concern, coordination may be difficult. For these couples, compromise in job choice and decisions involves pivotal areas of satisfaction and esteem, and adjustment of one partner to the other may be fraught with conflict and resentment.[5] On the other hand, when one or both of the partners places priority on nonwork aspects of life (for example, friends, sports, recreation), compromise in job choice and decisions is more palatable.

In explaining difficulties in job coordination, a third factor is the respective work stages of the partners. The most compatible combination of stages, however, is debatable. Some commentators maintain that partners who are both at the same stage in their jobs are able to provide understanding and support for each others' decisions. Yet the peership of shared statuses can breed comparison and an overflow of similar pressures. Hence, others would maintain that complementary, rather than parallel, stages are more compatible. In this way, a partner well established and senior in job status might provide security and support for the partner just beginning or changing a career. For example, researchers studying married partners who were both sociologists found that the husbands, who as a group were older and well-advanced in their careers, were in a position to pass on information and experience that facilitated their wives' careers (Martin, Berry, and Jacobsen, 1975).

Although difficulties of job seeking and coordination may vary with the factors discussed, dual-job couples do share some common work problems. A fundamental difficulty is simply that jobs, and especially careers (Papanek, 1973), have been designed around a traditional family with a full-time homemaker available to provide supportive services for the full-time worker. Dual-job couples, however, do not have the domestic and emotional aid of auxiliary partners. And this absence of backup help at home can make them less able and competitive at work (Hunt and Hunt, 1977; Rice, 1979). More specifically, while a person with a partner available to cook, clean, shop, and entertain is able to take on extra-heavy demands at work and do a good job with them, people without auxiliary help may be constrained in the number of clients they can meet, papers and reports they can write, or conferences they can attend (or in the case of blue-collar work, the number of hours they can work or jobs they can take on). In this way, dual-job partners may be handicapped at work and overburdened at home.

In addition, dual-job couples encounter problems because of inflexible work schedules requiring that they start and stop work at fixed hours—which may conflict with the children's schedule. If an employee has a partner available at home to tend to children's comings and goings and adjust to their vacations and breaks, a fixed work schedule may be quite feasible. But for dual-job couples without such a partner, a workday that starts a half hour before the school day may create ongoing tension and strain. As we shall see later in this chapter, employing institutions have been very slow to respond to these conflicts by providing "flex-time" and other scheduling options.

Relatedly, the absence of good part-time work creates a problem for dual-job couples. Part-time work would allow these people to better accommodate both family and work responsibilities. But currently, part-time opportunities are limited and the available jobs are concentrated in the poorest-paying employment sectors—clerical labor, retail sales, food service, and cleaning (U.S. Department of Labor, Employment and Training Administration, 1977). Furthermore, part-time work usually disadvantages employees by exempting them from fringe benefits such as insurance and pension plans and paid vacations.

Another problem for dual-job couples lies in "nepotism" rules that prohibit the hiring and employment of husband and wife in the same organization or department. These rules are particularly constraining for couples who live in communities with a single employing institution or for couples whose skills and specialties are likely to be appealing to the same employer —were it not for the bias against hiring both husband and wife.

Problems with Relationships

As the preceding might suggest, the coordination of work and family patterns among two-job couples results in certain power dynamics, and in turn, problems in managing their relationship, as well as the outside world.

To begin with, one must understand the association between marital power and work roles. A major perspective on this subject argues that power of marriage partners is based partly on their relative resources—their income, education, occupation, and organizational memberships (Blood and Wolfe, 1960; Heer, 1962). Since employment brings salary, occupational status, and organizational participation, it is said to be associated with resources, and hence power. Correspondingly, it is contended that employed wives have more power than unemployed wives. The data do show an association of employment and power and suggest that dual-worker couples are likely to have less traditional (less male-dominated) patterns of influence and decision making (Blood and Wolfe, 1960; Buric and Zecevic, 1967; Safilios-Rothschild, 1967; Weller, 1968).

Yet these patterns of power and employment can result in struggle and conflict, jealousy and competition; and this is especially the case in those marriages that depart the most from the traditional model in their occupational, and domestic, roles. Thus, pressures may be especially strong among partners with comparable occupational success, or among those couples in which wife's status and success are higher than husband's. Still, competition and problems with the marital relationship are subject to the particular orientations of the partners to their work. If the wife is more successful, yet the husband is less work-involved and indeed supportive of his wife's ambitions, competition tends to be minimal. However, if both partners are upwardly mobile, work-involved, and ambitious, the stage may be set for conflict and stress (Berger et al., 1978; Rice, 1979).

This mutually high work involvement may, in fact, be an especially frequent occurrence among dual-career couples, because psychological reports indicate that people who enter dual-career marriages are likely to be highly achieving men and women for whom goal attainment and recognition are extremely important (Rice, 1979). In pursuing the achievement and success they feel they deserve, however, these partners may be making paltry investments in each other, and while they work their way up the career ladder they may leave their marriage behind. Furthermore, these hard-driving spouses may have few resources left for reinforcing each others' efforts and attainments, and consequently their respective dependency needs may be frustrated. In describing the consequences of high work involvement on a relationship, one young man says, "We both worked long, hard hours and had high-pressure jobs. We were both eager to achieve. . . . It strained the relationship. It became so that working at the relationship was just too hard. . . . Having both a career and a relationship requires full commitment. We couldn't maintain both" (Hall and Hall, 1979:220).

In order for the marital relationship to survive, the problem becomes one of attaining a tolerable balance and mesh of achievements between dual-career partners (Rapoport and Rapoport, 1976). But this is easier said than done. First, while professional women might be better balanced, emotionally, with less work-involved husbands, the cultural emphasis on hypergamy (marriage at the same or higher social level for women) makes marriage to nonprofessional men a difficult option. Hence, 80 percent of the female physicians, for example, are married to men in professional positions (Berman, Sacks, and Leif, 1975).

Second, when the "balance" and "tempering" of achievement is negotiated, it has tended to be at the expense of female, rather than male, attainments. Earlier studies of dual-career partners (Garland, 1972; Poloma, 1972) demonstrated that conflict was minimized because the wives essentially subordinated their success to that of their husbands. And thus the negotiation of achievement has been subject to sex-role inequities that penalize women.

Third, the "balance" of achievement often translates into the issue of time management and organization for work as well as nonwork activities. Yet many couples, especially younger ones, are reluctant to structure and schedule leisure, and believe that with "goodwill" and "trust" everything will be accomplished (Rice, 1979). However, as we discuss further in the second half of the chapter, time management is indeed a "skill," and good faith and intentions simply are not sufficient for getting things done (Seiden, 1980). Successful time management involves certain practices, such as the identification of goals, ordering of priorities, and distinction between the "important" (qualitatively) versus merely "urgent" demands (Lakein, 1974; Mackenzie, 1975; Moskowitz, 1981). And it is through this explicit planning that people may be able to attain a balance of goals.

The next section of this chapter discusses, in some detail, certain strategies for coping with the conflicts of overloads of work, family, and relationship we have outlined thus far. But before proceeding, it is well to make these points: first, in spite of the stresses and strains in dual-job or career families, the marriage satisfaction of these couples tends to be at least as high as satisfaction among couples in more traditional families (Burke and Weir, 1976; Staines, Pleck, Shepard, and O'Connor, 1978). And second, the children born to dual-job couples do not appear to be adversely affected by their parents' work and family arrangements (Rice, 1979). The conflicts and overloads of nontraditional arrangements appear to be compensated by certain rewards (such as stimulation and satisfaction) in the work and family lives.

WORKING OUT THE PROBLEMS:
WHOSE RESPONSIBILITY?

How are the competing demands from work and family to be resolved? Who has the responsibility for resolving the conflict and tensions of work and family life? Must individual couples find ways of adapting their lives to fit a society whose institutions and values conform to a traditional family model? Or must society itself, and its institutional framework in particular, make changes in order to accommodate new family forms? Embedded in these questions are two different approaches to resolving the problem: an individual approach and a structural approach. Each approach suggests a different perspective of and resolution to the problem.

The individual approach accepts the traditional values and attitudes about work and family life as the normal and proper ones, and assumes that individual couples must make the changes in their lives in order to accommodate themselves to the traditional model—regardless of the costs involved. From this perspective, if conflicts fail to be resolved, the couples simply have themselves, or those close to them, to blame.

In the following account, a twenty-six-year-old female surgeon illustrates an individualistic response to the demands placed on a dual-worker family. Here, she describes how medical students with families have had to resolve their dual-career dilemma by changing their own lives and exhausting themselves in the process. The students do not question whether or not the medical profession might accommodate itself to the needs of a two-career family:

> A lot of women in my class still go meekly along with the superwoman act, and they get upset when I raise questions. Every woman who finished her residency last year got pregnant, had her baby in December, and is now back working full time. When one of the coolest superwomen quit because she couldn't take it, the rest got panicky. What is necessary is for medical training to change, to really work for women and men with little kids. Men in medicine, working one hundred and ten hours a week, have to be supermen, too. It's very hard to say at seven o'clock at night, "My kids are waiting for me." The man in the lab next to me leaves his lights on so they won't know he goes home to eat with his kids. (Friedan, 1981:630)

A structural resolution to this dilemma would stress, on the other hand, the rigidity and unresponsiveness of the medical profession. This perspective would emphasize the need of institutions such as the medical profession to adapt the demands of the work place to a labor force that is made up increasingly of women with children. The structural perspective rejects the notion that occupations must follow the traditional model of full-time worker and full-time homemaker, and proposes, instead, alternative scheduling and career patterns that provide greater flexibility in work and family lifestyles. The structuralist approach is radical, however. As the following statement illustrates, the approach requires basic changes in the current structure of work and society:

> It is easy to devise work schedules and arrangements that will allow both men and women to share in child-rearing and fully participate in the life of our time, if both desire to do so. But to bring these changes about for any large numbers of people will require more changes in social and economic arrangements than other oppressed groups have had to acomplish. It requires us to ask, not how can women fit in, and advance in, the institutions as organized for men, but how should these institutions be organized so as to include women. For example, the question is still asked of women: "How do you propose to answer the need for child care?" That is an attempt to structure the question in old terms. The questions are rather: If we as a human community want children, how does the total society propose to provide for them? How can it provide for them in such a way that women do not have to suffer or forfeit other forms of participation and power and opportunities for genuine leadership? How does society propose to organize so that men can benefit from equal participation in child care? (Miller, 1976:127–128)

In the following sections, we examine the individual and structural resolutions, and their respective costs and benefits, both for society and for the individual. We determine which individual resolutions are successful for the dual-worker couple and which result, on the other hand, in increased stress for these families. We then examine particular types of structural resolutions and their accessibility to the average couple. In this way, we aim to consider as many options as possible for the resolution of conflict in dual-worker families.

Individual Resolutions

One of the major problems faced by dual-worker families is the lack of time because of multiple role demands. The management of time then becomes a critical skill for men and women who are trying to fulfill work and family responsibilities. A number of researchers have suggested strategies such as limiting the number of obligations, learning to say no at home and on the job, delegating certain responsibilities, and managing and planning for events and changes in one's life (Bliss, 1976; Fensterheim and Baer, 1975; Hall and Hall, 1979; Lakein, 1974). Writers on time management especially stress the use of a daily "to do" list, which specifies and orders the tasks one would realistically hope to accomplish on a given day. Next to each task, one indicates its rank order importance as A, B, or C, where A is the most important category. One then starts to work with the A-1 task and continues with it until completion. If interrupted, one needs to weigh the interruption against the importance of the task, by asking "Can I afford to take time out?"

Although time-management strategies can help dual-worker couples, the schemes are often mechanistic in their approach. Many of the techniques were originally devised for business organizations in order to increase the efficiency of their employees. Treating the dual-worker couple like a business organization can promote the "superman" or "superwoman" notion that one can "have it all" if only time is managed more effectively and efficiently. However, in managing time one must address factors such as the couple's definition of work and commitment to each other. And considering these factors requires broader strategies in order to accommodate both work and family roles.

One set of strategies, offered by Bailyn (1978), categorizes patterns of accommodation as limitation, recycling, and segmentation. *Limitation* involves reduction of involvement in either work or family by both partners. This might include a decision to have no children (or fewer), or a decision to step out of the most rapid promotion track at work. *Recycling*, the second strategy, involves a shift in the staging of work and family events. One type of recycling strategy involves having a family later in life, after educational and initial career demands have been met. One dual-career woman puts the strategy this way: "Put in intensive work between the ages of twenty-five to thirty-five to advance your career and complete your education during this period. Establish credentials and understanding of job responsibilities early" (Kelly, 1981:56). A second type of recycling advocates just the opposite—having family when young, and postponing maximum work involvement until latter stages in life. This strategy is illustrated by a mother who says, "I strongly feel the family should take priority because the formative years pass too quickly. There are many years to continue with a career after your children are grown" (Kelly, 1981:56). Both recycling stages can be costly, however. Women who put off their careers until children are raised may find age discrimination a problem, while those who postpone having a family may end up waiting too long because the time never seemed quite right for childbearing.

The third strategy of accommodation, *segmentation*, involves a strengthening of the boundaries between work and family life. A very basic form of this strategy is simply to leave one's work at the office and to reserve time at home for family concerns. However, while this strategy may be useful for some dual-worker couples, it may be a problem for couples whose jobs require work outside of the nine-to-five schedule. For example, while academia is often considered to be an area that allows the flexibility to mesh family and work lives, it is also an occupational sphere in which segmentation of work and family concerns is almost impossible. Academic life puts heavy pressure on a professor to keep up with the field, do research, write, and often consult—and these activities are very difficult to segment into a nine-to-five work day (Bailyn, 1978:165).

A more complete form of segmentation is geographic separation and long-distance commuting. Farris (1978) describes how this arrangement compartmentalizes work and family life:

> During the few work days away from home, the commuter is totally involved in work—long hours, busy schedules, and full concentration on work without interference from family demands. During the weekend, however, time and attention are devoted to family-oriented activities spending time with husband/wife and children. (Farris, 1978:101)

Farris reported that those couples who choose this lifestyle do so basically because of career concerns. Although all the commuting couples studied would have preferred a career near home, such factors as monetary reward, prestige, personal challenge, attractive colleagues, and future potential in the "away job" led them to choose this extreme form of segmentation.

Although the benefits of commuting are clear in terms of career advancement, the costs for the family are also evident. These costs include concerns about infidelity, child care, and the management of housework. In addition, financial burdens are greatly increased by such factors as extra travel, phone bills, and rent. In fact, the commuting couple may spend an additional $10,000 a year on these expenses (Hall and Hall, 1979:209).

Clearly, it is not impossible to combine work and family lives. It does, however, take planning and consideration, as the preceding strategies suggest. Couples must be flexible in their careers and be willing to compromise their ideal aspirations. Within the family itself, the same type of flexibility and pragmatism must be applied to household-task division and to child care. This may involve lowering housekeeping standards and learning to share or exchange home roles and tasks—admitting, for instance, that one's husband is a more efficient housekeeper or that one's wife is a better business manager. Hiring help and paying for services can also be an aid to those who can afford it (Hall and Hall, 1979:114).

Learning to share parenting is another important factor for survival of the two-earner family (Bernard, 1974). Successful sharing of child care depends on the willingness of both partners to assume social and emotional responsibility for the child. In most dual-job families, the mother has automatically assumed primary responsibility; the father has been peripheral to child care. However, research indicates that if fathers become involved in the parenting process at the onset (from the beginning of the pregnancy), they are more likely to develop a sense of responsibility and bonding toward the child.

Regardless of which individualistic solutions couples choose, it is clear that the traditional family and work structures are no longer viable for either the dual-worker or the dual-career family and that any individual will be limited in capacity to provide a resolution to strains between work and

family. Individual resolutions have only gotten men and women so far, and
to some extent they have stretched the fiber of the family too thin. Hence,
we must go beyond individual solutions, and examine possibilities for structural change within the society itself.[6]

Structural Resolutions

Despite the ever-increasing numbers of women workers, institutional arrangements continue to be based on the assumption that women do not
work, and that if they do they are secondary earners with primary obligations to home and children. Outmoded structural arrangements such as the
nine-to-five workday, extensive travel policies, lack of child-care facilities,
nepotism rules, and tax and Social Security laws all assume the traditional
family model and serve to constrain a family's ability to combine work and
family life. The structural resolutions suggested here are directed at changing these arrangements in order to give working couples the opportunity to
share and accommodate work and family life. These structural resolutions
range from the more conservative—restructuring of certain practices and
policies in the workplace—to a more radical restructuring of the entire
work environment.

The more conservative strategies involve a redefinition of the total time,
and the particular hours, of the work schedule. One of these options, as
noted in Chapter 6, is flex-time, a program that requires employees to be
present during certain core hours, with additional times at the employees'
discretion. The John Hancock Mutual Life Insurance Company of Boston,
for example, allows employees to work any eight-hour period between 7:30
A.M. and 5:10 P.M., provided that they're present for the core hours of
9 A.M. to 3:40 P.M. (U.S. Department of Labor, Employment and Training
Administration, 1977). Flex-time allows parents greater freedom to arrange
the work day in order to accommodate the demands of both work and
home life. It is speculated, additionally, that flex-time could result in greater
father participation in child care (Kanter, 1977b). It can also result in benefits to employers, through increased services and longer hours without payments for overtime (Rubin, 1979) and through reduced absenteeism and
tardiness (Polit, 1978:39).

Yet some researchers are critical of flexible work hours and suggest that
although it reduces conflict between family and work, it still allows women
to continue to bear primary responsibility for family work. Others note
that while flex-time solves some difficulties for parents, it does not handle
"the fundamental problem of creating time for parenthood" (Greenwald,
1977:186).

Not enough research has yet been accomplished to ascertain the real
beneficiaries, if any, of flex-time, but recent research has begun to explore
some of the issues. Under the auspices of the Family Impact Seminar, Bohen

and Viveros-Long (1981) explored the central question concerning the use of flex-time: namely, does it make a difference, and if so, who benefits? Using survey research techniques, they studied employees in the U.S. Maritime Administration, who had been on flex-time for one year. Their findings were less than favorable for flex-time scheduling. They observed that the families who were most helped by flex-time were those with the fewest work/family conflicts—women without children and men with wives not in the labor force. No significant progress was made in shifting household responsibilities to both spouses. Bohen and Viveros-Long (1981) suggest that until cultural values about work and family roles for men and women are changed, flex-time will have no significant impact on work/family conflicts.

If women and men are to combine work and family obligations, part-time work is another possibility. There is nothing really new about part-time work, as such—particularly for women. Women are the great majority (70 percent) of all part-time workers (Barrett, 1979b). Yet women pay a high price for part-time work, because these jobs are concentrated in the lowest wage sectors of the economy and are usually exempt from fringe benefits and opportunities for promotion (Smith, 1978; Greenwald, 1977). Removing the stigma from part-time jobs and providing part-time opportunities for professionals could be an important step toward integration of work and family lives. In Sweden, for example, part-time work without economic penalty is available to all men and women during the childbearing years. Such a structural modification assumes that not only women but also men have family roles which they need time to fulfill (Safilios-Rothschild, 1976:56).

Job sharing is a particular type of part-time work that could also reduce the strain for dual-worker families. Under the job-sharing option, one job is split evenly between two individuals, either two people who are married or those without special connections. However, job sharing has not been accepted in the work world, and it has the disadvantage of other part-time work—namely, difficulty in finding high-paying professional work open to less than full-time employment. In addition, job-sharing couples find their income limited, because they have one salary, but the expenses of two workers in clothing, transportation, and so on.

In one study of job-sharing couples, Arkin and Dobrofsky (1978) reported that couples felt they were working more than their half-time employment each, and that they had to "overcompensate" in order to convince dubious employers that job sharing was advantageous:

> Many feel it is "unprofessional"—the main complaint it seems. I'm not sure what that means. It seems to have something to do with a fairly rigid notion of number of hours put in at the job, amount of time spent "in evidence" . . . as well as what I find to be a male definition of "professional." In academics the term is anything but clear. Whether more time is spent on committees than with

students, or in the classroom, than on writing articles is judged positively by some, negatively by others. I can say that combined, we spend more time on committees, with students, as advisors, etc. than most members of our department. (Arkin and Dobrofsky, 1978:131)

Employers also object to job sharing because of its economic disadvantages, because two workers sharing a job can result in higher expenses for fringe benefits and Social Security payments (Carver and Crossman, 1980). In addition, union leaders have opposed job sharing because it can eliminate full-time positions.

Clearly, there are many conflicting viewpoints regarding the advantages and disadvantages of job sharing. It does allow couples a certain flexibility in combining their work and family demands. However, people who share positions often need to overcome many hurdles, not the least of which is the existing prejudice of their employers toward any form of part-time work. And, ironically, job sharing may result in couples spending more, rather than fewer, hours working—without a sufficient salary to support a family.

Beyond part-time work, job sharing, and flex-time, additional scheduling options are possible. These include (1) working an average 80 hours in a two-week period without being bound to an 8-hour day, (2) doing some work at home, or (3) taking unpaid leaves of absence in order to devote time to family, leisure, or education. Another option is the four-day week, which reschedules work hours from five 8-hour days to four 10-hour days. However, it is questionable whether this latter option maintains or diminishes traditional sex-role expectations; if men use the extra day to pursue leisure activities and women use it for household chores, it is obvious that sex inequality will only be reinforced by compressed work schedules (Polit, 1978:38).

Other large-scale changes can include parental work-leave policies for both men and women, such as those which exist already in Sweden, France, and Norway (Bohen and Viveros-Long, 1981). Shorter workdays for parents represent another option; in Sweden, for example, parents may work six-hour days at lower pay, but with the same job security, until their child is eight years old. Another possibility is parental insurance to cover absences from work following the birth of a child.

In addition, private companies can reduce the strains in dual-worker families by revising travel and transfer policies and nepotism rules. The elimination of unnecessary travel and transfers and the revision of nepotism rules would help reduce the conflict between family and work life. Companies can also help their employees by providing services, such as marital counseling, day-care centers on the work site, and after-school programs and facilities to accommodate children of working parents during school holidays (Hall and Hall, 1979; Bohen and Viveros-Long, 1981).

SOCIAL ATTITUDES AND SOCIAL POLICY

The problems raised by dual-worker families demand a thorough rethinking of our ideas concerning work, family, and gender roles. Men's and women's attitudes about their gender roles will need to move closer toward a model of greater equality in the sharing of work and family roles.

These changes in attitudes and consciousness should come about, in part, by the increase in sheer numbers of dual-worker families who are individually dedicated to building a relationship in which both men and women share the work and family responsibilities. But legislative changes are also needed to push society toward structural solutions of work and family conflicts.

As we shall see further in the next chapter, social policies such as tax laws, Social Security legislation, and child-care policies do have an impact on the work and living decisions of American households. The federal income tax codes, for example, have created a "marriage penalty," whereby a married working couple pay more in income taxes than do two persons filing as single individuals. In 1979, the estimated tax liability of 16 million couples exceeded $8 billion, solely because of their marital status (Levitan and Belous, 1981:30).[7] Although this tax policy has not had a significant impact on marriage plans of individuals, it may encourage a married woman to stay out of the labor force.

In addition, the Social Security Act, which was introduced in the mid-1930s—at a time when the majority of women were outside of the labor force—carries assumptions that men are full-time workers and women full-time homemakers. Although the participation of working wives has increased dramatically, with the result that more and more women are paying Social Security taxes, most women face the prospect of receiving benefits no bigger than, or only slightly bigger than, those they would receive if they had elected to stay at home.

Furthermore, as we shall see in the next chapter, the United States needs a cohesive, well-thought-out federal child-care policy, instead of the existing patchwork of federally supported programs, which are inadequate in meeting the needs, current or future, of the working parent. Research indicates that women are frequently unable to take advantage of education and employment opportunities because they lack adequate child care, and hence suggests the importance of child care in women's attainment of equal opportunity (U.S. Commission on Civil Rights, 1981:8).

In conclusion, a range of structural options—flexible hours, child-care arrangements, outside services, reorganization of work environment, and new and amended legislation—are possible resolutions for the work and family conflict. It is difficult to speculate about the long-range effects of these structural resolutions for the dual-earner family, but it is clear that the slow adaptation of the work world is long overdue. It is also clear that traditional models of family life are no longer the current pattern for the majority of Americans; and we must bring sex-role attitudes and behavior into balance with the reality of labor-force participation for both sexes. The most necessary structural resolution involves adapting the institutions of work and family and our attitudes about them to the realities of modern life. With expectations more in tune with the actuality of the dual-worker family, the integration of work and family life will be a much easier task.

SUMMARY

We have observed that despite changes in women's labor-force patterns, social institutions are still geared to the traditional family model. Employment institutions continue to operate as though households had one full-time worker and a full-time wife and mother; sex-role values continue to emphasize the importance of men's compared to women's opportunities and aspirations; and housework and child care are allocated disproportionately to women whether they are employed or not. These lags result in stresses and strains, conflicts and overloads, in couples' work and family roles and relationship with each other.

The strain and problems in work, home, and relationship do vary, however, and depend on domestic factors such as personal housekeeping standards, the presence or absence of children, the availability of outside help, and the particular allocation of household tasks. They also depend on work factors, such as partners' specialization, involvement, and stage in work or career.

Still, nearly all dual-job couples are "caught" between traditional family values and the newly emerging dual-worker patterns. And they face common problems as the demands of new roles are added to, and often conflict with, traditional role obligations.

In resolving these strains and conflicts, strategies can focus on the individual or on the structure of work and society. The individual emphasis and approach tend to accept the traditional values and attitudes about work and family and to assume that individuals should make changes in their lives and accommodate to the traditional model. The structural approach rejects the notion that occupations must follow the traditional model of one full-time worker and one full-time homemaker, and proposes, instead, alterations in the organization of work and society.

On the individual level, the strategies often stress the importance of careful management of time. They also emphasize patterns of "accommodation" to work and family, such as (1) reduction of involvement in either work or family roles, (2) postponement of work involvement until children have grown, or (3) the strengthening of "boundaries" between work and family (the more extreme versions of which involve geographic separation of partners and long-distance commuting). Other individual patterns of resolution focus on a lowering of housekeeping standards and sharing of parenting.

Despite the usefulness of certain individual strategies, the approach tends to stretch the fiber of the family and leave couples with themselves to blame if adjustments are unsuccessful. In order to reduce the strain between work and family, we must ultimately introduce greater flexibility into the structure or organization of work. Specific proposals include the creation of flexible work schedules, job-sharing plans, and parental-leave policies. In addition, the expansion of part-time work with good pay and full benefits would permit both men and women greater opportunity to combine work and family obligations without the loss of fringe benefits, paid vacations, and health plans. Other possibilities include the development of federal child-care policy and abolition of restrictive legislation—which are analyzed further in the final chapter.

9 • Prospects and Strategies for Change: An Institutional Perspective

We have seen that women's experience and status at work reflect and connect with their position and plight in other organizations, institutions, and settings throughout the society. In order to understand women's position in the labor force, we have analyzed the particular linkages between work and society's other institutions—the family, the schools, and the government, as well as the economic system. In doing so, we have seen that women's status at work mirrors the constraints of family burdens, biased educational practices, and discriminatory employment structures and political and legal policies. Women's individual-level characteristics—their beliefs, attitudes, and behaviors—are never a sufficient explanation of their status in the work place. To understand women's status at work, we must examine institutional and organizational arrangements—including the settings in which women work, the jobs they hold, and other factors in the family, educational, and political systems in which they live and work.

In like manner, in order to change women's status at work—their pay, power, and prestige—we must understand the relationship between women, work, and the other institutional systems. Improvement in female occupational status entails more than change in the behavior of individual women—or even of men. It involves, instead, alterations and adjustments in the behavior and operation of each of society's basic institutions—its family, schools and colleges, employers and unions, laws, and political institutions. Moreover, there is probably no single point where we can exert pressure and expect the other institutions to follow suit (Schaeffer, 1976).[1] For example, we cannot simply alter educational practices, and expect hiring processes, wage policies, and legal standards to follow. Rather, in order to improve women's plight in one sphere, we must also make adjustments in the others. Hence, increasing female opportunities in management and professions will have only limited benefit if domestic responsibilities and arrangements continue to burden women. And equal access of the sexes to graduate education will do little good if the hiring of executives and professionals continues to be an informal process of recruitment through the "old-boy network." In this final chapter, we explore, then, the ways in which four major social institutions—family, education, economy, and political order—must alter and adjust together in order to achieve occupational equity for women.

More specifically, this chapter has two objectives. First, we aim to review and summarize the ways in which each of the four institutions have operated to disadvantage women in the labor force. Second, we propose specific ways in which each of the institutions can undergo change in order to improve the labor-force position of women. Although earlier chapters have offered strategies for improving the employment status of women in particular occupations and situations, this chapter offers a more comprehensive discussion of strategies to redress the disadvantaged position of women both within and between occupational classifications.

FAMILY AND HOUSEHOLD

Work outside the home is becoming the norm for American women as it is for men; and perhaps most notably, labor-force participation is becoming the norm for mothers as well. Since 1970, the greatest increases in female labor-force participation have been among women under age thirty-five and among mothers with preschool children (Kamerman and Kahn, 1981:25). By 1978, half of American mothers with children under age six, and 60 percent of the women in the prime childbearing and -caring years (ages twenty-five to twenty-nine) were working outside the home. These proportions are expected to be even larger in the next two decades—as each successive cohort of young women participates more fully in the labor force (Lloyd and Niemi, 1979; Smith, 1979). In addition, responses to national surveys indicate that women view work as central to their lives and that they would choose employment even if they could manage comfortably without earned income (Kamerman and Kahn, 1981:25). All this points toward a trend of permanent or lifetime labor-force commitment and attachment for women—similar to that of men.

However, these data also point to a fundamental problem—of tension between work and home for people who want or expect children, and for the whole society, which if it is to survive, needs these children (Kamerman and Kahn, 1981; Land, 1980). As we discussed in the previous chapter, the tensions between work and family have been managed in the past through a traditional family model, with one full-time worker who provides income and a full-time homemaker who provides the backup and support that make possible both the work involvement and the child and house care. To put it another way: both the organization of work and the traditional arrangement of the family have depended for their functioning on the subordination of women's interests to those of her home and children (see also Degler, 1980). But if women are to work outside the home and still bear children, the traditional assumptions and solutions are no longer tenable, and the resulting tensions indicate the need for a response and adaptation by the society at large.

Thus far, nothing has been done that would in any way indicate a rational response to or policy on the fundamental problem of child care and rearing for working parents. In fact, as Kahn and Kamerman (1981) point out, the reverse seems to be true, since although participation in preschool programs by children of working parents has increased, most of the care has been in private programs that have gone unnoticed. Although an estimated several million children need care, facilities are currently available for only about 900,000 children (U.S. Department of Labor, Employment and Training Administration, 1977).

The possible options for child-care policy fall broadly into two categories—benefits and services. The term *benefits* refers to cash or in-kind payments, such as cash maternity benefits, child-care allowances, social insurance, or tax benefits. These benefits are aimed to facilitate both parenting roles and responsibilities and the care and rearing of the young. One alternative is a six-month maternity leave that could be divided between parents, so that the mother takes the first three months and the father the second three months, or the mother the first part of the week and the father the second part of the week for the full six-month period. Maternity benefits such as these would legitimize shared parental responsibilities from the time of birth and would provide viable care for a child's first months of life (Safilios-Rothschild, 1974:22). The United States, however, is one of the few Western, industrialized nations without such benefits for parents and children. Among the six nations (France, Federal Republic of Germany [West], German Democratic Republic [East], Hungary, Sweden, and the United States) in Kamerman and Kahn's (1981) study, the United States was the only country without universal maternity benefits. And presently, the basic U.S. child-care benefit, Aid for Dependent Children, is restricted almost completely to single-parent, female-headed families; moreover, that benefit is designed primarily to support mothers who are *not* in the labor force (Kamerman and Kahn, 1981).

A second broad option for child-care policy centers not on such cash benefits or payments, but rather on out-of-home services for infants, toddlers, and children. The aim of the service is to encourage or make possible the employment of adults without endangering the socialization, development, and learning of children. Importantly, despite much myth and rhetoric to the contrary, out-of-home care does not appear to be harmful for either children or their families. In fact, current research indicates that day care has a "neutral" effect on children since "on all measures of intellectual, social, and emotional functioning, children attending day-care programs for several years did as well or better than equivalent samples of home-reared children" (Silverstein, 1981:295). The critical and current issue, then, is not *whether* day care is necessary or justifiable, but rather *how* and in what form it should be provided.

The day care needed can take two basic forms: care in a household (sometimes confusingly called "family care") and care in a center. Each of these two modes of child care have their relative costs and benefits. The advantages of household care are its flexible hours, similarity to the child's home, and possibilities for individualized attention; disadvantages include problems with quality control, less stimulating and interesting settings, poorer staff quality, and reinforcement of female stereotypes (since men almost never staff this type of care). The center care, on the other hand, offers advantages of peer interaction, better possibilities for equipment, materials, and resources, and a caretaking role that can be professionalized; disadvantages include the "collective" approach and less individualized attention of this care. In order to better evaluate these modes of child care, research is needed to determine the particular effects on children of such variables as child/staff ratio, group size, caretaker qualifications, educational and developmental services, nutritional standards, and parental involvement in the care (Kamerman and Kahn, 1981; Sander, Julian, Stechler, and Burns, 1972; Silverstein, 1981).

The national need for such investigation and provision of day care is becoming urgent. Yet there is no explicit policy either at the federal or state levels as to the place in our society of child-care services. Nor is there policy or direction as to the form that care should take (Kamerman and Kahn, 1981). The price of this nonpolicy is lack of standards, goals, and guidelines for benefits and services. Furthermore, "nonpolicy" is, tacitly, a support of existing laws and statutes—in areas of tax, pension, Social Security, and insurance—which implicitly or explicitly carry assumptions about the traditional roles of men and women. Under the Social Security law, for example, two-earner families have received smaller benefits, relative to payments they have made, than do one-earner families—reflecting the notion that men are the primary workers and that women's labor is only secondary (Gordon, 1979).

Laws such as these act in support of a traditional division of labor between the sexes and a traditional model of family and household. The failure to reformulate social policy so as to remove invidious distinctions between men and women (Ratner, 1979) simply supports the status quo. Specifically, "nonpolicy" supports the ideology that ascribes to women responsibility for family and domestic tasks—whether they are employed or not. These family and household burdens can draw on women's time and resources in such a way as to make them less competitive at work, and, reciprocally, their disadvantaged position in the marketplace can depress and restrict their employment aspirations. Policymakers voice a reluctance to intervene in the private and domestic sphere. But a "nonpolicy" on household and child care is, by default, a support of the traditional arrangements and institutions that constrain women's choices and opportunities.

The society can reallocate the child care, in various ways and degrees, through the operation, subsidy, regulation, and/or licensing of services and benefits. At the least, we need some systematic programming, policy debate, and leadership concerned with the issues. And ultimately we must face the fundamental concern with "development of alternative ways for adults, regardless of gender, to manage both family and work roles simultaneously, without undue hardship for themselves or their children" (Kamerman and Kahn, 1981:3). As long as women, alone, are allocated responsibility for children and household, and as long as that responsibility is taken for granted and undervalued, women's opportunities and position in the labor market will be limited (Land, 1980). Changes will not occur in either women's home or market status until the existing laws and statutes, which support and sustain gender divisions, are challenged by reformulated social policy.

EDUCATION

Educational trends over the past two decades show mixed prospects for women's educational future. On the positive side, female enrollment in colleges and universities has been increasing steadily over the past decades, and by 1978 women represented 50 percent of all postsecondary students, and half of all recipients of bachelor's degrees (Heyns and Bird, 1982). In addition, the educational concentrations and specializations of women are not as sex typed and traditional as formerly, and they do show some shifts away from teaching and toward technical and scientific areas. Yet men are still twice as likely as women to specialize in the physical science and business areas, and seven times more likely to concentrate in engineering. The vast proportion of undergraduate women continue to cluster in the humanities, in certain health sciences, and especially in education (Heyns and Bird, 1982).

Similarly, in postbaccalaureate education, women's attainments show mixed prospects. Fifteen years ago, women earned less than 5 percent of the professional degrees; the proportion rose to 12 percent in 1975, and to 19 percent in 1977. In doctoral degrees, also, the proportion earned by women rose from 11 percent in 1965 to 21 percent in 1975, so that by 1977 almost 25 percent of the nation's doctorates were awarded to women. Yet, as in undergraduate education, there are striking sex differences in graduate students' areas of concentration. Women tend to concentrate in areas aligned with poorer-paying, lower-status fields—the arts, education, and services. Men, on the other hand, pursue fields aligned with the better-paying and more powerful positions of business, science, and technology (see Fox, 1981a).

Moreover, as we discussed in Chapter 3, it is not simply that educational attainments and specializations vary for men and women. Rather, from grade school to graduate school, the whole experience and process of education differs for men and women. To summarize: the segregation and tracking of the sexes in activities and groups, the imagery and content of books, and the sex-biased structure of authority and patterns in student/faculty interaction result in different educational processes and different outcomes for males and females. Compared to males, females experience lowered esteem, stunted confidence, depressed aspirations, and restricted development in technical and scientific capacity. These experiences are, in turn, reflected in women's occupational "choices" and "preferences" and ultimately in their concentration in certain traditionally female-typed occupations—as secretaries, bookkeepers, schoolteachers, social workers, and nurses. In short, young women have extended their aspirations about as far as prevailing definitions of femininity, and moreover prevailing opportunities, permit (see Laws, 1978; Kanter, 1977a).

Social policies and strategies should be concerned, then, with the ways in which occupational options become known to women and with the particular educational supports that can foster increased possibilities for women (Laws, 1978). Likewise, strategies must confront the obstacles in education that currently hinder women's aspirations, efforts, and opportunities in the marketplace. In this way, strategies must redress the practices that directly segregate and track males and females into different curriculum groups and activities. Strategies must redress also the more indirect and implicit messages of texts, teachers, and staff that socialize the sexes into different occupational outcomes.

Segregation and Tracking in Education

In Chapter 3, we discussed the particular ways in which schools segregate males and females in their informal play and activities and in their formal classes and curriculum. To encourage occupational equity, we must redress this tracking of the sexes, and its reinforcement of the separations and divisions of men and women in the labor force at large. Among the various arrangements of educational segregation and tracking, two of the most important areas for occupational equity are vocational education and the mathematics curriculum.

Vocational education

Although females constitute over half of the students in vocational education, the great majority are concentrated in either homemaking or office-skills programs (see Chapters 3 and 6). Women are underrepresented in technical, industrial, and agricultural programs. And the small minority of women in the trade and industrial areas are concentrated in such traditionally feminine fields as cosmetology, textile production, and art (Rieder, 1978). Essentially, male students are being trained for the better-paying and more highly skilled jobs in technical fields and industrial trades, and females for low-paying and already overcrowded jobs in the clerical and retail areas. Moreover, the homemaking, clerical and retailing courses in which women are the majority have lower teacher/student ratios than do the technical programs in which males are the majority. And the programs in which men are concentrated have a higher proportion of funds allocated to them (Saario, 1976).

Because vocational education provides students with knowledge and skills, as well as placement into their first jobs, this education represents a critical juncture between school and work (Rieder, 1978). Thus educators have both the responsibility and the means to do something about these patterns of educational segregation and their occupational outcomes. Educators can take steps to broaden aspirations and break down vocational stereotypes by measures such as developing auxiliary materials on occupational options, inviting speakers currently engaged in fields atypical for their sexes, and forming student groups to discuss occupational alternatives (Wirtenberg and Nakamura, 1976). Another useful strategy would be an increase in the number of female teachers and administrators in male-typed courses, and the number of male teachers in female-typed programs—hence providing role models for nontraditional aspirations of both men and women.

A more controversial strategy for integrating curriculum is a policy of compulsory attendance for both males and females in certain prevocational courses in industrial arts, home economics, and handicraft areas. Compulsory attendance has been justified as a necessary measure for breaking sex stereotypes in a transition stage during which students are themselves unable to make stereotype-free decisions (Safilios-Rothschild, 1974). Compulsory measures have been further defended as a means of ultimately expanding, rather than restricting, educational and occupational choices. The goal, after all, is not to encourage every female student to choose a traditionally masculine field, but rather to develop human beings free to act in ways appropriate to their interests and abilities, rather than simply to their sex (Schlossberg, 1972).

Mathematics curriculum

Along with strategies to correct vocational segregation, measures are also needed to reduce the tracking of the sexes in math and science programs. Mathematics is critical as the "filter" subject necessary for continued education in 75 percent of all college and university majors, including business, medical, scientific, engineering, and architectural programs (Sell, 1974). Importantly, the study of mathematics is a structured sequence in which one must complete a given course in order to progress to the next. Once out of track and sequence, it is very difficult to catch up. And most women never do. At a tender age, females opt out of the math sequence, and in doing so they are shut out of the vast majority of better-paying occupations, including engineering, physical and biological sciences, financial management, and computer work.

In correcting this female pattern, a fundamental aim is to make clear the occupational and lifetime consequences of mathematical skills, and to remove numbers, logic, and problem solving from the dominantly male realm. Toward that end, particular strategies include removing from mathematics texts the sex-biased content of story problems that depict boys as enterprising figures who build things and go places and girls as more timid and domestic characters who illustrate problems by measuring ingredients, cutting fabrics, and shopping for food (Federbush, 1974; Frazier and Sadker, 1973). In addition, teachers and counselors need to be vigilant about providing encouragement and raising expectations for females compared to male students.[2] Traditional female socialization patterns, which have encouraged tension, panic, and anxiety about mathematics (Tobias, 1978), should be actively countered. Female students need support from their teachers and counselors in developing aspirations, confidence, and motivation for mathematical achievement.

Furthermore, although mathematics is indeed a structured sequence of study and although it is advantageous to correct sex-biased practices in the elementary and secondary schools, strategies need not be limited to young students. They can be applied also to adults (at college and postcollege level) who need to correct math deficiencies and increase their occupational options. Recently, in fact, a number of courses, workshops, and clinics have been organized to "recapture women (and others) who have long ago decided they were 'nonmathematical'" (Tobias, 1981:17).

Finally, scholars must confront the allegations in both the academic and popular press that the female mind inherently resists mathematical logic and problem solving. It would seem that confrontation of these allegations would be an easy and straightforward effort, since the previous "incriminating" research on sex differences in mathematical achievement has been poorly conducted and the supposedly "significant" sex differences have been largely discounted (Tobias, 1981:17). Yet, when the prestigious journal, *Science*, carried in its December 1980 issue a study (Benbow and Stanley, 1980) reporting that among gifted seventh- and eighth-grade students, the males consistently outperformed the females in mathematics, the news media immediately picked up the damaging evidence and produced such scathing headlines as "The Math Gene" (Tobias, 1981:17). This episode points to the enduring popular beliefs and attitudes about the "natural" mathematical ability of males compared to females (see Tobias, 1981) and to the need to confront allegations about "inherent" differences between the sexes. As we discussed in Chapter 3, it is not that biological or genetic factors are inconsequential. Rather, it is that any genetic factors are so conditioned by social expectations that the relative contribution of genetic differences—in mathematics or any other area—depends on the social setting and environment in which men and women interact.

Texts, Teachers, and Staff

Chapter 3 documented the particular ways in which textbooks and readers reinforce stereotypes of males as capable and industrious actors and of females as passive, ineffectual, and largely domestic characters. To correct these inequities, instructional materials must eliminate patronizing language and messages to females and must omit the stereotyped portrayal of the sexes. Instead, materials need to emphasize the actions and achievements of women, and the full range of human interests, traits, and capabilities of both sexes (Task Force on Women in Education, 1978b). To implement these aims, specific devices include (Task Force on Women in Education, 1978b:15–16):

1. The use of universal rather than masculine terms (such as *humanity*, *person*, or *people*, rather than *man*, and *s/he* rather than *he*)
2. The use of neutral rather than masculine terms for occupations (such as *firefighter* or *police officer* instead of *fireman* or *policeman*)
3. The use of parallel gender terms (such as *men and women* rather than *men and girls*)

4. Avoidance of gender personification of inanimate objects (such as female references for ships and hurricanes); and
5. Avoidance of gender modifications for occupations (such as *woman doctor*)

To induce publishers to implement these changes, several strategies are useful. First, protesting letters to publishers are helpful—probably because of publishers' sensitivity to the potential loss of income that unfavorable reviews can incur (Safilios-Rothschild, 1974). Second, the establishment of high-prestige rewards in all fields for stereotype-free texts and illustrations would be an incentive for authors to produce nonsexist materials (Safilios-Rothschild, 1974). Strategies such as these would help bring attention to, and correct, the language, role models, and cultural stereotypes in curricular materials that influence the occupational aspirations and possibilities of women.

Beyond the messages of texts and materials, the teachers themselves contribute to sexism in their higher regard for and more active instruction of male compared to female students (see Chapter 3). To some extent, these biases lie beneath teachers' level of awareness, but certain measures can increase consciousness of sexist attitudes and behaviors (Task Force on Women in Education, 1978b). One way to increase awareness is to have teachers evaluate the level of sex discrimination and sex-role stereotyping in their own schools and classes. Teachers can evaluate, specifically, the different standards of achievement they may apply to male and female students, the extent to which they award grades according to these expectations, and the different kinds of classroom activities they may organize for each sex. In developing teachers' objectivity about their own attitudes and behavior, it has been useful to have them observe and evaluate videotapes of classroom behavior (Task Force on Women in Education, 1978b). Moreover, it is important to caution that "liberation from sexism is not a definite state that, when reached, is free from backsliding" (Safilios-Rothschild, 1974:31). Even after training and awareness sessions, teachers and their schools have to continuously monitor themselves for perpetuation of sexist practices and procedures.

Along with teachers, counselors are especially crucial for students' occupational socialization, because they are the official resource people for help with educational plans and career options. Yet, because the counseling field has clung to practices based on male-centered psychology, theory, and thought (Verheyden-Hilliard, 1978), its operations help perpetuate sex inequity. Given such counseling practices, it is understandable that "young women seem to be low on information with regard to the range of possible occupations, what they entail, and the payoffs associated with them" (Laws, 1978:302). To break this reinforcement of restricted female options, the counseling profession needs to free the psychological and vocational tests of sex bias.[3] Moreover, the counseling field needs to examine and redress the theory and assumptions that underlie its messages as to what is "normal" and "appropriate" for women. As is, counselors have merely reinforced the restricted aspirations and options of women, and they have in turn, encouraged women's location in low-paying, overcrowded, and sex-typed jobs.

Throughout the educational system, from grade school through graduate school, women's aspirations would also be enhanced by the presence of females in positions of power and prestige. However, we find throughout educational levels that "the higher the rank, the fewer the women," and thus students learn implicitly about the subordinate position of women simply by virtue of exposure and observation in school. Research indicates that in those elementary and secondary schools that have women administrators, the self-image and career aspirations of female students are higher than usual (Task Force on Women in Education, 1978a).

In higher education, as well, female students experience broadened aspirations when they are exposed to female role models, whose presence suggests the real possibility of nontraditional attainments (Fox and Faver, 1981; Faver, Fox, and Shannon, 1982). The mere presence of women in nontraditional areas and positions is not sufficient, however. Female students also need the informal training and education and the interaction and support of faculty in these positions (see Chapter 6). Moreover, as organizational research indicates, employment aspirations are not simply a function of motivation and ability, but rather of available *opportunities* (Kanter, 1977a). Hence, we must consider in the following section the particular employment practices that would create and maintain those job opportunities for women. But before turning to that discussion, we need finally to examine Title IX statute in education and to evaluate how that legislation does and does not implement the strategies for sex equity in education.

Title IX

In June 1972, the Higher Education Act signed into law, and provided in its Title IX a mandate for sex equity in education. Title IX states that "No person in the United States shall, on the basis of sex, be excluded from participation in, be denied the benefits of, or be subjected to discrimination under any education program or activity receiving federal assistance." Thus, the law applies to almost all schools receiving federal grants, from preschools to graduate and professional schools.[4] It also applies to other groups related to education, such as boards of education, state departments of education, and federal bureaucratic personnel.

In barring sex discrimination in education, Title IX covers job access and promotion in education as well as almost every aspect of student life. The act prohibits practices such as requiring different courses for male and female students, allowing boys but not girls to be safety guards, awarding academic credit for athletics to boys but not girls, and requiring higher grades for college entrance from female compared to male applicants (Sandler, 1978: 3–4). However, while the act is broad, it does not cover discriminatory aspects of texts and instructional materials. The U.S. Department of Health, Education, and Welfare "recognized that sex stereotyping in curricula is a serious matter," but it concluded nonetheless, that "any specific regulatory provision in this area would raise grave constitutional questions under the First Amendment" (U.S. Department of Health, Education, and Welfare, 1974).

The legislative mandate of Title IX is broad, but legislation lives and dies, not by its mandate, but rather through its enforcement (Scott, 1974). And owing to the low priority placed on women's rights, public demand for enforcement of Title IX has been limited. Furthermore, implementation is hampered by ambiguities in the definition of both educational discrimination and remedial action. For example, if boys and girls enroll in equal numbers in a vocational class, but boys are the majority who seek employment, it is unclear whether the school has discriminated against females. Likewise, if a school board, facing a budget crisis, discontinues a music program in which male and female enrollments are roughly equal instead of an interscholastic sports program in which males predominate, it is unclear whether the school has discriminated against female students (Saario, 1976). School systems have few precedents or models available for resolving these problems.

In employment within education, the implementation of sex equity is also fraught with problems. To begin with, compliance decisions are generally in the hands of male administrators. But beyond this issue of administrators' protective self-interest, budget considerations also intrude (Saario, 1976). Purposeful affirmative action requires substantial reallocations of funds for training women and for remedying pay differentials. Yet in a budget in which 80 percent of the total is earmarked for salaries, affirmative action takes a low priority (Saario, 1976). And unions, caught between the interests of male teachers with years of seniority and the demands of those women and minority members hired as a result of affirmative-action programs, cannot be counted on for remedial action.

Hence, to implement equity in education, we do need clearer and less ambiguous definitions of discrimination. But we also need more vigorous enforcement and firm sanctions for noncompliance—neither of which are provided fully by Title IX.

EMPLOYMENT AND ECONOMY

Although the female component of the labor force has greatly expanded, we have seen that women's share of labor-force rewards remains limited. To summarize: In their employment, women are concentrated in low-ranking positions and in low-status, principally sex-typed, occupations. The majority of American women are employed at jobs in which at least 70 percent of their fellow workers are female (Blau, 1978), and this level of concentration is as high now as it was at the turn of the century. Specifically, one-quarter of all employed women are working in just five types of jobs—as secretary, household worker, bookkeeper, elementary-school teacher, and waitress. And if we add typist, cashier, nurse, and seamstress to this list, we have accounted for the occupational locations of 40 percent of all female workers in America (Blau, 1978). Furthermore, within every occupational group women's earnings are less than men's (U.S. Department of Commerce, Bureau of the Census, 1977). And across all occupations, women who work full time, year round, earn only 60 percent of that earned by men. Moreover, the size of this gap in men's and women's salaries has not decreased in the past thirty years.

To improve the labor-force status of women, certain socialization processes and family constraints must be altered, as we discussed in the previous sections. But alterations must occur also within the economic and employment structures, themselves. These alterations include modifications in salary policy, recruitment procedures, work structures, and labor unions.

Salary Policy

In a capital-based economy, such as ours, a salary is valued not only for the goods it buys but also for the success it reflects.[5] In such an economy, salary represents more than the payment for one's work; it is also a tacit statement of one's social worth (Williams, 1960; Wilson, 1971). Moreover, salary is a commodity that can be easily counted and assessed, while other employment rewards such as power or authority are not so quantifiable. Thus, in the struggle for equity between the sexes, salary equity—"equal pay for equal work"—is a fundamental issue. Salary inequity doesn't hurt only women; it also harms children and men. As we have seen in Chapter 2, the majority of women are either heads of household themselves (single, divorced, separated, or widowed), or they are married to men whose earnings are less than $10,000 a year. Inequitable wages for women, then, reduce family income and standard of living.

Since 1963, the United States has, in fact, had a federal law prohibiting wage discrimination between the sexes (see Chapter 4). This Equal Pay Act mandates equal pay for work that requires equal skill, effort, and responsibility and that is performed under similar working conditions in a given establishment. Salary differentials are permissible, however, if based on seniority, merit, or factors other than sex.

A great deal of litigation of the act, however, has dealt with the meaning of "equal work" (Greenberger, 1980). Under the act, equality does not require identical jobs, but rather "substantive equality" in the skill, effort, and responsibility of the jobs. Furthermore, these three criteria (skill, effort, and responsibility) are determined by the actual demands of the job, not simply by the description or classification of the position. Consequently, an employer cannot justify a higher salary for a man compared to a woman simply because the man has some capability that the woman lacks—unless the job really requires that skill (Greenberger, 1980). Moreover, employers may not automatically assign higher value and salary to jobs that require the physical effort more likely to be exerted by a man; under this law, physical and mental labor are both "substantively equal" efforts of a job (Greenberger, 1980).

The Equal Pay Act has certainly sharpened awareness and sensitivity to salary disparity between the sexes. And it has resulted in a number of suits and back-pay awards. The Wage and Hour Division of the Equal Employment Opportunity Commission reported that, between 1965 and 1976, $135,590,752 was due to employees underpaid according to the Equal Pay Act. Of this, only $29,562,135 (or 22 percent of the total amount) had been restored (see Greenberger, 1980: Table 4–3). However, even if vigorously enforced, the act has no effect on the salaries of the vast proportion of female workers who are employed in low-paying, low-status jobs, with no male counterparts. These female-typed jobs, into which the large proportion of working women are concentrated, have been underpaid and undervalued in comparison with male-typed positions. For example, positions such as nurse or secretary, which require considerable skill, effort, and responsibility, have been undervalued in relationship to male-typed jobs such as salesman (Greenberger, 1980). To truly achieve "equal pay for equal work," the female-typed jobs must be analyzed and evaluated according to some neutral principle.

In both the state of Washington and West Germany, studies using such job analysis and evaluation have, in fact, uncovered "significant disparities in the wage rates of men and women in comparable jobs" (Ratner, 1980: 430). However, in both situations, demands to raise the salaries of women have gone unheeded, and women workers included in these studies continue to be underpaid for work assessed as equivalent to better-paying male jobs. And to date, little can be said for the U.S. government effort to spearhead action toward standards and enforcement of equal pay for work of comparable value.[6] Yet, as long as the labor force remains sex segregated, and women remain in sex-typed positions, salary equity will depend on neutral assessment of "women's jobs" and payment according to comparable values of effort, skill, and responsibility. For this reason, the drive for equal payment for comparable worth has been called "the civil rights issue of the 80s for working women" (E. H. Norton, quoted in Jacobson, 1981:5).

Recruitment and Hiring Procedures

Traditionally, hiring for jobs, especially for the better-paying ones, has been an informal process in which search and selection is made through a "male network" on the basis of loosely defined, unwritten, and subjective criteria. Because women are outsiders to these networks, they have not even had the chance to compete for certain positions. Hence, the open posting (or advertising) of jobs is a critical factor in employment equity for women.

To provide a basis for these postings, it is necessary for organizations to assess and specify the qualifications and competencies needed for successful performance of a given job. Organizations and firms, however, have resisted such specification and have defended shifting criteria as a "flexible" standard. "Flexibility" may be a favored organizational norm, but the problem for women and minorities is that this flexibility "keeps other things from being equal" (Huber, 1973). When standards are unclear, unwritten, and flexible, white males tend to be perceived and evaluated as better qualified than women (Fox, 1978:ch. 7). Under these conditions, ascribed characteristics such as sex are especially likely to determine rewards (Epstein, 1970).

Employment equity requires more, however, than open posting and standardized criteria. Equity in employment requires affirmative action to advance women and to break the preferential hiring of white males. An affirmative-action policy for employment of "underutilized groups" is required, under the law, by Executive Order 1126 (see Chapter 4). But this order covers and sanctions only those employers who receive federal contracts of $50,000 or more and who have fifty or more employees. Furthermore, those businesses that are indeed covered by affirmative action have resisted, avoided, and procrastinated implementation of the order. For example, employers have frequently filed affirmative-action programs that they never intend to follow, and have held hundreds of interviews with women but made few job offers. Or they may set demanded credentials at such a level that, owing to earlier discriminatory practices, women cannot meet the qualifications (Safilios-Rothschild, 1974:55). In addition, businesses have restricted their compliance with Executive Order 1126 to the most blatant tokenism—appointment of a sole woman to a "high position" that has been stripped of its former power and prestige, or appointment to a high-ranking title robbed of the backup needed to effect any consequence in the organization.

Not only have businesses failed to comply with affirmative action— government agencies have also failed to enforce the order. The report of the General Accounting Office found that compliance agencies seldom investigated or monitored the affirmative-action goals and timetables of business and industries (Greenberger, 1980). And rarely have strong sanctions been imposed. In fact, although some federal contracts have been delayed because organizations' affirmative-action plans were unacceptable, no federal funds have actually been withheld because of sex discrimination (Raffel, 1979:113).

This is not to say that Executive Order 1126 has made no gains for women. It has prodded certain businesses to develop affirmative-action plans, and it has provoked remedial settlements.[7] Affirmative action has acted, in some sense, as a "protective shield" against discrimination in employment (Benokraitis and Feagin, 1978:194). But in general, victories have been isolated, and advances have been small.

Work Structures: Hierarchies and Schedules

Among women in the labor force, the largest proportion (35 percent) are clerical workers; in comparison, only 6 percent of male employees are in these occupations. As we saw in Chapter 5, in most companies, lines of mobility from clerical occupations to higher-level jobs simply do not exist. And the women in these clerical positions are stuck in jobs with short promotion ladders, low ceilings on pay and prestige, and few possibilities for development. As long as females remain concentrated in such positions, and as long as these jobs remain low paying, there is little likelihood that the status of employed women will improve.[8]

To advance the possibilities of clerical workers (and hence the majority of employed women), tracks of mobility into other jobs and functions must be recognized and created (Kanter, 1976). Clericals need the opportunity to prepare for and move into these jobs. Once located in new positions, they also require training and supervision to develop career plans and managerial skills. In addition, because organizations are created, maintained, and dominated by men and because women are outsiders to this world, females need special access to the support and communication—the people and resources—which can help them do the job and accomplish their goals. (For more detailed discussion of these strategies to improve women's status in management, specifically, see Chapter 6.)

Women's employment status will improve not only from movement *out* of clerical ranks but also from modifications *within* these positions. Importantly, the secretary/boss relationship could be changed from a personal relationship to a more rationalized position with job descriptions and performance appraisals (Kanter, 1976). These modifications would create a "work contract" for clerical employees, enabling them to be evaluated for the work they do, rather than for the personal relationship they are able to form. In addition, these periodic appraisals of performance would be helpful in sharpening skills and identifying potential for mobility.

Along with these modifications in the organization of clerical work, women's employment status would be fundamentally improved by alterations in the evaluation and rewards of part-time work. The part-time issue is critical because most employed women are, in fact, part-time workers. Only 40 percent of all female workers and 10 percent of all married female employees work full time the year around. The remainder hold part-time employment for either the whole or part of the year, or they work part time for some fraction of the year (Kreps and Leaper, 1976).

We have seen in previous chapters that part-time work carries heavy penalties—low pay, little job security, and few benefits. Most part-time jobs are concentrated in clerical work, retail sales, food services, and cleaning—all poor-paying areas. Furthermore, only half of all part-time workers receive holiday or vacation benefits, and these workers rarely receive health benefits or pension plans (U.S. Department of Labor, Employment and Training Administration, 1977). Part-time workers have been regarded by employers as a marginal labor force, used to meet temporary overload, expand customer service, and minimize costs by avoiding overtime salaries for full-time workers (U.S. Department of Labor, Employment and Training Administration, 1977).

To improve the status of the females, who constitute the bulk (70 percent) of part-time workers, we must remove this link between part-time work and an inferior market position. Industries should establish flexible work schedules and part-time options in better paying areas and positions; and they should provide part-time workers with the benefits of full-time work, including pensions and insurance, as well as seniority, vacations, and leaves of absence. Specific options include (1) alternatives of work during part of the year, the month, the week, or the day; (2) flex-time, which provides for flexible starting and finishing times, but requires workers to be on the job during certain core hours; (3) job sharing, which allows one position to be allocated between two persons; and (4) child-care leaves for both men and women. (More detailed discussion of these particular scheduling options can be found in Chapters 6 and 8.) Measures such as these will not only broaden employment options but also integrate part-time work into the organization, and thereby will help to remove the marginal employment status of these workers.

Labor Unions

Within labor unions, women do not fare any better than they do in the society at large (see Chapter 5). In 1974, women comprised 21 percent of all union members, but only 7 percent of the office holders. Even in unions with predominately female membership, such as Amalgamated Clothing and

Textile Workers, women are not in top positions as national executive board members or vice presidents (Wertheimer, 1980). Moreover, women's interests and concerns have been traded off at the bargaining table, if they get there at all (Wertheimer, 1980).

To improve the status of women workers, it will be necessary to organize more women into unions and to introduce women and their interests into union leadership. The labor union is a critical locus of concern because each of the functions of the union—collective bargaining, political action, and worker education—carry the potential for furthering the priorities of women workers (Ratner, 1979; Wertheimer, 1980). Hence, in collective bargaining, issues such as flex-time, parental leaves, and child-care provisions can and should be negotiated and promoted at contract time. Through political action, women can be provided with invaluable skills and leadership training. And with worker education, attitudes conducive to sex equity can be advanced.

Economic Conditions

Women's labor-force prospects depend on certain practices of recruitment, hiring, and reward in employment, as we have discussed. But these employment practices are, in turn, contingent on aggregate conditions of the economy. A strong economy, by itself, will not generate employment equity for women, but such an economy does provide a more favorable environment for equal employment practices (Smith, 1980). Upgrading the salaries of female-typed jobs and expanding opportunities and rewards to part-time workers, for example, requires a growing economy. And the movement of women out of low-paying, low-status positions and into jobs with greater possibilities requires the creation of new jobs—unless our goal is to replace them with women and put men into an unemployed group (Norwood, 1976). Therefore, "without a healthy labor market, it becomes all the more difficult to increase women's share of employment" (Smith, 1980:364).

Yet current economic conditions foretell recession rather than growth. Not since the Great Depression of the 1930s has unemployment been so high for such a sustained period of time. And in the 1980s workers are facing fewer options than those available in the 1960s and early 1970s. Under these conditions of decreasing options and reduced opportunities, workers with weaker roots in the labor force are likely to be singled out as those who should be "at the end of the queue" and at the bottom of the payroll (Smith, 1980:364). Despite the increase in women's labor-force participation and the growth in the number of female-headed households, a scarcity of jobs could, then, resurface the earlier view that women are secondary workers who should stay out of, and marginal to, the labor force—leaving the better jobs and the higher pay to men (Barrett, 1976). For example, when U.S. District Judge Fred Winner turned down the claim of nurses in Denver, Colorado, that they should be paid as much as the male tree trimmers working for the city, he said that the nurses' claim was "pregnant with the possibility of disrupting the entire economic system of the country" (see Jacobson, 1981:5). Thus, as we shall see further in our subsequent and final section, strategies for equity in employment depend, in part, on the awareness, support, and action of the public.

POLITICAL INSTITUTIONS

Throughout this chapter, we have seen (1) that strategies toward occupational equity for women involve reorganizations of family, education, and employment, and (2) that these adjustments necessarily involve political and legislative action. We observed, for example, that existing laws and statutes in areas of tax, pension, and social security implicitly and explicitly support assumptions about the traditional roles and labor divisions of men and women. The reallocation of women's household and family burdens will, then, require redress of these laws and a reconstruction of social policy that expands opportunities for men to participate more actively at home and for women to participate more fully and equitably at work and in the society at large. In education, likewise, we explained that equity for the sexes depends, in part, on legislation that helps to identify and correct the educational practices that currently hinder women's opportunities in the marketplace. In employment, as well, we saw that any substantial change in economic and employment structures will require public analysis, redress, and enforcement.

Integral to this political evaluation and action, is the prevailing definition and conception of "discrimination." In the early days of the 1964 Civil Rights Act, discrimination was simply viewed as a "human problem" of ill will toward women and minorities. Thus, enforcement focused on eradication of bias and bigotry, and the government's compliance strategy emphasized "skillful persuasion through conciliation" (Robertson, 1980:128). Such an enforcement strategy, emphasizing elimination of prejudice, did little to redress the practices and policies that actually disadvantage women and minorities. The Equal Employment Opportunity Commission (EEOC) next focused on the behavior rather than the attitudes of employers, and discrimination was defined in terms of "unequal treatment" because of race, religion, national origin, or sex. The third and subsequent stage, however, shifted attention from unequal treatment toward the practices that gave rise to the disadvantaged status of the minority group in the first place (Robertson, 1980). This then shifts focus toward the *impact* of practices, or the different ways, for example, in which institutions recruit, hire, and promote men compared to women. In this way, we concentrate *not* on remedy for the individual, but rather on change throughout the entire system. And, in fact, it is a "systemic perspective" that has guided (1) our analysis and explanation of women's employment status and (2) our proposals and strategies for correction of this disadvantaged female status.

Specific solutions for redress of women's employment status do begin with a particular definition and perspective of discrimination. But beyond this, solutions require vigorous and consistent monitoring and enforcement of the law. Such enforcement is, however, restricted by certain political attitudes and realities. First, the Congress and administrative agencies responsible for enforcement of occupational equity have perceived sex discrimination as "less invidious" than other types of discrimination (Walum, 1977). Consequently, programs have been poorly coordinated and weakly enforced. This laxness is attributable in part to a belief that sex stratification is a "natural and necessary" part of a social order in which men and women have different—and unequal—roles, responsibilities, and options. In addition, awareness of sex discrimination is limited by domestic arrangements in which men and women living together have been unable to look beyond private issues toward public concerns. Hence, although women are the largest and fastest-growing constituency in America, they still lack strong political advocacy. As Jessie Bernard (1981) points out, politics is a "male preserve."

Enforcement of employment equity is constrained not only by political attitudes that are tolerant of sex discrimination but also by a political tradition that relies on individual litigation as a means of redress. Of all the strategies for sex equity in employment, individual lawsuits are probably the most inefficient and ineffective (Ratner, 1980). Judicial proceedings are expensive, time consuming, and often frustrating, because judges vary in their commitment to equal-employment policy (see Dunlap, 1977). Individual litigation should not, on the other hand, be abandoned altogether, because at an early stage in policy development it is useful in stimulating political action and providing a viable means of redress for employees (Ratner, 1980). However, for large-scale and systemic change, we must look beyond redress of individual cases and focus, instead, on modification of the structure of work and society.

As we have emphasized, improvement in women's position in the labor force depends not simply on change in the behavior of individual men or women, but rather on alteration in the operation of society's basic institutions. Every major institution in society—the family, the schools, the polity, and the economy—carries assumptions about the traditional roles of the sexes and thus contributes to women's subordination by restricting their opportunities and promoting their marginal status in work and employment.

Equity for women in employment will depend, then, on certain alterations in household burdens, educational processes and practices, and employment structures and political policies. Only by altering basic institutional arrangements will we lift the constraints on both the aspirations and efforts and the opportunities of American women at work.

STRATEGIES FOR CHANGE: SUMMARY AND CONCLUSION

Throughout this book, we have emphasized that work and employment are not isolated aspects of women's lives, and that in order to understand women's status in employment we must analyze the linkages between women's work and their plight and position in society's other institutions—the family, schools, and the political system, as well as the economy. Likewise, in order to change the labor-force status of women, we must alter the structure and operations of each of these institutions.

To begin with, we must alleviate the family burdens that fall disproportionately on women. As long as women are expected to manage the children and household, and as long as those responsibilities are undervalued in the society at large, women's status and opportunities in the labor force will be limited. Basically, we need to develop alternative ways for adults of both sexes to manage family and work roles without damage to themselves or the children. Specific strategies to facilitate parenting include social benefits such as six-month maternity leaves that can be divided among parents, thus legitimizing shared parenting from the start.

A second strategy centers on services for the out-of-home care of infants, toddlers, and children. Although half of American mothers with children under age six are in the labor force, and although an estimated several million children need care, facilities are available for only about 900,000 children. This points to a pressing national need for the investigation and provision of child care—either through the operation, subsidy, regulation, and/or licensing of these services.

In education, strategies must redress the practices and arrangements that currently constrain women's aspirations, efforts, and opportunities in the labor force. Specific areas for redress include

1. The elimination of sex segregation, stereotyping, and tracking in vocational education and mathematics curriculum, and increased opportunities for women in these areas
2. Elimination of the patronizing messages and stereotyped portrayals of the sexes in texts and materials
3. Increased consciousness and correction of sexist practices and proce-

dures in classroom and counseling office, such as differential standards of achievement, activities, and vocational supports for male versus female students

4. Concerted efforts to alter the sex-biased structure of authority and to increase the proportion of females in positions of power and prestige throughout elementary, secondary, and higher education

Along with adjustments in the family and in education, alterations must be made in the economic and employment structures themselves. Particular strategies include

1. The development of salary policies and standards of equal pay for comparable effort, skill, and responsibility
2. Open posting and standardized criteria for the recruitment, hiring, and promotion of personnel
3. Affirmative action to advance women and break the preferential hiring of men
4. Open lines of mobility from clerical and other jobs that currently have short promotion ladders and low ceilings on pay and prestige
5. Introduction of flexible work schedules and part-time options
6. The organization of women into unions and introduction of women and their causes into union leadership

These strategies for sex equity in family, education, and employment rely, in turn, on the behavior of political institutions. Alterations of household burdens, educational arrangements, and employment opportunities will depend on political action to help identify the practices and arrangements that restrict women. Moreover, it is the political institution that must monitor and enforce the laws and statutes necessary for correction of women's disadvantaged status in the work place. As early civil rights legislation has indicated, attitudes are an important part of the movement toward equality and opportunity for groups, but attitudes often follow rather than precede behavioral adaptations of both individuals and organizations and institutions. For this reason, the political institution—and its active identification, monitoring, and enforcement of equity—is a critical area for intervention in the movement toward equity for women in work and society.

Notes

1 · Introduction: The Study of Work

1. The following historical discussion of work values draws on Tilgher (1962).

2. However, while the participation of women in the labor force is increasing, that of men has been decreasing. The decrease in men's rate of participation is attributable to the trends of longer educational training and younger retirement age over the century.

3. This perspective is most apparent in the stratification theories of the functionalists (see Parsons, 1942, 1953), who maintain that social arrangements stem from inherent needs of the society and that the parts of a social system are basically in harmony with each other. But this perspective of the family is also characteristic of Marxists and other nonfunctionalists (Machonin, 1970; Wesolowski and Slomczynski, 1968), who maintain generally that social relations are characterized by conflict and dissension among competing groups in the society.

2 · Women in the Work Force: Past and Present

1. Scharf (1980) notes that the Depression's impact on women in the professions had long-lasting effects:

The replacement of women by men in colleges and universities produced a multiplier effect. The absence of models of achievement in visible academic pursuits reinforced a sense of futility where female aspirations and goals were concerned. Fewer women, therefore, obtained the training necessary for attaining high professional status in the future. (Scharf, 1980:93)

3 · Family and Educational Context: Socialization for Work

1. For an analysis of the other ways in which professional structures disadvantage women, see Chapter 6, on women in professional and managerial occupations.

2. This does not explain *why* the feminine-typed occupations are poor-paying jobs. For that discussion, see the economic arguments in Chapter 4.

4 · Working Women: Economic and Legal Context

1. This description of occupational differences reflects what is known as the "functionalist" perspective, which assumes that inequalities such as unequal rewards are necessary for society because they motivate individuals to work hard and to aspire to difficult work that requires talents and skills not distributed equally among individuals. The functionalist perspective assumes that some positions in society are "more important" than others and should therefore be more highly rewarded. This perspective differs from a "conflict" perspective, which argues that inequalities result not from the fact that some jobs are more important than others (a claim it disallows) but from the ability of those in control (of the political and economic structures of society) to maintain their privileged positions. For a detailed presentation of the functionalist perspective, see Davis and Moore, 1945; for a detailed criticism of the functionalist perspective, see Tumin, 1953.

2. Even when women enter male-dominated occupations such as medicine, gender roles and family responsibilities may influence the specialty areas women select. Kosa and Coker (1965) state that "women doctors tend to manage their professional careers by selecting for work those fields of practice which are least likely to offer work duties incompatible with the female task" (1965:295). They cite as illustrations women's preference for pediatrics (which combines the nurturing role within the work context) and the tendency of male physicians to be primarily in private practice (with its unscheduled hours) and of female physicians to be concentrated in salaried (regular hours) positions.

Yet there are problems with this argument. Although socialization may influence women's selection of specialty areas, other factors are also important. Primary among these are the semiexclusionary practices of the medical profession itself, as was noted in a recent study of sex typing in medicine (Quadagno, 1976).

3. According to this perspective, a segmented labor market promotes employee stability in jobs that require an extensive manpower investment in human capital (the primary sector), while retaining the ability to expand and contract employment in other jobs as economic conditions or technology require. Creating and manipulating sexual divisions within the labor force is one important way to accomplish this. For example, introducing new female occupations in previously all-male fields is a means of overcoming male opposition to de-skilling, or reducing the level of skill—and pay—needed for a job (Beechey, 1977:54–55). Another way involves the creation of factions within the working class (such as ethnic subdivisions). By doing this, employers reduce the potential for class conflict at the work place and prevent the formation of a unified working-class consciousness. Usually an employer will differentially reward some employees (the most militant and best organized groups within the working class) while increasing their power over less vocal, poorly organized groups (Burris and Wharton, 1981:10).

4. Confusion over the legality of quotas and other forms of affirmative action remains widespread. This confusion is exemplified by the *Bakke* decision. Allen P. Bakke, a thirty-eight-year-old white engineer, claimed that the minority-admissions plan of the University of California Medical School at Davis had made him a victim of reverse discrimination. In 1978, the U.S. Supreme Court ruled (in a 5–4 ruling) on this case that (1) the minority-admissions program of the University of California Medical School at Davis had discriminated illegally against a white male applicant but (2) that the university could legally consider race a factor in admissions.

5 · The "Ordinary" Woman at Work: Clerical and Blue-Collar Occupations

1. A word processor is a computerized machine with a keyboard like a typewriter. Most word processors have a CRT (cathode-ray tube) screen on which a page of the text being typed appears, memory storage on floppy disk, and a printer for printing out the final copy (some printers can print 425 lines per minute). The text can be edited and corrected on the screen before being printed out, eliminating the need for retyping whole pages when changes in the text are to be made.

2. Personal communication from an office worker.

6 · Women in Professional and Managerial Occupations

1. Women in the professions are also the focus of numerous scholarly works (for example, see Astin, 1969; Epstein, 1970; Rossi and Calderwood, 1973; Theodore, 1971).

2. Here, Hennig and Jardim's work (1977) is contradicted by other research (for example, Kegan, 1964; Bardwick, 1970; and Marciano, 1981, discussed in Chapter 3) contending that compared to men, women depend more directly on, and react more directly to, the responses of others.

3. Ascriptive characteristics are personal attributes (such as age, sex, and national origin) that are relatively fixed and unalterable.

4. For examples of the formation of such groups, see Bowker (1981) and Candy (1981).

7 · The Minority Woman at Work

1. The Bureau of the Census sometimes groups women of Spanish origin with whites; its figures concerning minority and nonminority populations should be interpreted accordingly.

8 · Problems and Strategies for Dual-Worker Families

1. The decline is attributable also to the growth in the proportion of childless and single-parent households, but those family arrangements are, in turn, strongly associated with female employment (although, of course, the cause-and-effect relationships are uncertain). For discussion of the effects of women's employment on marriage patterns, see Hofferth and Moore, 1979.

2. Careers are occupations characterized by continuous participation, strong commitment, and involvement as a life's work.

3. The term *social roles* refers to the expectations—rights and duties—of the social positions we occupy (see Chapter 3).

4. Early research maintained that children do suffer from the mother's employment (Bowlby, 1953; Spitz, 1945), but that research has been discredited. The error of the earlier research lay in extrapolating data on apathy and retardation among institutionalized children and in misapplying those data to children separated from their parents simply by their parents' daily employment.

5. The issue of work centrality is particularly critical among professional and managerial employees with high career commitment. But it is pertinent also in certain craft and operative areas, where work involvement can be very high.

6. Correspondingly, Betty Friedan (1981) has called for a movement toward a "second stage" in development of equality for the sexes. She notes that the first stage of change aimed to break down the bastions of male exclusivity—to have women fully participate in the political, economic, and social institutions. In the second stage, however, she says that we must reexamine the work demands of corporations, education, and government, and must restructure these institutions so that men and women are able to organize their lives to achieve an equitable balance between success in work and gratification in personal life (Friedan, 1981).

7. Recent legislation passed by Congress has given some relief for the two-wage family. To soften the "marriage penalty," a special deduction for two-earner married couples was passed by Congress. For 1982, the initial limit was 5 percent of the first $30,000 earned by the lower income spouse, for a minimum of $1,500. By 1983, the deduction was 10 percent or a maximum of $3,000.

9 · Prospects and Strategies for Change: An Institutional Perspective

1. On the other hand, the cycle of women's subordinate position can be modified by certain "systemic jolts" such as war or a new method of organizing labor. Major social "jolts" can act to change both the demand for labor and the goals and values of the society (Strober, 1976:296). Thus in Chapter 2, on historical trends, we observed changes in women's labor-force position as a function of war and technological revolution.

2. In the following subsection, we further discuss strategies for sex equity in texts and in the behavior of teachers and counselors as they apply to curriculum *in general*, rather than to mathematics specifically.

3. New testing forms have been developed, but old sex-biased procedures continue to linger (see Chapter 3).

4. The statute exempts military schools if the school's primary purpose is to actually train students for military service. It also exempts religious institutions if the antidiscrimination provisions are inconsistent with religious custom or practice. In addition, it excuses admissions to private preschool, elementary, and secondary schools and to single-sex undergraduate institutions.

5. The term *salary* here refers to all forms of pay, including hourly wages and piecework rates of payment.

6. In 1979, the Equal Employment Opportunity Commission did offer a brief as friend of the court for a case (*International Union of Electrical, Radio, and Machine*

Workers v. *Westinghouse*) appealing equal payment for work of comparable value performed by women and by men.

7. The most notable settlement was American Telephone and Telegraph Company's payment in back wages to thousands of women and minorities who had been denied pay and promotion opportunities.

8. Upgrading the salaries of clerical positions to reflect their level of skill, responsibility, and effort is another option for improving women's employment status, as discussed in the previous section on salary policy.

References

Abbott, Edith. *Women in Industry*. New York: Appleton, 1910.

Abrams, Mary. "Title IX—A Modest Success." *Graduate Woman* 76 (January–February 1982):23–25.

Abromowitz, Stephen I., Weitz, Lawrence J., Schwartz, Joseph M., Amira, Stephen, Gomes, Beverly, and Abromowitz, Christine Z. "Comparative Counselor Inferences Toward Women with Medical School Aspirations." *Journal of College Student Personnel* 16 (March 1975):128–130.

Acker, Joan. "Women and Social Stratification: A Case of Intellectual Sexism." *American Journal of Sociology* 78 (January 1973):936–945.

Acker, Joan. "Introduction: Women and Work." *International Journal of Sociology* 5(Winter 1976):3–13.

Acker, Joan. "Issues in the Sociological Study of Women's Work." In Ann H. Stromberg and Shirley Harkess, eds., *Women Working: Theories and Facts in Perspective*, pp. 134–161. Palo Alto, Calif.: Mayfield, 1978.

Aldridge, Delores. "Black Women in the Economic Marketplace: A Battle Unfinished." *Journal of Social and Behavioral Sciences* 21(Winter 1975):48–62.

Alexander, Vicki. "The Nature of Professional Training for Minority Women: An Overview." In Lucy Ann Geiselman, ed., *The Minority Woman in America: Professionalism at What Cost?*, pp. 15–25. Proceedings of the Program for Women in Health Sciences Conference at University of California, San Francisco, March 1979. San Francisco: University of California, August 1979.

Almquist, Elizabeth M. *Minorities, Gender, and Work*. Lexington, Mass.: Heath, 1979.

Almquist, Elizabeth M., and Wehrle-Einhorn, Juanita L. "The Doubly Disadvantaged: Minority Women in the Labor Force." In Ann H. Stromberg and Shirley Harkess, eds., *Women Working: Theories and Facts in Perspective*, pp. 63–88. Palo Alto, Calif.: Mayfield, 1978.

Amsden, Alice. *The Economics of Women and Work*. New York: St. Martin's Press, 1980.

Anderson, Karen. *Wartime Women: Sex Roles, Family Relations, and the Status of Women During World War II*. Westport, Conn.: Greenwood Press, 1981.

Angrist, Shirley S., and Almquist, Elizabeth M. *Careers and Contingencies: How College Women Juggle with Gender*. New York: Dunellen, 1975.

Anthony, Susan B. *Out of the Kitchen—Into the War*. New York: Daye, 1943.

Arkin, William, and Dobrofsky, Lynne. "Job Sharing." In Rhona and Robert N. Rapoport, eds., *Working Couples*, pp. 122–137. New York: Harper & Row, 1978.

Astin, Helen S. *The Woman Doctorate in America*. New York: Russell Sage Foundation, 1969.

Astin, Helen S. "Factors Affecting Women's Scholarly Productivity." In Helen S. Astin and Walter S. Hirsch, eds., *The Higher Education of Women*, pp. 133–157. New York: Praeger, 1978.

Astin, Helen S., and Bayer, Alan E. "Pervasive Sex Differences in the Academic Reward System: Scholarship, Marriage, and What Else?" In Darrell R. Lewis and William E. Becker, eds., *Academic Rewards in Higher Education*, pp. 211–229. Cambridge, Mass.: Ballinger, 1979.

Axelson, Leland J. "Marital Adjustment and Marital Role Definitions of Husbands of Working and Nonworking Wives." *Marriage and Family Living* 25 (May 1963): 189–195.

Backhouse, Constance, and Cohen, Leah. *Sexual Harassment on the Job*. Englewood Cliffs, N.J.: Prentice-Hall, 1981.

Baer, Judith A. *The Chains of Protection: The Judicial Response to Women's Labor Legislation*. Westport, Conn.: Greenwood Press, 1978.

Bahr, Howard M., Chadwick, Bruce, and Strauss, Joseph. "Discrimination Against Urban Indians in Seattle." *Indian Historian* 5(4), (Winter 1972): 4–11.

Bailyn, Lotte. "Accommodation of Work to Family." In Rhona and Robert N. Rapoport, eds., *Working Couples*, pp. 159–174. New York: Harper & Row, 1978.

Baird, Leonard. *The Graduates*. Princeton, N.J.: Educational Testing Service, 1973.

Baker, Elizabeth F. *Technology and Women's Work*. New York: Columbia University Press, 1964.

Baker, Mary Anne, Berheide, Catherine W., Greckel, Fay R., Gugin, Linda C., Lipetz, Marcia J., and Segal, Marcia T. *Women Today: A Multidisciplinary Approach to Women's Studies*. Monterey, Calif.: Brooks/Cole, 1980.

Baker, Sally Hillsman. "Women in Blue-Collar and Service Occupations." In Ann H. Stromberg and Shirley Harkess, eds., *Women Working: Theories and Facts in Perspective*, pp. 339–376. Palo Alto, Calif.: Mayfield, 1978.

Baker, Sally Hillsman, and Levenson, Bernard. "Job Opportunities of Black and White Working-Class Women." *Social Problems* 2 (April 1975): 510–533.

Bandura, Albert. "Social-Learning Theory of Identification Process." In David A. Goslin, ed., *Handbook of Socialization Theory and Research*. Chicago: Rand McNally, 1969.

Bandura, Albert, and Walters, Richard H. *Social Learning and Personality Development*. New York: Holt, Rinehart, & Winston, 1963.

Bardwick, Judith, "Psychological Conflict and the Reproductive System." In Judith Bardwick, ed., *Feminine Personality and Conflict*, pp. 3–28. Belmont, Calif.: Brooks/Cole, 1970.

Barnett, Rosalind C., and Baruch, Grace K. *The Competent Woman: Perspectives on Development*. New York: Irvington, 1978.

Barrett, Nancy Smith. "The Economy Ahead of Us: Will Women Have Different Roles?" In Juanita M. Kreps, ed., *Women and the American Economy*, pp. 155–171. Englewood Cliffs, N.J.: Prentice-Hall, 1976.

Barrett, Nancy S. "Women in the Job Market: Unemployment and Work Schedules." In Ralph E. Smith, ed., *The Subtle Revolution: Women at Work*, pp. 63–98. Washington, D.C.: Urban Institute, 1979b.

Barrett, Nancy S. "Women in the Job Market: Unemployment and Work Schedules." In Ralph E. Smith, ed., *The Subtle Revolution*, pp. 63–98. Washington, D.C.: Urban Institute, 1979b.

Barron, R. D., and Norris, G. M. "Sexual Divisions and the Dual Labor Market." In Diana L. Barker and Sheila Allen, eds., *Dependence and Exploitation in Work and Marriage*, pp. 47–69. London: Longman, 1976.

Baruch, Grace K. "Maternal Influences upon College Women's Attitudes Toward Women and Work." *Developmental Psychology* 6(January 1972):32–37.

Baxandall, Rosalyn, Gordon, Linda, and Reverby, Susan. *America's Working Women: A Documentary History—1600 to the Present*. New York: Vintage Books, 1976.

Bayer, Alan E., and Astin, Helen S. "Sex Differentials in the Academic Reward System." *Science* 188(May 23, 1975):796–802.

Beale, Francis. "Double Jeopardy: To Be Black and Female." In Toni Cade, ed., *The Black Woman: An Anthology*, pp. 90–100. New York: New American Library, 1970.

Beck, E. M., Horan, Patrick, and Tolbert, Charles. "Stratification in a Dual Economy: A Sectoral Model of Earnings Determination." *American Sociological Review* 43(October 1978):704–720.

Becker, Gary S. *The Economics of Discrimination*. Washington, D.C.: Brookings Institute, 1957. (2nd edition, 1971.)

Becker, Gary S. *Human Capital*. National Bureau of Economic Research General Series, no. 80. New York: Columbia University Press, 1964.

Becker, Gary S. *Human Capital: A Theoretical and Empirical Analysis, with Special Reference to Education*. New York: National Bureau of Economic Research, 1975.

Bednarzik, Robert W., and Klein, Deborah P. "Labor Force Trends: A Synthesis and Analysis." *Monthly Labor Review* 100(October 1977):3–12.

Beechey, Veronica. "Female Wage Labour in Capitalist Production." *Capital and Class* 3(1977):45–66.

Bell, Duran, Jr. "Why Participation Rates of Black and White Wives Differ." *Journal of Human Resources* 9(Fall 1974):465–479.

Beller, Andrea H. "The Impact of Equal Employment Opportunity Laws on the Male/Female Earnings Differential." Paper presented at the Department of Labor and the Barnard College Conference on Women in the Labor Market, Barnard College, New York, September 29–30, 1977.

Benbow, Camille P., and Stanley, Julian C. "Sex Differences in Mathematical Ability: Fact or Artifact?" *Science* (December 12, 1980), pp. 1262–1264.

Benenson, Harold. "Family Success and Sexual Equality: The Limits of the Dual-Career Family Model." Paper presented at the annual meetings of the American Sociological Association, Toronto, Canada, August 1981.

Benet, Mary K. *The Secretarial Ghetto*. New York: McGraw-Hill, 1972.

Benjamin, Lois. "Black Women Achievers: An Isolated Elite." *Sociological Inquiry* 52(2), (Spring 1982):141–151.

Benokraitis, Nijole V., and Feagin, Joe R. *Affirmative Action and Equal Opportunity: Action, Inaction, and Reaction*. Boulder: Colo.: Westview Press, 1978.

Berger, Michael, Foster, Martha, and Wallston, Barbara Strudler. "Finding Two Jobs." In Rhona and Robert N. Rapoport, eds., *Working Couples*, pp. 23–35. New York: Harper & Row, 1978.

Bergmann, Barbara. "The Effect on White Incomes of Discrimination in Employment." *Journal of Political Economy* 79(March–April 1971):294–313.

Berman, Ellen, Sacks, S., and Leif, H. "Two-Profession Marriage: New Conflict Syndrome." *Journal of Sex and Marital Therapy* 1(1975):242–253.

Bernard, Jessie. *Marriage and Family Among Negroes*. Englewood Cliffs, N.J.: Prentice-Hall, 1966.

Bernard, Jessie. *The Future of Motherhood*. New York: Dial Press, 1974.

Bernard, Jessie. *The Female World*. New York: Free Press, 1981.

Bibb, Robert, and Form, William F. "The Effects of Industrial, Occupational, and Sex Stratification on Wages in Blue-Collar Markets." *Social Forces* 55(June 1977):974–996.

Blau, Francine. *Equal Pay in the Office*. Lexington, Mass.: Heath, 1977.

Blau, Francine. "The Data on Women Workers, Past, Present, Future." In Ann H. Stromberg and Shirley Harkess, eds., *Women Working: Theories and Facts in Perspective*, pp. 29–62. Palo Alto, Calif.: Mayfield, 1978.

Blau, Francine D., and Jusenius, Carol L. "Economists' Approaches to Sex Segregation in the Labor Market: An Appraisal." In Martha Blaxall and Barbara Reagan, eds., *Women and the Workplace: The Implications of Occupational Segregation*, pp. 181–199. Chicago: University of Chicago Press, 1976.

Blauner, Robert. "Work Satisfaction and Industrial Trends in Modern Society." In Walter Galenson and Martin S. Lipset, eds., *Labor and Trade Unionism*, pp. 339–369. New York: Wiley, 1960.

Blauner, Robert. *Alienation and Freedom*. Chicago: University of Chicago Press, 1964.

Bliss, E. C. *Getting Things Done*. New York: Scribners, 1976.

Block, Jeanne H. "Issues, Problems, and Pitfalls in Assessing Sex Differences." *Merrill-Palmer Quarterly* 22(January 1976):283–308.

Blood, Robert, and Wolfe, Donald. *Husbands and Wives*. New York: Free Press, 1960.

Bock, E. Wilbur. "Farmer's Daughter Effect: The Case of the Negro Female Professional." In Athena Theodore, ed., *The Professional Woman*, pp. 119–131. Cambridge, Mass.: Schenkman, 1971.

Bohen, Halcyone, and Viveros-Long, Anamaria. *Balancing Jobs and Family Life*. Philadelphia: Temple University Press, 1981.

Bonacich, Edna. "A Theory of Ethnic Antagonism: The Split Labor Market." *American Sociological Review* 37(5), (October 1972):547–559.

Bowker, Joan. "An Attempt at Collectivity: Professional Confirmation and Support." In Barbara L. Forisha and Barbara H. Goldman, eds., *Outsiders on the Inside: Women and Organizations*, pp. 223–230. Englewood Cliffs, N.J.: Prentice-Hall, 1981.

Bowlby, J. A. "Some Pathological Processes Engendered by Early Mother-Child Separation." In Milton Senn, ed., *Infancy and Childhood*. New York: Josiah Macy Jr. Foundation, 1953.

Brager, George, and Michael, John A. "The Sex Distribution in Social Work: Causes and Consequences." *Social Casework* 50(December 1969):595–601.

Braverman, Harry. *Labor and Monopoly Capital*. New York: Monthly Labor Review Press, 1974.

Brief, Arthur P., and Oliver, Richard L. "Male-Female Differences in Work Attitudes Among Retail Sales Workers." *Journal of Applied Psychology* 61(August 1976):526–528.

Briggs, Norma. "Apprenticeship." In Ann Foote Cahn, ed., *American Women Workers in a Full Employment Economy*, pp. 225–233. A compendium of papers submitted to the Subcommittee on Economic Growth and Stabilization of the Joint Committee of Congress. U.S. Congress, Joint Economic Committee Hearing, September 16, 1977. Washington, D.C.: U.S. Government Printing Office, 1977.

Broverman, Inge, Vogel, Susan R., Broverman, Donald M., Clarkson, Frank E., and Rosenkrantz, Paul S. "Sex Role Stereotypes: A Current Appraisal." *Journal of Social Issues* 28(2), (1972):59–78.

Brown, Linda Keller. *The Woman Manager in the United States*. Washington, D.C.: Business and Professional Women's Foundation, 1981.

Brown, Scott Campbell. "Moonlighting Increased Sharply in 1977, Particularly Among Women." *Monthly Labor Review* 101(January 1978):27–30.

Brownlee, W. Elliot, and Brownlee, Mary M. *Women in the American Economy: A Documentary History, 1675–1929*. New Haven, Conn.: Yale University Press, 1976.

Bruner, Jerome. *Toward a Theory of Instruction*. Cambridge, Mass.: Belknap Press, 1966.

Bularzik, Mary. "Sexual Harassment at the Workplace: Historical Notes." *Radical America* 12(4), (July–August 1978):25–43.

Buric, Olivera, and Zecevic, Andjelka. "Family Authority, Marital Satisfaction, and the Social Network in Yugoslavia." *Journal of Marriage and the Family* 29(May 1967):325–336.

Burke, Ronald J., and Weir, Tamara. "Relationship of Wives' Employment Status to Husband, Wife, and Pair Satisfaction and Performance." *Journal of Marriage and the Family* 38(May 1976):278–287.

Burnham, James. *The Managerial Revolution.* New York: Day, 1941.

Burris, Val, and Wharton, Amy. "Sex Segregation in the U.S. Labor Force, 1950–1979." Paper presented at the annual meeting of the Society for the Study of Social Problems, Toronto, Ontario, August 1981.

Cahn, Ann Foote. "Summary." In Ann Foote Cahn, ed., *American Women Workers in a Full Employment Economy,* pp. 1–22. A compendium of papers submitted to the Subcommittee on Economic Growth and Stabilization of the Joint Economic Committee. U.S. Congress, Joint Economic Committee Hearing, September 16, 1977. Washington, D.C.: U.S. Government Printing Office, 1977.

Cain, Glen. "The Challenge of Segmented Labor Market Theories to Orthodox Theory: A Survey." *Journal of Economic Literature* 14(December 1976):1215–1257.

Candy, Sandra E. "Women, Work, and Friendship: Personal Confirmation and Support." In Barbara L. Forisha and Barbara H. Goldman, eds., *Outsiders on the Inside: Women and Organizations,* pp. 188–198. Englewood Cliffs, N.J.: Prentice-Hall, 1981.

Carver, Carol, and Crossman, Linda J. "Job Sharing: It May be Right for You." *American Journal of Nursing* 80(1980):676–678.

Cashman, James, Dansereau, Fred, Green, George, and Haga, William J. "Organizational Understructure and Leadership: A Longitudinal Investigation of the Managerial Role-Making Process." *Organizational Behavior and Human Performance* 15(2), (April 1976):278–296.

Chafe, William. *The American Woman: Her Changing Social, Economic, and Political Roles, 1920–1970.* New York: Oxford University Press, 1972.

Chafe, William. "Looking Backward in Order to Look Forward: Women, Work, and Social Values in America." In Juanita M. Kreps, ed., *Women and the American Economy,* pp. 6–30. Englewood Cliffs, N.J.: Prentice-Hall, 1976.

Chafe, William. *Women and Equality: Changing Patterns in American Culture.* New York: Oxford University Press, 1977.

Clawson, Augusta. "Shipyard Diary of a Woman Welder." *Radical America* 9(July–August 1975):134–138.

Coleman, Richard P., and Rainwater, Lee. *Social Standing in America.* New York: Basic Books, 1978.

Collins, A. M., and Selacke, W. E. "Counselor Ratings of Male and Female Clients." ERIC Document No. ED 071597, 1972.

Collins, Sharon. "Making Ourselves Visible: Evolution of Career Status and Self-Image of Minority Professional Women." In Lucy Ann Geiselman, ed., *The Minority Woman in America: Professionalism at What Cost?* pp. 4–14. Proceedings of the Program for Women in Health Sciences Conference at the University of California, San Francisco, March 1979. San Francisco: University of California, August 1979.

Cook, A. H. "Working Women: European Experience and American Need." In Ann Foote Cahn, ed., *American Women Workers in a Full Employment Economy,* pp. 271–306. A compendium of papers submitted to the Subcommittee on Economic Growth and Stabilization of the Joint Economic Committee. U.S. Congress, Joint Economic Committee, Hearing, September 16, 1977. Washington, D.C.: U.S. Government Printing Office, 1977.

Corcoran, Mary, and Duncan, Gregory J. "Work History, Labor Force Attachment, and Earnings Differences Between the Races and Sexes." *Journal of Human Resources* 14(Winter 1979):3–20.

Coser, Lewis. *Greedy Institutions: Patterns of Undivided Commitment.* New York: Free Press, 1974.

Coser, Rose Laub, and Rokoff, Gerald. "Women in the Occupational World: Social Disruption and Conflict." *Social Problems* 18(4), (Spring 1971):535–554.

Cott, Nancy, and Pleck, Elizabeth H. *A Heritage of Her Own: Toward a New Social History of American Women.* New York: Simon & Schuster, 1979.

Crandall, Vaughn, and Robson, Alice. "Children's Repetition Choices in an Intellectual Achievement Situation Following Success and Failure." *Journal of Genetic Psychology* 97(1960):161–168.

Davidson, Laurie, and Gordon, Laura Kramer. *The Sociology of Gender.* Chicago: Rand McNally, 1979.

Davies, Margery. "Women's Place Is at the Typewriter: The Feminization of the Clerical Work Force." In Richard C. Edwards, Michael Reich, and David Gordon, eds., *Labor Market Segmentation,* pp. 279–296. Lexington, Mass.: Heath, 1975.

Davis, Angela Y. "Reflections on the Black Women's Role in the Community of Slaves." *Black Scholar,* special edition: The Best of *The Black Scholar*: The Black Woman (November–December 1981), pp. 3–15.

Davis, Kingsley, and Moore, Wilbert. "Some Principles of Stratification." *American Sociological Review* 10(April 1945):242–249.

Deckard, Barbara Sinclair. *The Women's Movement: Political, Socioeconomic, and Psychological Issues.* New York: Harper & Row, 1979.

Degler, Carl N. *At Odds: Woman and the Family in America from the Revolution to the Present.* New York: Oxford University Press, 1980.

Dexter, Elizabeth A. *Colonial Women of Affairs: A Study of Women in Business and the Professions in America Before 1776.* Boston: Houghton Mifflin, 1924.

Diamond, Esther. *Issues of Sex Bias and Sex Fairness in Career Interest Measurement.* Washington, D.C.: National Institute of Education, 1975.

Doeringer, Peter B., and Piore, Michael. *Internal Labor Markets and Manpower Analysis.* Lexington, Mass.: Heath, 1971.

Douglas, Priscilla Harriet. "Black Working Women: Factors Affecting Labor Market Experience." Working paper. Wellesley, Mass.: Center for Research on Women, Wellesley College, March 1980.

Duncan, Gregory, and Hoffman, Saul. "Training and Earnings." In Gregory Duncan and James Morgan, eds., *Five Thousand American Families: Patterns of Economic Progress,* vol. 6, pp. 105–150. Ann Arbor: University of Michigan, Institute for Social Research, 1978.

Dunlap, Mary C. "The Legal Road to Equal Opportunity: A Critical View." In Ann Foote Cahn, ed., *American Women Workers in a Full Employment Economy,* pp. 61–74. A compendium of papers submitted to the Subcommittee on Economic Growth and Stabilization of the Joint Economic Committee. U.S. Congress, Joint Economic Committee Hearing, September 16, 1977. Washington, D.C.: U.S. Government Printing Office, 1977.

Eastwood, Mary. "Legal Protection Against Sex Discrimination." In Ann H. Stromberg and Shirley Harkess, eds., *Women Working: Theories and Facts in Perspective*, pp. 108–123. Palo Alto, Calif.: Mayfield, 1978.

Edgeworth, Francis. "Equal Pay to Men and Women for Equal Work." *Economic Journal* 32(December 1922):431–447.

Edwards, Richard C. *Contested Terrain: The Transformation of the Workplace in America*. New York: Basic Books, 1979.

Edwards, Richard C., Reich, Michael, and Gordon, David, eds. *Labor Market Segmentation*. Lexington, Mass.: Heath, 1975.

Eichler, Margrit. *The Double Standard: A Feminist Critique of Feminist Social Science*. New York: St. Martin's Press, 1980.

Emmerich, Walter. "Complexities in Human Development." *Science* 190(October 10, 1975):140–141.

England, Paula. "The Failure of Human Capital Theory to Explain Occupational Sex Segregation." *Journal of Human Resources* 17(3), (Summer 1982):358–370.

Epstein, Cynthia Fuchs. *Woman's Place: Options and Limits in Professional Careers*. Berkeley: University of California Press, 1970.

Epstein, Cynthia Fuchs. "Positive Effects of the Multiple Negative: Explaining the Success of Black Professional Women." *American Journal of Sociology* 78(4), (Summer 1973):912–935.

Epstein, Cynthia Fuchs. "Bringing Women in: Rewards, Punishments, and the Structure of Achievement." In Ruth B. Kundsin, ed., *Women and Success: The Anatomy of Achievement*, pp. 13–21. New York: Morrow, 1974a.

Epstein, Cynthia Fuchs. "A Different Angle of Vision: Notes on the Selective Eye of Sociology." *Social Science Quarterly* 55(December 1974b):645–656.

Epstein, Cynthia Fuchs. "Institutional Barriers: What Keeps Women Out of the Executive Suite?" In Francine E. Gordon and Myra H. Strober, eds., *Bringing Women into Management*, pp. 7–21. New York: McGraw-Hill, 1975.

Farley, Lyn. *Sexual Shakedown: The Sexual Harassment of Women on the Job*. New York: McGraw-Hill, 1978.

Farris, Agnes. "Commuting." In Rhona and Robert Rapoport, eds., *Working Couples*, pp. 100–107. New York: Harper & Row, 1978.

Faver, Catherine A., Fox, Mary Frank, and Shannon, Colleen. "The Educational Process and the Occupational Outcomes: Toward Job Equity for the Sexes in Social Work." Forthcoming, *Journal of Education for Social Work*.

Featherman, David, and Hauser, Robert. "Sexual Inequalities and Socioeconomic Achievement in the U.S., 1962–1973." *American Sociological Review* 41(June 1976):462–483.

Federbush, Marsha. "The Sex Problems of School Math Books." In Judith Stacey, Susan Bereaud, and Jean Daniels, eds., *And Jill Came Tumbling After*, pp. 178–184. New York: Dell, 1974.

Feldman, Saul D. *Escape from the Doll's House: Women in Graduate and Professional School Education.* New York: McGraw-Hill, 1974.

Fensterheim, H., and Baer, J. *Don't Say Yes When You Want to Say No.* New York: McKay, 1975.

Ferber, Marianne A., and Kordick, Betty. "Sex Differentials in the Earnings of Ph.Ds." *Industrial and Labor Relations Review* 31(January 1978): 227–238.

Ferree, Myra Marx. "Working-Class Jobs: Housework and Paid Work as Sources of Satisfaction." *Social Problems* 23(April 1976): 431–441.

Fisher, Elizabeth. "Children's Books: The Second Sex, Junior Division." In Judith Stacey, Susan Bereaud, and Jean Daniels, eds., *And Jill Came Tumbling After*, pp. 116–122. New York: Dell, 1974.

Flexner, Eleanor. *Century of Struggle: The Women's Rights Movement in the U.S.* Cambridge, Mass.: Belknap Press, 1959.

Flowers, Lorna K. "Being a Minority Professional Woman." In Lucy Ann Geiselman, ed., *The Minority Woman in America: Professionalism at What Cost?* pp. 39–51. Proceedings of Program for Women in Health Sciences Conference at the University of California, San Francisco, March 1979. San Francisco: University of California, August 1979.

Fogarty, Michael P., Rapoport, Rhona, and Rapoport, Robert N. *Sex, Career, and Family.* Beverly Hills, Calif.: Sage Publications, 1971.

Foner, Philip. *The Factory Girls.* Urbana: University of Illinois Press, 1978.

Forisha, Barbara L., and Goldman, Barbara H., eds. *Outsiders on the Inside: Women and Organizations.* Englewood Cliffs, N.J.: Prentice-Hall, 1981.

Form, William. "Auto Workers and Their Machines: A Study of Work, Factory, and Job Satisfaction in Four Countries." *Social Forces* 52(September 1973): 1–15.

Fox, Mary Frank. "Achievement, Ascription, and Reward: An Analysis of Academic Sex-Wage Variation." Unpublished doctoral dissertation, University of Michigan, 1978.

Fox, Mary Frank. "Sex, Salary, and Achievement: Reward-Dualism in Academia." *Sociology of Education* 54(April 1981a): 71–84.

Fox, Mary Frank. "Sex Segregation and Salary Structure in Academia." *Sociology of Work and Occupations* 8(February 1981b): 39–60.

Fox, Mary Frank, and Faver, Catherine A. "Achievement and Aspiration: Patterns Among Male and Female Academic-Career Aspirants." *Sociology of Work and Occupations* 8(November 1981): 439–463.

Foxworth, Jo. *Wising Up: The Mistakes Women Make in Business and How to Avoid Them.* New York: Dell, 1980.

Frazier, Nancy, and Sadker, Myra. *Sexism in School and Society.* New York: Harper & Row, 1973.

Friedan, Betty. *The Feminine Mystique.* New York: Norton, 1963.

Friedan, Betty. *The Second Stage.* New York: Summit Books, 1981.

Frieze, Irene H., Parsons, Jacquelynne E., Johnson, Paula, Ruble, Diane M., and Zellman, Gail. *Women and Sex Roles.* New York: Norton, 1978.

Fuchs, Victor. "Differences in Hourly Earnings Between Men and Women." *Monthly Labor Review* 94(May 1971): 9–15.

Garland, T. Neal. "The Better Half? The Male in the Dual-Profession Family." In Constantina Safilios-Rothschild, ed., *Toward a Sociology of Women*, pp. 199–215. Lexington, Mass.: Xerox College Publishing, 1972.

Gates, Margaret J. "Occupational Segregation and the Law." In Martha Blaxall and Barbara Reagan, eds., *Women and the Workplace: The Implications of Occupational Segregation*, pp. 61–74. Chicago: University of Chicago Press, 1976.

Gibbs, Jewelle Taylor. "Cultural Conflicts in Professional Training." In Lucy Ann Geiselman, ed., *The Minority Woman in America: Professionalism at What Cost?* pp. 28–38. Proceedings of Program for Women in Health Sciences Conference at the University of California, San Francisco, March 1979. San Francisco: University of California, August 1979.

Glazier-Malbin, Nona. "The Division of Labor in the Husband-Wife Relationship." A paper presented at the Merrill-Palmer Institute on Sex Roles and the Family, Detroit, Michigan, November 1975.

Glenn, Evelyn, and Feldberg, Rosalyn. "Degraded and Deskilled: The Proletarianization of Clerical Work." *Social Problems* 25(July 1977): 52–64.

Glenn, Evelyn, and Feldberg, Rosalyn. "Clerical Work: The Female Occupation." In J. Freeman, ed., *Women: A Feminist Perspective*, pp. 313–338. 2nd ed. Palo Alto, Calif.: Mayfield, 1979.

Glick, Paul C. "Updating the Life Cycle of the Family." *Journal of Marriage and the Family* 39(1977): 5–13.

Goldin, Claudia. "Female Labor Force Participation: The Origins of Black and White Differences, 1870 and 1880." *Journal of Economic History* 37(March 1977): 87–108.

Golembiewski, Robert, and Proehl, Carl. "Public Sector Applications of Flexible Workhours: A Review of Available Experiences." *Public Administrative Review* 40(January 1980): 72–85.

Good, Thomas L., Sikes, J. Neville, and Brophy, Jere E. "Effects of Teacher Sex and Student Sex on Classroom Interaction." *Journal of Educational Psychology* 65(August 1973): 74–87.

Gordon, Ann, Buhle, Mari Jo, and Schrom, Nancy. "Women in American Society: An Historical Contribution." *Radical America* 5(4), (July–August 1971): 3–66.

Gordon, David M. *Theories of Poverty and Underemployment*. Lexington, Mass.: Lexington Books, 1972.

Gordon, Nancy. "Institutional Response: The Social Security System." In Ralph E. Smith, ed., *The Subtle Revolution: Women at Work*, pp. 223–255. Washington, D.C.: Urban Institute, 1979.

Gordon, Nancy, Morton, Thomas E., and Braden, Ina C. "Faculty Salaries: Is There Discrimination by Sex, Race, and Discipline?" *American Economic Review* 64(1974): 419–427.

Goy, Robert W. "Early Hormonal Influences on the Development of Sexual and Sex-Related Behavior." In Francis O. Schmitt, ed., *Neurosciences: Second Study Program*, pp. 197–207. New York: Rockefeller University Press, 1970.

Greenberger, Marcia. "The Effectiveness of Federal Law Prohibiting Sex Discrimination in Employment in the United States." In Ronnie Steinberg Ratner, ed., *Equal Employment Policy for Women*, pp. 108–128. Philadelphia: Temple University Press, 1980.

Greenwald, Carol S. "Part-Time Work." In Ann Foote Cahn, ed., *American Women Workers in a Full Employment Economy*, pp. 182–191. A compendium of papers submitted to the Subcommittee on Growth and Stabilization of the Joint Economic Committee. U.S. Congress, Joint Economic Committee Hearing, September 16, 1977. Washington, D.C.: U.S. Government Printing Office, 1977.

Greenwald, Carol S., and Liss, Judith. "Part-Time Workers Can Bring Higher Productivity." *Harvard Business Review* 51(September–October 1973):20–21, 166.

Greenwald, Maurine Weiner. *Women, War, and Work: The Impact of World War I on Women Workers in the United States*. Westport, Conn.: Greenwood Press, 1980.

Grimm, James W. "Women in Female-Dominated Professions." In Ann H. Stromberg and Shirley Harkess, eds., *Women Working: Theories and Facts in Perspective*, pp. 293–315. Palo Alto, Calif.: Mayfield, 1978.

Grimm, James W., and Stern, Robert N. "Sex Roles and the Internal Labor Market Structures: The 'Female' Semi-Professions." *Social Problems* 21(June 1974): 690–705.

Grossman, Allyson Sherman. "Women in the Labor Force: The Early Years." *Monthly Labor Review* 98(11), (November 1975):3–9.

Gruber, James E., and Björn, Lars. "Blue-Collar Blues: The Sexual Harassment of Women Autoworkers." *Work and Occupations* 9(3), (August 1982):271–298.

Gurin, Patricia, and Epps, Edgar. *Black Consciousness, Identity and Achievement*. New York: Wiley, 1975.

Gurin, Patricia, and Gaylord, Carolyn. "Educational and Occupational Goals of Men and Women at Black Colleges." *Monthly Labor Review* 99(6), (June 1976):10–16.

Hall, Francine, and Hall, Douglas T. *The Two-Career Couple*. Reading, Mass.: Addison-Wesley, 1979.

Hall, Richard H. *Occupations and the Social Structure*. 2d ed. Englewood Cliffs, N.J.: Prentice-Hall, 1975.

Hare, Nathan, and Hare, Julie. "Black Woman, 1970." *Transaction* 8(December 1970):65–68, 90.

Harlan, Anne, and Weiss, Carol L. "Sex Differences in Factors Affecting Managerial Career Advancement." Working Paper No. 56. Wellesley, Mass.: Center for Research on Women, Wellesley College, 1980

Harlan, Sharon L., and O'Farrell, Brigid. "After the Pioneers: Prospects for Women in Nontraditional Blue-Collar Jobs." *Work and Occupations* 9(3), (August 1982):363–368.

Harmon, Lenore W. "Technical Aspects: Problems of Scale Development, Norms, Item Differences by Sex, and the Rate of Change in Occupational Group Characteristics." In Esther Diamond, ed., *Issues of Sex Bias and Sex Fairness in Career Interest Measurement*, pp. 45–64. Washington, D.C.: National Institute of Education, 1975.

Hartmann, Heidi. "Capitalism, Patriarchy, and Job Segregation by Sex." *Signs* 1(Spring 1976, pt. 2):137–169.

Havener, Helen. "Prepare for Peace." *Independent Woman* 19(December 1940): 394–395.

Heer, David. "Husband and Wife Perceptions of Family Power Structure." *Marriage and Family Living* 24(February 1962):65–67.

Hennig, Margaret, and Jardim, Anne. *The Managerial Woman*. New York: Pocket Books, 1977.

Henry, Alice. *Trade Union Woman*. New York: Appleton, 1915.

Hesse, Sharlene J. "Women Working: Historical Trends." In Karen Feinstein, ed., *Working Women and Families*, pp. 35–62. Beverly Hills, Calif.: Sage Publications, 1979.

Hesse, Sharlene, Burstein, Ira, and Atkins, Geri. "Sex Role Bias in Public Opinion Questionnaires." *Social Policy* 10(November–December 1979):51–56.

Hesse-Biber, Sharlene J. "Male and Female Perceptions of the Coeducational Environment." A paper presented at the Skidmore Conference on Coeducation: Toward an Equitable Education for Women and Men: Models from the Past Decade. Saratoga Springs, 1983.

Hesselbart, Susan. "An Evaluation of Sex Role Theories: The Clash Between Idealism and Reality." Paper presented at the annual meetings of the Association for Consumer Research, Arlington, Virginia, October 1980.

Hesselbart, Susan. "Some Underemphasized Issues About Men, Women, and Work." Paper presented at the annual meetings of the American Sociological Association, San Francisco, August 1978.

Heyns, Barbara, and Bird, Joyce Adair. "Recent Trends in the Higher Education of Women." In Pamela Perun, ed., *The Undergraduate Woman: Issues in Educational Equity*, ch. 3. Lexington, Mass.: Lexington Books, 1982.

Hodge, Robert, and Hodge, Patricia. "Occupational Assimilation as a Competitive Process." *American Journal of Sociology* 71(November 1965):249–264.

Hofferth, Sandra L., and Moore, Kristin A. "Women's Employment and Marriage." In Ralph E. Smith, ed., *The Subtle Revolution: Women at Work*, pp. 99–124. Washington, D.C.: Urban Institute, 1979.

Hoffman, Lois Wladis. "Effects of the Employment of Mothers on Parental Power Relations and the Division of Household Tasks." *Marriage and Family Living* 22(February 1960):27–35.

Hoffman, Lois Wladis. "Effects on Child." In Lois Wladis Hoffman and Francis I. Nye, eds., *Working Mothers*, pp. 126–166. San Francisco: Jossey-Bass, 1974.

Holmstrom, Engininel, and Holmstrom, Robert. "The Plight of the Woman Doctoral Student." *American Educational Research Journal* 11(Winter 1974): 1–17.

Horner, Matina S. "Toward an Understanding of Achievement Motivation and Performance in Competitive and Non-Competitive Situations." Unpublished doctoral dissertation, University of Michigan, 1968.

Horner, Matina S. "Toward an Understanding of Achievement-Related Conflicts in

Women." *Journal of Social Issues* 28(2), (1972):157–175.

Hornig, Lilli S. *Climbing the Academic Ladder: Doctoral Women Scientists in Academe.* Washington, D.C.: National Academy of Sciences, 1979.

Howe, Louise K. *Pink Collar Workers: Inside the World of Women's Work.* New York: Putnam, 1977.

Huber, Joan. "Criteria for Hiring, Promotion, and Tenure." *A.S.A. Footnotes* (American Sociological Association), (March 1973), p. 3.

Hunt, Janet, and Hunt, Larry. "Dilemmas and Contradictions of Status: The Case of the Dual-Career Family." *Social Problems* 24(April 1977):407–416.

Jackson, Jacquelyne J. "A Critique of Lerner's Work on Black Women and Further Thoughts." *Journal of Social and Behavioral Sciences* 21(Winter 1975): 63–89.

Jacobson, Beverly. "Comparable Worth: The Working Woman's Issue for the 80s." *National Forum* 61(Fall 1981):5–6.

Jelinek, Mariann, and Harlan, Anne. "MBA Goals and Aspirations: Potential Predictors of Later Success Differences Between Males and Females." Working paper. Wellesley, Mass.: Center for Research on Women, Wellesley College, 1979.

Joffe, Carole. "As the Twig Is Bent." In Judith Stacey, Susan Bereaud, and Jean Daniels, eds., *And Jill Came Tumbling After*, pp. 91–109. New York: Dell, 1974.

Johnson, Beverly L. "Women Who Head Families, 1970–1977: Their Numbers Rose, Income Lagged." *Monthly Labor Review* 101(February 1978):32–37.

Johnson, Colleen L., and Johnson, Frank A. "Role Strain in High-Commitment Career Women." *Journal of American Academy of Psychoanalysis* 4(1976): 13–36.

Johnson, Colleen L., and Johnson, Frank A. "Attitudes Toward Parenting in Dual-Career Families." *American Journal of Psychiatry* 134(1977):391–395.

Johnson, Colleen L., and Johnson, Frank A. "Parenthood, Marriage, and Careers: Situational Constraints and Role Strain." In Fran Pepitone-Rockwell, ed., *Dual-Career Couples*, pp. 143–161. Beverly Hills, Calif.: Sage Publications, 1980.

Jones, Jacqueline. "My Mother Was Much of a Woman: Black Women, Work, and the Family Under Slavery." Wellesley, Mass.: Center for Research on Women, Wellesley College, 1980.

Josefowitz, Natasha. *Paths to Power.* Reading, Mass.: Addison-Wesley, 1980.

Kamerman, Sheila. *Parenting in an Unresponsive Society.* New York: Free Press, 1981.

Kamerman, Sheila B., and Kahn, Alfred J. *Child Care, Family Benefits, and Working Parents: A Study in Comparative Policy.* New York: Columbia University Press, 1981.

Kanter, Rosabeth Moss. "The Policy Issues: Presentation VI." In Martha Blaxall and Barbara Reagan, eds., *Women and the Workplace*, pp. 282–291. Chicago: University of Chicago Press, 1976.

Kanter, Rosabeth Moss. *Men and Women of the Corporation.* New York: Basic Books, 1977a.

Kanter, Rosabeth Moss. *Work and Family in the United States: A Critical Review and Agenda for Research and Policy.* New York: Russell Sage Foundation, 1977b.

Kanter, Rosabeth Moss. "The Impact of Organizational Structure: Models and Methods for Change." In Ronnie Steinberg Ratner, ed., *Equal Employment Policy for Women*, pp. 311–327. Philadelphia: Temple University Press, 1980.

Katz, Joseph. "The New and Old Lives of Men and Women Undergraduates." In Office of the Provost, Brown University, ed., *Men and Women Learning Together: A Study of College Students in the Late 70s*, pp. 145–167. Report of the Brown Project (Carole Leland, Director). Providence, R.I.: Brown University, 1980.

Katz, Phyllis A. "The Development of Female Identity." *Sex Roles* 5(April 1979): 155–178.

Katzman, David M. *Seven Days a Week: Women and Domestic Service in Industrializing America.* New York: Oxford University Press, 1978.

Kegan, Jerome. "Acquisition and Significance of Sex-Typing and Sex-Role Identity." In Martin L. Hoffman and Lois Wladis Hoffman, eds., *Review of Child Development Research*, pp. 137–167. New York: Russell Sage Foundation, 1964.

Kelly, Ellen. "Power Structure, Task Division, and Stress in the Dual-Career Family." Unpublished senior honors thesis, Department of Sociology, Boston College, April 1981.

Kemp, Alice Abel. "Black Females in the Labor Force: A Further Test of the Double Negative Hypothesis." Paper presented at the annual meeting of the Society for the Study of Social Problems, Toronto, Canada, August 1981.

Kessler-Harris, Alice. "Stratifying by Sex: Understanding the History of Working Women." In Richard C. Edwards, Michael Reich, and David Gordon, eds., *Labor Market Segmentation*, pp. 217–242. Lexington, Mass.: Heath, 1975.

Kessler-Harris, Alice. *Women Have Always Worked: A Historical Overview.* Old Westbury, N.Y.: Feminist Press, 1981.

Kilson, Marion. "Black Women in the Professions: 1890–1990." *Monthly Labor Review* 100(May 1977): 38–41.

King, Lourdes. "Puertoriqueñas in the United States: The Impact of Double Discrimination." *Civil Rights Digest* 6(Spring 1974): 21–27.

King, Mae C. "Oppression and Power: The Unique Status of the Black Woman in the American Political System." *Social Science Quarterly* 56(June 1975): 116–128.

Kjerulff, Kristen, and Blood, Milton R. "A Comparison of Communication Patterns in Male and Female Graduate Students." *Journal of Higher Education* 42(November 1973): 623–632.

Kohlberg, L. "A Cognitive-Developmental Analysis of Children's Sex-Role Concepts and Attitudes." In Eleanor E. Maccoby, ed., *The Development of Sex Differences.* Stanford, Calif.: Stanford University Press, 1966.

Kohn, Melvin, and Schooler, Carmi. "Occupational Experience and Psychological Functioning: Assessment of Reciprocal Effects." *American Sociological Review* 30(1973): 97–118.

Komarovsky, Mirra. *Blue-Collar Marriage.* New York: Vintage Books, 1967.

Korda, Michael. *Male Chauvinism: How It Works*. New York: Random House, 1972.

Kosa, John, and Coker, Robert E. "The Female Physician in Public Health: Conflict and Reconciliation of the Professional and Sex Roles." *Sociology and Social Research* 49(April 1965):294–305.

Kosinar, Patricia. "Socialization and Self-Esteem: Women in Management." In Barbara L. Forisha and Barbara H. Goldman, eds., *Outsiders on the Inside: Women and Organizations*, pp. 31–41. Englewood Cliffs, N.J.: Prentice-Hall, 1981.

Kravetz, Diane. "Sexism in a Woman's Profession." *Social Work* 21(November 1976):421–426.

Kreps, Juanita. *Sex in the Marketplace: American Women at Work*. Baltimore, Md.: Johns Hopkins University Press, 1971.

Kreps, Juanita, and Leaper, R. John. "House Work, Market Work, and the Allocation of Time." In Juanita M. Kreps, ed., *Women and the American Economy*, pp. 61–81. Englewood Cliffs, N.J.: Prentice-Hall, 1976.

Kutner, Nancy, and Brogan, Donna. "Occupational Role Innovation and Secondary Career Choice Among Women Medical Students." Paper presented at the annual meetings of the American Sociological Association, Boston, August 1979.

Ladner, Joyce. *Tomorrow's Tomorrow: The Black Woman*. New York: Doubleday, 1971.

Ladner, Joyce A. "The Black Woman Today." *Ebony* (August 1977), pp. 32–42.

Lakein, Alan. *How to Get Control of Your Time and Your Life*. New York: New American Library, 1974.

Land, Hilary. "Social Policies and the Family: Their Effect on Women's Employment in Great Britain." In Ronnie Steinberg Ratner, ed., *Equal Employment Policy for Women*, pp. 366–388. Philadelphia: Temple University Press, 1980.

Lapidus, Gail W. "Occupational Segregation and Public Policy: A Comparative Analysis of American and Soviet Patterns." In Martha Blaxall and Barbara Reagan, eds., *Women and the Workplace*. Chicago: University of Chicago Press, 1976.

Laws, Judith Long. "Work Aspirations of Women: False Leads and New Starts." *Signs: Journal of Women in Culture and Society* 1(Spring 1976):33–49.

Laws, Judith Long. "Work Motivation and Work Behavior of Women: New Perspectives." In Jean A. Sherman and Florence L. Denmark, eds., *Psychology of Women: Future Directions in Research*, pp. 287–348. New York: Psychological Dimensions, Inc., 1978.

Lee, R. E. *A Lawyer Looks at the Equal Rights Amendment*. Provo, Utah: Brigham Young University Press, 1980.

Leggon, Cheryl Bernadette. "Black Female Professionals: Dilemmas and Contradictions of Status." In La Frances Rodgers-Rose, ed., *The Black Woman*, pp. 189–202. Beverly Hills, Calif.: Sage Publications, 1980.

Leland, Carole. "Declarations About the Future: Career Goals and Plans of a College Generation." In Office of the Provost, Brown University, ed., *Men and Women Learning Together: A Study of College Students in the Late 70s*, pp.

107–144. Report of the Brown Project (Carole Leland, Director). Providence, R.I.: Brown University, 1980.

Leon, Carol Boyd, and Rones, Philip L. "Employment and Unemployment During 1979: An Analysis." *Monthly Labor Review* 103(February 1980):3–10.

Leonard, Eugenie Andruss, Drinker, Sophie Hutchinson, and Holden, Miriam Young. *The American Women in Colonial and Revolutionary Times, 1565–1800.* Philadelphia: University of Pennsylvania Press, 1962.

Lerner, Gerda. *Black Women in White America: A Documentary History.* New York: Vintage Books 1972.

Lerner, Gerda. "The Lady and the Mill Girl: Changes in the Status of Women in the Age of Jackson." *Midcontinent American Studies Journal* 10(1969):5–15. (Reprinted in J. E. Friedman and W. G. Shade, eds., *Our American Sisters*, pp. 120–132. 2nd ed. Boston: Allyn & Bacon, 1976.)

Lerner, Gerda. *The Majority Finds Its Past: Placing Women in History.* New York: Oxford University Press, 1979.

Lever, Janet. "Sex Differences in the Games Children Play." *Social Problems* 23(April 1976):478–487.

Levitan, Sar A., and Belous, R. S. "Working Wives and Mothers: What Happens to Family Life?" *Monthly Labor Review* 104(9), (September 1981):26–31.

Levitan, Sar A., Johnson, William B., and Taggart, Robert. *Still a Dream.* Cambridge, Mass.: Harvard University Press, 1975.

Lewis, Michael. "Parents and Children: Sex-Role Development." *School Review* 80(February 1972a):229–239.

Lewis, Michael. "State as an Infant-Environment Interaction: An Analysis of Mother-Infant Interaction as a Function of Sex." *Merrill-Palmer Quarterly* 18(April 1972b):95–121.

Lewis, Michael, and Brooks, Jeanne. "Infants' Social Perception: A Constructivist View." In Leslie Cohen and Philip Salapatek, eds., *Infant Perception: From Sensation to Cognition*, pp. 101–143. New York: Academic Press, 1975.

Lewis, Michael, and Cherry, L. "Social Behavior and Language Acquisition." In Michael Lewis and R. Rosenblum, eds., *Interaction, Conversation, and the Development of Language*, vol. 2. New York: Wiley, 1977.

Lewis, Michael, and Weinraub, Marsha. "Origins of Early Sex-Role Development." *Sex Roles* 5(April 1979):135–153.

Liebow, Elliot. *Talley's Corner.* Boston: Little, Brown, 1967.

Lindsey, Karen. "Sexual Harassment on the Job and How to Stop It." *Ms.* Magazine (November 1977), pp. 47–49.

Lloyd, Cynthia B., and Niemi, Beth T. *The Economics of Sex Differentials.* New York: Columbia University Press, 1979.

Lockwood, David. *The Blackcoated Worker.* London: Allen & Unwin, 1958.

Lofland, Lyn H. "The 'Thereness' of Women: A Selective Review of Urban Sociology." In Marcia Millman and Rosabeth Moss Kanter, eds., *Another Voice: Feminist Perspectives on Social Life and Social Science*, pp. 144–170. New York: Anchor Press, 1975.

Looft, W. R. "Sex Differences in the Expression of Vocational Aspirations by Elementary School Children." *Developmental Psychology* 5(September 1971):366.

Lorenzana, Noemi. "La Chicana." In Eloise C. Snyder, ed., *The Study of Women: Enlarging Perspectives of Social Reality*, pp. 336–341. New York: Harper & Row, 1979.

Lott, Bernice E. "Who Wants the Children?" In Arlene Skolnick and Jerome Skolnick, eds., *Intimacy, Family, and Society*, pp. 390–406. Boston: Little, Brown, 1974.

Lyle, Jerolyn L., and Ross, Jane L. *Women in Industry.* Lexington, Mass.: Lexington Books, 1973.

Lynn, David B. "The Process of Learning Parental and Sex-Role Identification." *Journal of Marriage and the Family* 28(November 1966): 466–470.

Maccoby, Eleanor E., and Jacklin, Carol Nagy. *The Psychology of Sex Differences.* Stanford, Calif.: Stanford University Press, 1974.

Machonin, Pavel. "Social Stratification in Contemporary Czechoslovakia." *American Journal of Sociology* 75(March 1970): 725–741.

Mackenzie, R. Alec. *The Time Trap.* New York: McGraw-Hill, 1975.

MacKinnon, Catharine A. *Sexual Harassment of Working Women: A Case of Sex Discrimination.* New Haven, Conn.: Yale University Press, 1979.

Malveaux, Julianne. "Three Views of Black Women: The Myths, The Statistics, and a Personal Statement." *Heresies* (Winter 1979): 50–55.

Marciano, Teresa Donati. "Socialization and Women at Work." *National Forum* 61(Fall 1981): 24–25.

Marini, Margaret Mooney, and Greenberger, Ellen. "Sex Differences in Occupational Aspirations and Expectations." *Sociology of Work and Occupations* 5(May 1978): 151–174.

Martin, Thomas W., Berry, Kenneth W., and Jacobsen, R. Brooke. "The Impact of Dual-Career Marriages on Female Professional Careers." *Journal of Marriage and Family* 37(November 1975): 734–742.

Matthaei, Julie A. *An Economic History of Women in America: Women's Work, the Sexual Division of Labor, and the Development of Capitalism.* New York: Schocken, 1982.

McGregor, Douglas. *The Professional Manager.* New York: McGraw-Hill, 1967.

McIlwee, Judith S. "Work Satisfaction Among Women in Nontraditional Occupations." *Work and Occupations* 9(3), (August 1982): 299–335.

McNally, Fiona. *Women for Hire: A Study of the Female Office Worker.* New York: St. Martin's Press, 1979.

Meece, Judith L., Parsons, Jacquelynne, Kaczala, Caroline, Goff, Susan, and Futterman, Robert. "Sex Differences in Math Achievement: Toward a Model of Academic Choice." *Psychological Bulletin* 91(March 1982): 324–348.

Meissner, Martin, Humphreys, Elizabeth, Meis, Scott, and Scheu, William J. "No Exit for Wives: Sexual Division of Labour and the Cumulation of Household Demands." *Canadian Review of Sociology and Anthropology* 12(1975): 424–439.

Metoyer, Cheryl A. "The Native American Woman." In Eloise C. Snyder, ed., *The Study of Women: Enlarging Perspectives of Social Reality*, pp. 329–335. New York: Harper & Row, 1979.

Milkman, Ruth. "Organizing the Sexual Division of Labor: Historical Perspectives on 'Women's Work' and the American Labor Movement." *Socialist Review* 49(1980):95–105.

Miller, Jean B. *Toward a New Psychology of Women*. Boston: Beacon, 1976.

Miller, Shirley Matile. "Effects of Maternal Employment on Sex Role Perception, Interest, and Self-Esteem in Kindergarten Girls." *Developmental Psychology* 11(May 1975):405–406.

Millman, Marcia, and Kanter, Rosabeth Moss. "Introduction." In Marcia Millman and Rosabeth Moss Kanter, eds., *Another Voice: Feminist Perspectives on Social Life and Social Science*, pp. xii–xvii. New York: Anchor Press, 1975.

Mills, C. Wright. *White Collar: The American Middle Class*. New York: Oxford University Press, 1951.

Mincer, Jacob. "Labor Force Participation of Married Women: A Study of Labor Supply." In H. Gregg Lewis, ed., *Aspects of Labor Economics*, pp. 63–105. A Report of the National Bureau of Economic Research. Princeton, N.J.: Princeton University Press, 1962.

Mincer, Jacob, and Polachek, Solomon W. "Family Investments in Human Capital: Earnings of Women." *Journal of Political Economy* 82(March–April 1974) Pt. 2:S76–S108.

Minority Women Lawyers' Regional Seminar. Session on "Surviving as a Minority Woman Lawyer: Developing Coping Skills." NAACP Legal Defense and Educational Fund, Inc. Stanford University, Stanford, California, July 6, 1979.

Mischel, Walter. "A Social Learning View of Sex Differences in Behavior." In Eleanor E. Maccoby, ed., *The Development of Sex Differences*, pp. 56–81. Stanford, Calif.: Stanford University Press, 1966.

Monteiro, Joseph. "Women at Top Colleges Show Lower Self-Esteem Than Men." *Foster's Daily Democrat* (Dover, New Hampshire), December 4, 1978, p. 12.

Moore, Kristin A., and Hofferth, Sandra L. "Women and Their Children." In Ralph E. Smith, ed., *The Subtle Revolution: Women at Work*, pp. 125–157. Washington, D.C.: Urban Institute, 1979.

Morgall, Janine. "Typing Our Way to Freedom: Is It True That New Office Technology Can Liberate Women?" *Feminist Review* (9), (October 1981), pp. 87–101.

Morgan, David. "Men, Masculinity, and the Process of Sociological Inquiry." In Helen Roberts, ed., *Doing Feminist Research*, pp. 83–113. London: Routledge & Kegan Paul, 1981.

Morgan, James. *Productive Americans*. Ann Arbor: University of Michigan, 1966.

Moroney, R. "Note from the Editor." *Urban and Social Change Review* 11(1, 2), (1978):2.

Morse, Nancy C., and Weiss, R. S. "The Function and Meaning of Work and the Job." In Sigmund Nosow and William H. Form, eds., *Man, Work, and Society*, pp. 29–35. New York: Basic Books, 1962.

Moskowitz, Robert. *How to Organize Your Work and Your Life*. New York: Doubleday, 1981.

Moss, H. A. "Sex, Age, and State as Determinants of Mother-Infant Interaction." *Merrill-Palmer Quarterly* 13(1967):19–36.

Myers, Lena Wright. *Black Women: Do They Cope Better?* Englewood Cliffs, N.J.: Prentice-Hall, 1980.

Nadelson, Carol C., and Nadelson, Theodore. "Dual-Career Marriages: Benefits and Costs." In Fran Pepitone-Rockwell, ed., *Dual-Career Couples*, pp. 81–109. Beverly Hills, Calif.: Sage Publications, 1980.

Nelson, Charmeynne D. "Myths About Black Women Workers in Modern America." *Black Scholar* 6(6), (March 1975):11–15.

Neugarten, Bernice, and Brown-Rezanka, Lorill. "Midlife Women in the 1980s." In Anne Foote Cahn, ed., *Women in Mid-Life: Security and Fulfillment*, pt. 7. A compendium of papers submitted to the Select Committee on Aging and the Subcommittee on Retirement Income and Employment. U.S. House of Representatives, Ninety-Fifth Congress, Second Session. Washington, D.C.: U.S. Government Printing Office, 1978.

Neugarten, Dail A., and Shafritz, Jay M., eds. *Sexuality in Organizations: Romantic and Coercive Behaviors at Work.* Oak Park, Ill.: Moore, 1980.

Newland, Kathleen. *Women, Men, and the Division of Labor.* Worldwatch Institute, May 1980.

Newman, Winn. "The Policy Issues: Presentation III." In Martha Blaxall and Barbara Reagan, eds., *Women and the Workplace*, pp. 265–272. Chicago: University of Chicago Press, 1976.

Nieto, Consuelo. "The Chicana and the Women's Rights Movement: A Perspective." *Civil Rights Digest* 6(Spring 1974):36–42.

Norton, Mary Beth. *Liberty's Daughter: The Revolutionary Experience of American Women, 1750–1800.* Boston: Little, Brown, 1980.

Norwood, Janet. "The Policy Issues: Presentation V." In Martha Blaxall and Barbara Reagan, eds., *Women and the Workplace*, pp. 278–281. Chicago: University of Chicago Press, 1976.

O'Farrell, Brigid. *Women and Blue Collar Work.* A paper presented at the Industrial Liaison Symposium, Massachusetts Institute of Technology, Cambridge, January 20, 1978.

O'Farrell, Brigid. "Women and Nontraditional Blue Collar Jobs in the 1980s: An Overview." In Phyllis A. Wallace, ed., *Women in the Workplace*, pp. 135–165. Boston, Mass.: Auburn, 1982.

O'Farrell, Brigid, and Harlan, Sharon. "Craftworkers and Clerks: The Effect of Male Co-Worker Hostility on Women's Satisfaction with Nontraditional Jobs." Working Paper. Wellesley, Mass.: Center for Research on Women, Wellesley College, 1980.

O'Hara, Robert. "The Roots of Careers." *Elementary School Journal* 62(February 1962):277–280.

Olesen, Virginia, and Katsuranis, Frances. "Urban Nomads: Women in Temporary Clerical Services." In Ann H. Stromberg and Shirley Harkess, eds., *Women Working: Theories and Facts in Perspective*, pp. 316–338. Palo Alto, Calif.: Mayfield, 1978.

Oppenheimer, Valerie Kincade. *The Female Labor Force in the United States.* Berkeley: University of California Press, 1970.

Oppenheimer, Valerie Kincade. "The Sociology of Women's Economic Role in the Family." *American Sociological Review* 42(June 1977):387–406.

Osburn, Richard N., and Vicars, William N. "Sex Stereotypes: An Artifact in Leader Behavior and Subordinate Satisfaction Analysis?" *Academy of Management Journal* 19(1976):439–449.

Papanek, Hanna. "Men, Women, and Work: Reflections on the Two-Person Career." *American Journal of Sociology* 78(January 1973):852–872.

Parelius, Ann Parker, and Parelius, Robert. *The Sociology of Education.* Englewood Cliffs, N.J.: Prentice-Hall, 1978.

Parnes, Herbert, and Nestel, Gilbert. "Factors in Career Orientation and Occupational Status." In U.S. Department of Labor, Manpower Administration, ed., *Dual Careers*, vol. 4, ch. 3. Washington, D.C.: U.S. Government Printing Office, 1975.

Parsons, Talcott. "Age and Sex in the Social Structure of the United States." *American Sociological Review* 7(October 1942):604–616.

Parsons, Talcott. "A Revised Analytical Approach to the Theory of Social Stratification." In Richard Bendix and Martin S. Lipset, eds., *Class, Status, and Power.* New York: Free Press, 1953.

Parsons, Talcott, and Bales, Robert. *Family, Socialization, and Interaction Process.* New York: Free Press, 1956.

Patterson, Michelle, and Engelberg, Laurie. "Women in Male-Dominated Professions." Ann H. Stromberg and Shirley Harkess, eds., in *Women Working: Theories and Facts in Perspective*, pp. 266–292. Palo, Alto, Calif.: Mayfield, 1978.

Pavalko, Ronald. *Sociology of Occupations.* Ithaca, Ill.: Peacock, 1971.

Petty, M. M., and Lee, Gordon K. "Moderating Effects of Sex of Supervisor and Subordinate on Relationships Between Supervisory Behavior and Subordinate Satisfaction." *Journal of Applied Psychology* 60(October 1975):624–628.

Petty, M. M., and Miles, H. "Leader Sex-Role Stereotyping in Social Service Organizations." *Academy of Management Proceedings* (1976):467–471.

Phelps, Edmund S. "The Statistical Theory of Racism and Sexism." *American Economic Review* 62(September 1972):659–661.

Pifer, Alan. "Women and Working: Toward a New Sociology." *Urban and Social Change Review* 11(1–2), (1978):3–11.

Piore, Michael J. "Notes for a Theory of Labor Market Stratification." Working paper No. 95. Cambridge: Department of Economics, Massachusetts Institute of Technology, 1972.

Piore, Michael J. "Notes for a Theory of Labor Market Stratification." In Richard C. Edwards, Michael Reich, and David Gordon, eds., *Labor Market Segmentation*, pp. 125–150. Lexington, Mass.: Heath, 1975.

Pitcher, Evelyn G. "Male and Female." In Judith Stacey, Susan Bereaud, and Jean Daniels, eds., *And Jill Came Tumbling After*, pp. 79–90. New York: Dell, 1974.

Pleck, Elizabeth H. "A Mother's Wages: Income Earning Among Married Italian and Black Women, 1896–1911." In Nancy Cott and Elizabeth Pleck, eds., *A Heri-*

tage of Her Own: Toward a New Social History of American Women, pp. 367–392. New York: Simon & Schuster, 1979.

Pleck, Joseph H. "The Work-Family Role System." *Social Problems* 24(April 1977): 417–427.

Pleck, Joseph H. "The Work-Family Problem: Overloading the System." In Barbara L. Forisha and Barbara H. Goldman, eds., *Outsiders on the Inside: Women and Organizations*, pp. 239–254. Englewood Cliffs, N.J.: Prentice-Hall, 1981.

Polachek, Solomon. "Occupational Segregation: An Alternative Hypothesis." *Journal of Contemporary Business* 5(Winter 1976): 1–12.

Polachek, Solomon. "Sex Differences in Education: An Analysis of the Determinants of College Major." *Industrial and Labor Relations Review* 31(4), (1978): 498–508.

Polachek, Solomon. "Occupational Segregation: Theory, Evidence, and a Prognosis." In Cynthia B. Lloyd, Emily Andrews, and Curtis L. Gilroy, eds., *Women and the Labor Market*, pp. 137–157. New York: Columbia University Press, 1979.

Polit, Denise F. "Implications of Nontraditional Work Schedules for Women." *Urban and Social Change Review* 11(1, 2), (1978): 37–42.

Poloma, Margaret M. "Role Conflict and the Married Professional Woman." In Constantina Safilios-Rothschild, ed., *Toward a Sociology of Women*, pp. 187–198. Lexington, Mass.: Xerox College Publishing, 1972.

Quadagno, Jill. "Occupational Sex-Typing and Internal Labor Market Distributions: An Assessment of Medical Specialties." *Social Problems* 23(4), (April 1976): 442–453.

Raffel, Norma K. "Federal Laws and Regulations Prohibiting Sex Discrimination." In Eloise S. Snyder, ed., *The Study of Women: Enlarging Perspectives of Social Reality*, pp. 103–123. New York: Harper & Row, 1979.

Rapoport, Rhona, and Rapoport, Robert N. *Dual-Career Families*. Baltimore: Penguin, 1971.

Rapoport, Rhona, and Rapoport, Robert N. *Dual-Career Families Re-Examined*. New York: Harper Colophon, 1976.

Ratner, Ronnie Steinberg. "Themes in Equal Employment Policy: Fruitful Areas for Research and Exchange." Paper prepared for conference on "Work and Environment: Toward What Kind of Society?" Lisbon, Portugal, January 1979.

Ratner, Ronnie Steinberg. "Equal Employment Policy for Women: Summary of Themes and Issues." In Ronnie Steinberg Ratner, ed., *Equal Employment Policy for Women*, pp. 419–440. Philadelphia: Temple University Press, 1980.

Reskin, Barbara F. "Sex Differentiation and the Social Organization of Science." *Sociological Inquiry* 48(1978): 6–37.

Rheingold, Harriet L., and Cook, Kaye V. "The Concepts of Boys' and Girls' Rooms as an Index of Parents' Behavior." *Child Development* 46(June 1975): 459–563.

Rice, David G. *Dual-Career Marriage: Conflict and Treatment*. New York: Free Press, 1979.

Richardson, Laurel Walum. *The Dynamics of Sex and Gender.* 2nd ed. Boston: Houghton Mifflin, 1981.

Ricks, Frances A., and Pike, S. W. "Teacher Perceptions and Attitudes That Foster or Maintain Sex Role Differences." *Interchange* 4(1973):26–33.

Rieder, Corinne H. "Work, Women, and Vocational Education." In National Project on Women in Education, ed., *Taking Sexism Out of Education*, pp. 69–79. Washington, D.C.: U.S. Government Printing Office, 1978.

Rima, Ingrid H. *Labor Markets, Wages, and Employment.* New York: Norton, 1981.

Robertson, Peter C. "Strategies for Improving the Economic Situation of Women in the United States: Systemic Thinking, Systemic Discrimination, and Systemic Enforcement." In Ronnie Steinberg Ratner, ed., *Equal Employment Policy for Women*, pp. 128–142. Philadelphia: Temple University Press, 1980.

Roby, Pamela A. *The Conditions of Women in Blue Collar, Industrial, and Service Jobs: A Review of Research and Proposals for Research Action and Policy.* New York: Russell Sage Foundation, 1974.

Roby, Pamela A. "The Condition of Women in Blue-Collar Jobs." In Jane Roberts Chapman, ed., *Economic Independence for Women: The Foundation for Equal Rights*, pp. 155–181. Beverly Hills, Calif.: Sage Publications, 1976.

Roby, Pamela A. "Vocational Education." In Ann Foote Cahn, ed., *American Women Workers in a Full Employment Economy*, pp. 203–224. A compendium of papers submitted to the Subcommittee on Economic Growth and the Stabilization of the Joint Economic Committee. U.S. Congress, Joint Economic Committee Hearing, September 16, 1977. Washington, D.C.: U.S. Government Printing Office, 1977.

Rodgers, Harrell R., Jr., and Bullock, Charles S. *Law and Social Change: Civil Rights and Their Consequences.* New York: McGraw-Hill, 1972.

Rodgers-Rose, La Frances. "Some Demographic Characteristics of the Black Woman: 1940 to 1975." In La Frances Rodgers-Rose, ed., *The Black Woman*, pp. 29–41. Beverly Hills, Calif.: Sage Publications, 1980.

Roper Organization. *The 1980 Virginia Slims American Women's Opinion Poll: A Survey of Contemporary Attitudes.* Storrs: Roper Center, University of Connecticut, 1980.

Rosen, Ellen. "Hobson's Choice: Employment and Unemployment Among Factory Workers in New England." Report submitted to the U.S. Department of Labor, 1981. Available from author, Social Welfare Research Institute, Boston College, Chestnut Hill, Massachusetts.

Rosen, Ellen. "The Changing Jobs of American Women Factory Workers." A paper presented at the conference on the Changing Jobs of American Women Workers, sponsored by the Professional and Business Women's Foundation, George Washington University, and the Service Employees in the Union, Washington, D.C., January 1982.

Rossi, Alice, and Calderwood, Ann. *Academic Women on the Move.* New York: Russell Sage Foundation, 1973.

Roussell, Cecile. "Relationship of Sex of Department Head to Department Climate." *Administrative Science Quarterly* 19(June 1974):211–220.

Rowe, B. *The Private Secretary.* London: Museum Press, 1958.

Rozen, Frieda S. "Women and the Work Force: The Interaction of Myth and Reality." In Eloise S. Snyder, ed., *The Study of Women: Enlarging Perspectives of Social Reality*, pp. 79–102. New York: Harper & Row, 1979.

Rubin, Jeffrey, Provenzano, Frank, and Luria, Zella. "The Eye of the Beholder: Parents' Views on Sex of Newborns." *American Journal of Orthopsychiatry* 44(1974):512–519.

Rubin, Lillian B. *Worlds of Pain: Life in the Working-Class Family*. New York: Basic Books, 1976.

Rubin, Richard S. "Flextime: Its Implementation in the Public Sector." *Public Administrative Review* 39(May 1979):277–282.

Ryan, William. *Blaming the Victim*. New York: Pantheon Books, 1971.

Saario, Terry Tinson. "Title IX: Now What?" In A. C. Ornstein and S. I. Miller, eds., *Policy Issues in Education*. Lexington, Mass.: Lexington Books, 1976.

Sachs, Albie, and Wilson, Joan Hoff. *Sexism and the Law: A Study of Male Beliefs in Britain and the United States*. Oxford, England: Robertson, 1978.

Safilios-Rothschild, Constantina. "A Comparison of Power Structure and Marital Satisfaction in Urban Greek and French Families." *Journal of Marriage and the Family* 29(May 1967):345–352.

Safilios-Rothschild, Constantina. *Women and Social Policy*. Englewood Cliffs, N.J.: Prentice-Hall, 1974.

Safilios-Rothschild, Constantina. "Dual Linkages Between the Occupational and Family Systems." *Signs* 1(1976):51–60.

Safrain, Claire. "What Men Do to Women on the Job: A Shocking Look at Sexual Harassment." *Redbook* 149(November 1976):217–224.

Sander, L. W., Julian, H. L., Stechler, G., and Burns, P. "Continuous 24-Hour Interactional Monitoring in Infants Reared in Two Caretaking Environments." *Psychosomatic Medicine* 34(1972):270–282.

Sandler, Bernice. "The Policy Issues: Presentation IV." In Martha Blaxall and Barbara Reagan, eds., *Women and the Workplace*, pp. 273–277. Chicago: University of Chicago Press, 1976.

Sandler, Bernice. "Title IX: Antisexism's Big Legal Stick." In National Project on Women in Education, ed., *Taking Sexism out of Education*, pp. 1–12. Washington, D.C.: U.S. Government Printing Office, 1978.

Sawhill, Isabel V. "The Economics of Discrimination Against Women: Some New Findings." *Journal of Human Resources* 8(Summer 1973):383–396.

Sawhill, Isabel V. "On the Way to Full Equality." In Ann Foote Cahn, ed., *American Women Workers in a Full Employment Economy*, pp. 40–57. A compendium of papers submitted to the Subcommittee on Growth and Stabilization of the Joint Economic Committee. U.S. Congress, Joint Economic Committee hearing, September 16, 1977. Washington, D.C.: U.S. Government Printing Office, 1977.

Schaeffer, Ruth G. "The Policy Issues: Presentation I." In Martha Blaxall and Barbara Reagan, eds., *Women and the Workplace*, pp. 253–258. Chicago: University of Chicago Press, 1976.

Scharf, Lois. *To Work and to Wed: Female Employment, Feminism, and the Great Depression*. Westport, Conn.: Greenwood Press, ,1980.

Schein, Virginia Ellen. "The Relationship Between Sex Role Stereotypes and Requisite Management Characteristics." *Journal of Applied Psychology* 57(April 1973):95–100.

Schein, Virginia Ellen. "Relationships Between Sex Role Stereotypes and Management Characteristics Among Female Managers." *Journal of Applied Psychology* 60(June 1975):340–344.

Schiller, Anita. "Characteristics of Professional Personnel in College and University Libraries." Illinois State Library. Research Series No. 16, 1969.

Schiller, Anita. "Women in Librarianship." In Melvin J. Voight, ed., *Advances in Librarianship*, vol. 4, pp. 103–147. New York: Academic Press, 1974.

Schlossberg, Nancy K. "A Framework for Counseling Women." *Personnel and Guidance Journal* 51(October 1972):137–143.

Schwartz, Felice N. "New Work Patterns for Better Use of Woman Power." *Management Review* 63(5), (May 1974):4–12.

Scott, Ann. "It's Time for Equal Education." In Judith Stacey, Susan Bereaud, and Jean Daniels, eds., *And Jill Came Tumbling After*, pp. 399–409. New York: Dell, 1974.

Scott, Joan W., and Tilly, Louise A. "Women's Work and the Family in Nineteenth-Century Europe." In Alice H. Amsden, ed., *The Economics of Women and Work*, pp. 91–124. New York: St. Martin's Press, 1980.

Sears, Pauline S., and Feldman, David H. "Teacher Interactions with Boys and with Girls." In Judith Stacey, Susan Bereaud, and Jean Daniels, eds., *And Jill Came Tumbling After*, pp. 147–158. New York: Dell, 1974.

Seavey, Carole A., Katz, Phyllis A., and Zalk, Sue Rosenberg. "Baby X: The Effect of Gender Labels on Adult Responses to Infants." *Sex Roles* 1(June 1975): 102–109.

Seiden, Anne M. "Time Management and the Dual-Career Couple." In Fran Pepitone-Rockwell, ed., *Dual-Career Couples*, pp. 163–189. Beverly Hills, Calif.: Sage Publications, 1980.

Seidman, Ann. *Working Women: A Study of Women in Paid Jobs.* Boulder, Colo.: Westview Press, 1978.

Seifer, Nancy. *Absent from the Majority: Working Class Women in America.* New York: American Jewish Committee, National Project on Ethnic America, 1973.

Seifer, Nancy. *"Nobody Speaks for Me!" Self-Portraits of American Working Class Women.* New York: Simon & Schuster, 1976.

Sell, Lucy. "High School Math as a Vocational Filter for Women and Minorities." University of California, Berkeley, 1974.

Siegel, Clarre L. "Sex Differences in the Occupational Choices of Second Graders." *Journal of Vocational Behavior* 3(January 1973):15–19.

Silberman, Melvin. "Classroom Rewards and Intellectual Courage." In Melvin Silberman, ed., *The Experience of Schooling*, pp. 191–195. New York: Holt, Rinehart, & Winston, 1971.

Silverman, Dierdre. "Sexual Harassment: Working Women's Dilemma." *Quest: A Feminist Quarterly* 3(3), (1976–1977):15–24.

Silverstein, Louise. "A Critical Review of Current Research on Infant Day Care." In Sheila Kamerman and Alfred J. Kahn, eds., *Child Care, Family Benefits, and Working Parents*, pp. 265–315. New York: Columbia University Press, 1981.

Simpson, Richard L., and Simpson, Ina Harper. "Women and Bureaucracy in the Semi-Professions." In Amitai Etzioni, ed., *The Semi-Professions and Their Organization*, pp. 196–265. New York: Free Press, 1969.

Slocum, Walter. *Occupational Careers*. Chicago: Aldine, 1966.

Smith, Dorothy E. "Women's Perspective as a Radical Critique of Sociology." *Sociological Inquiry* 44(January 1974): 7–13.

Smith, Dorothy E. "A Personal Eclipsing: Women's Exclusion from Men's Culture." *Women's Studies International Quarterly* 1(1978): 281–296.

Smith, James P. "The Convergence to Racial Equality in Women's Wages." In C. Lloyd, E. Andrews, and C. Gilroy, eds., *Women in the Labor Market*, pp. 173–215. New York: Columbia University Press, 1979.

Smith, Ralph E. "The Effects of Hours Rigidity on the Labor Force Status of Women." *Urban and Social Change Review* 11(1, 2), (1978): 43–47.

Smith, Ralph E. "The Movement of Women into the Labor Market." In Ralph E. Smith, ed., *The Subtle Revolution: Women at Work*, pp. 1–29. Washington, D.C.: Urban Institute, 1979.

Smith, Ralph E. "Women's Stake in a High-Growth Economy in the United States." In Ronnie Steinberg Ratner, ed., *Equal Employment Policy for Women*, pp. 350–365. Philadelphia: Temple University Press, 1980.

Smuts, Robert. *Women and Work in America*. New York: Schocken, 1971.

Snyder, David, and Hudis, Paula. "Occupational Income and the Effects of Minority Competition and Segregation: A Reanalysis and Some New Evidence." *American Sociological Review* 41(April 1976): 209–234.

Snyder, Eloise S. "The Selective Eye of Sociology." In Eloise S. Snyder, ed., *The Study of Women: Enlarging Perspectives of Social Reality*, pp. 39–78. New York: Harper & Row, 1979.

Spitz, Rene A. "Hospitalism: An Inquiry into the Genesis of Psychiatric Conditions in Early Childhood." *Psychoanalytic Studies of the Child: An Annual* 1(1945): 53–74.

Stacey, Judith, Bereaud, Susan, and Daniels, Jean, eds. *And Jill Came Tumbling After*. New York: Dell, 1974.

Staines, Graham L., Pleck, Joseph H., Shepard, Linda J., and O'Connor, Pamela. "Wives' Employment Status and Marital Adjustment: Yet Another Look." *Psychology of Women Quarterly* 3(Fall 1978): 90–120.

Staples, Robert. "The Myth of the Black Matriarchy." *Black Scholar* 1(3–4), (January-February 1970): 8–16.

Stein, Aletha Houston. "The Effects of Maternal Employment and Educational Attainment on the Sex-Typed Attributes of College Females." *Social Behavior and Personality* 1(no. 2), (1973): 111–114.

Stevenson, Joanne Sabol. "The Nursing Profession: From the Past Into the Future." *National Forum* 61(Fall 1981): 9–10.

Stevenson, Mary. "Internal Labor Markets and the Employment of Women in Complex Organizations." Wellesley, Mass.: Wellesley College, Center for Research on Women, 1975a.

Stevenson, Mary. "Relative Wages and Sex Segregation by Occupation." In Cynthia B. Lloyd, ed., *Sex, Discrimination, and the Division of Labor*, pp. 175–200. New York: Columbia University Press, 1975b.

Stevenson, Mary. "Women's Wages and Job Segregation." In Richard C. Edwards, Michael Reich, and David Gordon, eds., *Labor Market Segmentation*, pp. 243–255. Lexington, Mass.: Heath, 1975c.

Stockard, Jean, and Johnson, Miriam M. *Sex Roles: Sex Inequality and Sex Role Development*. Englewood Cliffs, N.J.: Prentice-Hall, 1980.

Strober, Myra. "Bringing Women Into Management: Basic Strategies." In Francine E. Gordon and Myra H. Strober, eds., *Bringing Women into Management*, pp. 77–96. New York: McGraw-Hill, 1975.

Strober, Myra H. "Toward Diamorphics: A Summary Statement to the Conference on Occupational Segregation." In Martha Blaxall and Barbara Reagan, eds., *Women and the Workplace*, pp. 293–302. Chicago: University of Chicago Press, 1976.

Suter, Larry, and Miller, Herman. "Income Differences Between Men and Career Women." *American Journal of Sociology* 78(January 1973):962–974.

Suttles, Gerald D. *The Social Order of the Slum*. Chicago: University of Chicago Press, 1968.

Task Force on Women in Education. "No Room at the Top." In National Project on Women in Education, ed., *Taking Sexism Out of Education*, pp. 50–63. Washington, D.C.: U.S. Government Printing Office, 1978a.

Task Force on Women in Education. "Toward a Nonsexist School." In National Project on Women in Education, ed., *Taking Sexism out of Education*, pp. 13–21. Washington, D.C.: U.S. Government Printing Office, 1978b.

Task Force on Working Women. *Exploitation from 9 to 5*. Report of the Twentieth-Century Fund Task Force on Women and Employment. Lexington, Mass.: Heath, 1975.

Tepperman, Jean. "Two Jobs: Women Who Work in Factories." In Robin Morgan, ed., *Sisterhood Is Powerful*, pp. 115–124. New York: Vintage Books, 1970.

Tepperman, Jean. *Not Servants, Not Machines: Office Workers Speak Out*. Boston: Beacon Press, 1976.

Tepperman, Jean. *60 Words a Minute and What Do You Get?* Somerville, Mass.: New England Free Press (n.d.).

Terborg, James R. "Women in Management: A Research Review." *Journal of Applied Psychology* 62(December 1977):647–664.

Theodore, Athena. "The Professional Woman: Trends and Prospects." In Athena Theodore, ed., *The Professional Woman*, pp. 1–35. Cambridge, Mass.: Schenkman, 1971.

Thomas, Arthur, and Stewart, Norman. "Counselor Response to Female Clients with Deviate and Conforming Career Goals." *Journal of Counseling Psychology* 18(July 1972):352–357.

Tilgher, Adriano. "Work Through the Ages." In Sigmund Nosow and William H. Form, eds., *Man, Work, and Society*, pp. 11–23. New York: Basic Books, 1962.

Tilly, Louise A. "Comments on the Yans-McLaughlin and Davidoff Papers." *Journal of Social History* 7(1974):452–459.

Tittle, Carole. "The Use and Abuse of Vocational Tests." In Judith Stacey, Susan Bereaud, and Jean Daniels, eds., *And Jill Came Tumbling After*, pp. 241–248. New York: Dell, 1974.

Tobias, Sheila. *Overcoming Math Anxiety*. New York: Norton, 1978.

Tobias, Sheila. "The Mathematics Filter." *National Forum* 61(Fall 1981): 17–18.

Treiman, Donald, and Hartmann, Heidi. *Women, Work, and Wages: Equal Pay for Jobs of Equal Value*. Washington, D.C.: National Academy Press, 1981.

Treiman, Donald J., and Roos, Patricia. "Sex and Earnings in Industrial Society: A Nine Nation Comparison." A paper presented at the Seminar on Social Stratification and Intellectual Skills, sponsored by the Research Committee on Stratification, International Sociological Association, Austin, Texas, February 4–7, 1980.

Treiman, Donald J., and Terrell, Kermitt. "Women, Work, and Wages." In Kenneth Land and S. Spillerman, eds., *Social Indicator Models*, pp. 157–199. New York: Russell Sage Foundation, 1975.

Trey, Joan Ellen. "Women in the War Economy—World War II." *Review of Radical Political Economics* 4(3), (1972): 40–57.

Tsuchigane, Robert, and Dodge, Norton. *Economic Discrimination Against Women in the United States: Measures and Changes*. Lexington, Mass.: Lexington Books, 1974.

Tumin, Melvin. "Some Principles of Stratification: A Critical Analysis." *American Sociological Review* 18(August 1953): 287–294.

Union for Radical Political Economics. *Women Organizing the Office*. New York: Union for Radical Economics, 1978.

U.S. Commission on Civil Rights. *Child Care and Equal Opportunity for Women*. Clearinghouse Publication No. 67. Washington, D.C.: U.S. Government Printing Office, June 1981.

U.S. Department of Commerce, Bureau of the Census. *Current Population Reports*, Series P-60, No. 118. Washington, D.C.: U.S. Government Printing Office, 1977.

U.S. Department of Commerce, Bureau of the Census. *A Statistical Portrait of Women in the United States: 1978*. Current Population Reports, Special Studies, Series P-23, No. 100. Washington, D.C.: U.S. Government Printing Office, 1980.

U.S. Department of Education, National Center for Education Statistics. "Bulletin." October 17, 1980.

U.S. Department of Health, Education, and Welfare. "Fact Sheet." Washington, D.C.: U.S. Department of Health, Education, and Welfare, June 18, 1974.

U.S. Department of Health, Education, and Welfare, Public Health Service. *Vital and Health Statistics, Current Estimates from the Health Interview Study*. Public Health Service. Washington, D.C.: U.S. Government Printing Office, 1967.

U.S. Department of Labor. *Women in Apprenticeship: Why Not?* Manpower Research Monograph No. 35. Washington, D.C.: U.S. Government Printing Office, 1974.

U.S. Department of Labor. *Women Workers Today*. Washington, D.C.: U.S. Government Printing Office, 1976.

U.S. Department of Labor. "Women Managers." Washington, D.C.: Employment Standards Administration, November 1977.

U.S. Department of Labor. *The Employment of Women: General Diagnosis of Developments and Issues.* Washington, D.C.: U.S. Government Printing Office, 1980.

U.S. Department of Labor, Bureau of Labor Statistics. "Employment and Earnings." Washington, D.C.: U.S. Department of Labor, Bureau of Labor Statistics, January 1979.

U.S. Department of Labor, Bureau of Labor Statistics. *Perspectives on Working Women: A Databook.* Bulletin 2080. Washington, D.C.: U.S. Government Printing Office, October 1980.

U.S. Department of Labor, Employment and Training Administration. *Dual Careers: A Longitudinal Study of the Labor Market Experience of Women.* Vol. 4. Washington, D.C.: U.S. Government Printing Office, 1976.

U.S. Department of Labor, Employment and Training Administration. *Women and Work.* R&D Monograph 46. Washington, D.C.: U.S. Government Printing Office, 1977.

U.S. Department of Labor, Employment Standards Administration, Women's Bureau. *1975 Handbook on Women Workers.* Washington, D.C.: U.S. Government Printing Office, 1975.

U.S. Department of Labor, Employment Standards Administration, Women's Bureau. *Minority Women: A Statistical Overview.* Washington, D.C.: U.S. Government Printing Office, 1977.

U.S. Department of Labor, Women's Bureau. *A Working Woman's Guide to Her Job Rights.* Leaflet 55. Washington, D.C.: U.S. Government Printing Office, 1978.

U.S. Department of Labor, Women's Bureau. *Employment Goals of the World Plan of Action: Developments and Issues in the United States.* Washington, D.C.: U.S. Government Printing Office, 1980a.

U.S. Department of Labor, Women's Bureau. *Women in Management.* Washington, D.C.: U.S. Government Printing Office, 1980b.

Urban Associates. *A Study of Selected Socio-Economic Characteristics of Ethnic Minorities Based on the 1970 Census: American Indians.* Washington, D.C.: U.S. Government Printing Office, 1974.

Vanek, Joann. "Time Spent in Housework." *Scientific American* 23(November 1974):116–120.

Veevers, J. E. "Voluntarily Childless Wives: An Exploratory Study." *Sociology and Social Research* 57(April 1973):356–366.

Verheyden-Hilliard, Mary Ellen. "Counseling: Potential Superbomb Against Sexism." In National Project on Women in Education, ed., *Taking Sexism Out of Education*, pp. 27–40. Washington, D.C.: U.S. Government Printing Office, 1978.

Veroff, Joseph, Douvan, Elizabeth, and Kulka, Richard. *The Inner American.* New York: Basic Books, 1981.

Vroom, Victor. *Work and Motivation.* New York: Wiley, 1964.

Wachter, Michael. "Primary and Secondary Labor Markets: A Critique of the Dual Approach." *Brookings Papers on Economic Activity* 3(1974):637–693.

Waite, Linda J. "U.S. Women at Work." *Population Bulletin*, vol. 36, no. 2. Washington, D.C.: Population Reference Bureau, 1981.

Walker, Kathryn. "Household Work Time: Its Implications for Family Decisions." *Journal of Home Economics* 65(October 1973):7–11.

Wallace, Phyllis. *Equal Employment Opportunity and the AT&T Case*. Cambridge, Mass.: M.I.T. Press, 1976a.

Wallace, Phyllis A. "Impact of Equal Employment Opportunity Laws." In Juanita M. Kreps, ed., *Women and the American Economy*, pp. 123–145. Englewood Cliffs,. N.J.: Prentice-Hall, 1976b.

Wallace, Phyllis. "Sex Discrimination." In Eli Ginzberg and Alice Yohalem, eds., *Corporate Lib: Women's Challenge to Management*, pp. 69–84. Baltimore, Md.: Johns Hopkins University Press, 1973.

Wallace, Phyllis. *Black Women in the Labor Force*. Cambridge, Mass.: M.I.T. Press, 1980.

Walsh, Mary R. *Doctors Wanted—No Women Need Apply: Sexual Barriers in the Medical Profession*. New Haven, Conn.: Yale University Press, 1977.

Walshok, Mary Lindenstein. "Occupational Values and Family Roles: A Descriptive Study of Women Working in Blue-Collar and Service Occupations." *Urban and Social Change Review* 11(1,2), (1978):12–20.

Walshok, Mary Lindenstein. *Blue-Collar Women: Pioneers on the Male Frontier*. New York: Anchor Books, 1981.

Walum, Laurel Richardson. *The Dynamics of Sex and Gender: A Sociological Perspective*. New York: Rand McNally, 1977.

Wandersee, Winifred. *Women's Work and Family Values, 1920–1940*. Cambridge, Mass.: Harvard University Press, 1981.

Watson, J. S. "Operant Conditioning of Visual Fixation in Infants Under Visual and Auditory Reinforcement." *Developmental Psychology* 1(September 1969): 408–416.

Weisskoff, Francine Blau. "Women's Place in the Labor Market." *American Economic Review—Proceedings* 62(May 1972):161–166.

Weisstein, Naomi. "How Can a Little Girl Like You Teach a Great Big Class of Men?" In S. Ruddick and P. Daniels, eds., *Working It Out*, pp. 241–250. New York: Pantheon Books, 1977.

Weller, R. H. "The Employment of Wives, Dominance, and Fertility." *Journal of Marriage and Family* 30(August 1968):437–442.

Wertheimer, Barbara Mayer. *We Were There: The Story of Working Women in America*. New York: Pantheon Books, 1977.

Wertheimer, Barbara M[ayer]. "Leadership Training for Union Women in the United States." In Ronnie Steinberg Ratner, ed., *Equal Employment Policy for Women*, pp. 226–241. Philadelphia: Temple University Press, 1980.

Wertheimer, Barbara Mayer, and Nelson, Anne H. *Trade Union Women*. New York: Praeger, 1975.

Wesolowski, Wlodzimierz, and Slomczynski, Kazimierz. "Social Stratification in Polish Cities." In John Archer Jackson, ed., *Social Stratification*. Cambridge, England: Cambridge University Press, 1968.

West, Jackie. "New Technology and Women's Office Work." In Jackie West, ed.,

Work, Women, and the Labour Market, pp. 61–79. London: Routledge & Kegan Paul, 1982.

Wetherby, Terry. *Conversations: Working Women Talk About Doing a "Man's Job."* Millbrae, California: Les Femmes, 1977.

Whitt, Mary, and Naherny, Patricia K. *Women's Work—Up from 878: Report on the DOT Research Project.* Women's Educational Resources, University of Wisconsin Extension, Madison, 1975.

Whyte, William F. "Social Organization in the Slums." *American Sociological Review* 8(February 1943):34–39.

Whyte, William F. *Street-Corner Society.* Chicago: University of Chicago Press, 1955.

Williams, Robin M., Jr. *American Society: A Sociological Interpretation.* New York: Knopf, 1960.

Willis, Sherry, and Brophy, Jere. "Origins of Teachers' Attitudes Toward Young Children." *Journal of Educational Psychology* 66(August 1974):520–529.

Wilson, Everett. *Sociology: Rules, Roles, Relationships.* Homewood, Ill.: Dorsey Press, 1971.

Wirtenberg, T. Jeana, and Nakamura, Charles Y. "Education: Barrier or Boon to Changing Occupational Roles of Women?" *Journal of Social Issues* 32(no. 3), (1976):165–199.

Women on Words and Images. *Dick and Jane as Victims: Sex Stereotyping in Children's Readers.* Princeton, N.J.: Central New Jersey NOW [National Organization of Women], 1972. (Revised edition, 1975.)

Working Women United Institute. *Project Statement: Sexual Harassment on the Job.* New York: Working Women United Institute, 1980.

Wright, James D. "Are Working Women Really More Satisfied? Evidence from Several National Surveys." *Journal of Marriage and the Family* 40(4), (May 1978):301–313.

Wylie, Ruth C. "Children's Estimates of Their Schoolwork Ability as a Function of Sex, Race, and Socioeconomic Level." *Journal of Personality* 63(June 1963):202–224.

Yans-McLaughlin, Virginia. *Family and Community: Italian Immigrants in Buffalo, 1880–1930.* Ithaca, N.Y.: Cornell University Press, 1977.

Young, Anne McDougall. "Median Earnings in 1977 Reported for Year-Round Full-Time Workers." *Monthly Labor Review* 102(June 1979):35–39.

Young, Ruth, and Shouse, Catherine F. "The Woman Worker Speaks." *Independent Woman* 24 (October 1945):274–275.

Zeno, Ken. "Caring and Curing: Women in Medicine." *Whole Life Times* (April–May 1982), pp. 21–25.

Zuckerman, Harriet. "Women and Blacks in American Science." Paper presented at the Symposium of Women in American Science and Engineering, California Institute of Technology, 1971.

Name Index

Subject Index